FAITH OF OUR
FOUNDING FATHERS

FAITH OF OUR FOUNDING FATHERS

Tim LaHaye

First printing: 1994
Second printing: October 1996
Third printing: October 1999

ISBN: 0-89051-201-9
Library of Congress Catalog Card Number: 94-77270

Printed in the United States of America.

Please visit our website for other great titles:
www.masterbooks.net

To Reverend William Lyons

This book is dedicated to Rev. William Lyons, faithful missionary to Free China for twenty years and Pastor of Missions at Scott Memorial Baptist Church of San Diego, California for twelve years, where he also served as Director of Missions at Christian Heritage College.

Without his careful research of over 600 books in the Library of Congress, this book would not have been written. I am proud to acknowledge him, not only as my pastoral associate for many years, but also as my brother-in-law and treasured friend.

CONTENTS

ACKNOWLEDGMENTS

With deepest appreciation I acknowledge the able assistance of Dr. James DeSaegher, my faithful grammarian and friend who has edited all my books, Rolland Goree and my other staff members who labored so carefully to guarantee the accuracy of this book, and the hundreds of authors who included in their record of history the Christian beliefs and influences of our Founding Fathers.

PREFACE

THE FOUNDING FATHERS SIGNING THE CONSTITUTION
(SEPTEMBER 17, 1787)

The untold story in American history (at least in the books written during the past fifty years) relates to the debt the people of this nation owe to the Christian faith. For, as this book will prove, the overwhelming majority of the Founding Fathers of this nation were raised in and believed the Christian faith.

Washington's Prayer for the United States of America
Almighty God; We make our earnest prayer that Thou wilt keep the United States in Thy Holy protection; and Thou wilt incline the hearts of the citizens to cultivate a spirit of subordination and obedience to government; and

entertain a brotherly affection and love for one another and for their fellow citizens of the United States at large.

And finally that Thou wilt most graciously be pleased to dispose us all to do justice, to love mercy, and to demean ourselves with that charity, humility, and pacific temper of mind which were the characteristics of the Divine Author of our blessed religion, and without a humble imitation of whose example in these things we can never hope to be a happy nation. Grant our supplication, we beseech Thee, through Jesus Christ our Lord. Amen.

The original source of the prayer is the concluding paragraph in Washington's farewell circular letter sent to the governors of the thirteen states from his headquarters in Newburgh, New York, June 8, 1783. This altered version appears on a plaque in St. Paul's Chapel in New York City and is used at Pohick Church, Fairfax County, Virginia, where Washington was a vestryman from 1762 to 1784.

ONE

HELP! WE'VE BEEN ROBBED!

A U.S. federal judge was fascinated by the testimony of the expert witness on the stand as he described the distortion of history in the state-approved textbooks. The judge had always been led to believe that students and their parents could trust their schoolbooks. Consequently, it was difficult for him to believe that the religious history of America had been systematically stolen from our nation's texts.

Dr. Paul C. Vitz, New York University psychology professor, had just finished a research project for the U.S. Department of Education on sixty of the most popular textbooks in our public schools. It is estimated that 87 percent of the nation's elementary school children use the books. "The most striking thing about these texts," stated Dr. Vitz in Judge Brevard Hand's court in Mobile, Alabama, "is the total absence of the Christian religion in them." He went on to point out that other beliefs were mentioned—the Jewish, Amish, Mormon, and Catholic faiths—but little or no mention was made of the evangelical Protestants who founded this nation.

Secularism is taught in those same textbooks, a life and world view for children and young people that little resembles the one taught in this nation for the first 150 years of its history. Almost no mention is made of the public schools that represented education at the time the Founding Fathers gathered in Philadelphia to draft our nation's Constitution. Consequently, a whole generation of school children is being robbed of its country's religious heritage in the learning process.

A group of high school students in Lubbock, Texas, was denied access to a school classroom before or after school because conducting a Bible study would supposedly violate the first amendment. The school provided such a room for groups to study politics, social activism, athletics, or almost anything else — but for religious purposes? "Absolutely not!" said school officials.

The outrage of U.S. congressmen caused them to pass "the equal access bill" in 1985 to rectify this problem. But even after it became federal law, making it legal for Christian students to have "equal access" to such rooms before and after school, many hostile school authorities still refuse to cooperate. Some obsessively secular school superintendents have chosen to cancel all such special meetings so that Christian students are not given the opportunity to use school facilities. In many cases, students or their parents have had to file lawsuits to get a classroom assigned for their use. According to one student, "It is easier at our school for Marxists to get a room to hold meetings in than for Christians."

There was a day when Bibles were freely distributed in our public schools — and no one complained about the separation of church and state or "the wall of separation." In fact, (as you will see in Chapter 6), one of the appropriations of the first U.S. Congress was for the printing of Bibles for the conversion of the Indians. How things have changed! In Columbus, Ohio, for example, a veteran teacher was forbidden her fifteen-year-long practice of giving a Bible to every family in her class. Even though she went to the homes *on weekends, on her own time,* to get acquainted with the parents of each of her new students, in the process presenting them with a Bible that she purchased personally, that was forbidden. She didn't force the Bible on the parents; she merely offered it. To date, none of the parents has complained. Yet the school board, at the recommendation of the superintendent of education, decided that "even when on her own time, she is an agent of the public school; therefore, it is a violation of the separation of church and state principle."

What happened to the citizenship rights of a teacher? Apparently, they don't exist if one is a Christian. The National Education Association (NEA), the most powerful union in the nation and an organization that is supposed to protect its dues paying members, is not interested in protecting Christians. Instead, it is committed to the secularization of our schools, as are the

American Civil Liberties Union (ACLU) and other secularist organizations.

Who would have believed that the Supreme Court in 1980 would uphold the decision of a Kentucky school board (in *Stone v. Graham*) that the Ten Commandments, the basis of English law and the most important code of laws ever written, were illegal to display on the walls of the public schools because they represented a religious symbol? Ironically, just a few weeks before the court's decision, some Polish high school students had demonstrated openly against their country's communist authorities for ordering the removal of the Catholic crucifix that still adorned the walls of their public schools — and the government backed down. Americans cheered the courage of those young people for speaking out against their repressive government. Yet when our atheistically dominated Supreme Court removed the Ten Commandments from our halls, not a whimper was heard from the 95 million Christians in this country, who still don't realize that their religious freedoms are being systematically removed without a fight.

Not just the Ten Commandments and religious history have been stripped from our textbooks and classroom walls, but all religious symbols and remembrances. Christmas and Easter classics have been removed from literature; some of the greatest anthems and hymns of the holiday season are no longer permitted to be sung. The "Christmas holidays" of my youth have been changed to "winter break," and "Easter vacation" is now called "spring break" in deference to the children of atheists, Jews, and other minorities. Of course, it is permissible to teach Hanukkah during the Christmas season, but don't review the Christmas story. One Florida child was discriminated against when she provided a manger scene in response to her teacher's request that she "draw a picture of what you think of when you consider Christmas." Santa Claus was appropriate, evergreen trees and presents were acceptable, and trips to "Grandma's house" were welcomed, but the original Christmas scene was forbidden.

We Have Been Robbed of Our Moral Values

The removal of religion as history from our schoolbooks betrays the intellectual dishonesty of secular humanist educators and reveals their blind hostility to Christianity. Hatred that overrules academic integrity ought to disqualify them from the public educational process. Unfortunately, however, they run the process. As a history major in college, I cannot conceive how any honest scholar can put together a history book without mentioning the powerful influence of the Puritans, the Calvinists, and the revivals of the eighteenth century that produced the Great Awakening, on the founding of this nation. But as Dr. Vitz's still-unchallenged report indicates, that is exactly what they have done. They have systematically removed religious history from a nation of children at a time when humanism's antimoral philosophy has created such an emptiness in our children that sexual permissiveness, unwed pregnancy, and venereal disease are rampant among junior and senior high schoolers, and suicide is the second highest cause of death among our nation's youth.

Whom do you blame? Don't blame the church; we still warn young people about the consequences of such activities. Don't blame parents! They don't want their children living like humanistic animals who have evolved from lower life forms. I blame the secular humanists, who have expelled traditional American moral values that were an integral part of our school curriculum for the first 150 years of our nation's history. Since the humanists gained virtual control of education in this country (about fifty years ago), not only have academic levels declined but moral levels have radically deteriorated as well. Doing away with moral absolutes, they introduced "situation ethics" and "moral relativism," helping to create a wave of permissiveness that has given them the excuse to further attack our nation's youth by teaching a radical and explicit form of sex education in mixed classes without benefit of moral values. The ensuing moral holocaust could well destroy America if a cure is not found.

To illustrate the bizarre nature of this blind attack on Christianity and its moral values, note the reaction of the avid secular humanists when President Reagan openly called for the teaching of "sexual abstinence before marriage as the best preventive against AIDS and other social diseases." Immediately, they railed against the suggestion as an "unconstitutional mixing of religion and state in violation of the first amendment." With such thinkers setting educational and social policy, it is no wonder this nation is on the verge of being transformed into the U.S. of Sodom and Gomorrah.

The Deliberate Rape of History

When I first saw a painting of George Washington framed by a toilet seat, hanging on the walls of a local junior college, I realized that the history revisionists had gone too far. That 1975 disrespect was the direct result of a plan set in motion by "experts" on the Carnegie Foundation board of trustees back as early as 1903.

Norman Dodd, director of research for the Reece Committee, established by the U.S. Congress in 1954, revealed that a study of the activities of tax-free foundations in this country during the past fifty years indicated that some of their enormous resources had been used ($30 million a year from Carnegie alone, plus the Rockefeller and Ford Foundations) to change the perception of history. Instead of presenting our national heroes like George Washington, Thomas Jefferson, Benjamin Franklin, and others as men of integrity and virtue, they were purposely presented as crass human beings who used their public notoriety for personal advantage.

This gave substance to the report of the 1950s that textbooks were purposely changed to include moral indiscretions, suggesting even that Thomas Jefferson had fathered children by one of his slave girls—a report that rests on very dubious "evidence." This reduction of national heroes was what caused some of the angry parental outcries of the '60s and '70s to the effect that textbooks gave more space to Joseph Stalin, Mao Tse Tung, and Marilyn Monroe than to our Founding Fathers. Thus, a whole generation of young people grew up without the knowledge of American heroes, which contributed to a loss of patriotism and the reluctance of young men to serve in our military service.

Norman Dodd, in a private video testimony to a Dallas doctor, explained how the Carnegie Foundation board had planned the rewriting of history. At first they tried to hire scholars to design new books that emphasized the fallacies about the national heroes our children have traditionally studied. To the credit of scholars in 1904-1910, the Carnegie board couldn't find any who were willing. But the board did find bright, young collegians, sent them to graduate school, and then financed them to rewrite history to conform to what is today called "a contemporary view of history."

As bizarre as that may sound, it does support an observation I have made in my research of over 600 books in the Library of Congress: If you wish to find the Christian views of our Founding Fathers, you must go back to books written more than fifty years ago. Those closest to the scene carried freely the accounts of their faith, if available, but such is almost never mentioned in contemporary texts.

Dr. Cleon Skousen, a careful research scholar, pointed out that his investigations showed no derogatory accounts of our national heroes prior to 1913. Such statements were all but non-existent. This leads a normal person to ask, "Where did today's scholars get their information?" Perhaps from the recent technique called "faction"—that is, fiction written to resemble facts. The tragedy is that such "faction" is pervasively used in our nation's texts as if it were the true record of history. Consequently, our young grow up without national heroes whom they can respect and admire.

Fortunately, that started to change during the bicentennial celebrations of the Declaration of Independence in 1976, followed by the conservative and patriotic rhetoric of President Ronald Reagan from 1976 (his first attempt to win the presidency) to 1988. Doubtless, the positive results of the bicentennial celebration of the Constitution under the direction of former U.S. Supreme Court Chief Justice Warren Burger will also help set the record straight. Any scholarly works presented during that time, however, should be examined carefully to see if the author uses quotations from the period when history was deliberately raped by left-wing scholars for hire, or if he went back to more reliable sources—those closest to the events they describe.

It has been my observation that left-wing scholars tend to lionize and exalt the statements of those who agree with them and ignore those who hold a religious or conservative viewpoint. That is why selected statements by Thomas Jefferson, Thomas Paine, Benjamin Franklin, and James Madison are frequently used and statements of a conservative tone by other patriots are ignored. For example, have you ever read anything positive about Patrick Henry except his "Give me liberty or give me death" speech? Instead, he is presented as unpopular and extremely out of step with his countrymen. Some even suggest he was lazy, not a good lawyer, and of dubious scholarship. He is particularly portrayed by contemporary historians as opposed to the progressive ideas of Jefferson, his fellow Virginian.

The truth is, however, that Patrick Henry, who vehemently opposed almost everything Thomas Jefferson stood for, particularly after he returned from France with his Enlightenment ideas, was a very popular and brilliant attorney. Even Jefferson acknowledged that his brilliance at oratory had never been surpassed. And as far as popularity is concerned, what school child has ever learned that Patrick Henry was the only governor in American history to be elected and reelected five times? And that much of his popularity was sparked by his being the most activist attorney in the colonies on religious freedom issues? Many times he voluntarily defended the dissident ministers of his state against the attacks of the established clergy.

One story about Henry that never appears in today's history books relates to the origin of his oratory. He is acknowledged by most (even some of his detractors) as the greatest orator of his day and possibly in all our nation's history. But how he learned his oratory is seldom mentioned. His mother was an active Christian of a dissident sect in Virginia, Scottish Presbyterians. She drove her son out of town to services to hear the Reverend Samuel Davies, considered the greatest pulpiteer in colonial history. Young Patrick was assigned the task of taking notes of Davies's sermons and was required to repeat them to his mother on the buggy ride back into town — ideal training at ages ten to thirteen for a great orator and defender of religious freedoms.

While he refused to attend the Constitutional Convention because he opposed a strong federal government (for the very reasons that make big government too big today), and while he vigorously opposed the ratification of the document after it was completed, Henry and George Mason were largely responsible for extracting from James Madison the promise that the Bill of Rights would be added during the first session of Congress. But this kind of fact does not fit in with the "faction" of contemporary historians, who would rather delete Christian leaders like Patrick Henry from our textbooks.

What About Television and Radio?

One may ask, "Aren't you forgetting about the impact of television, radio, movies, and the entertainment industry on society?" Not for a moment. Their programming, which during the last ten years has degraded our society with its frequent ridicule of morality while resorting to explicit sex and even perversion, is a result of this kind of education. Where do you think the two or three thousand morally perverted screenwriters, playwrights, producers, directors, and others who make the shows received their education? The all-pervasive antimoral values of secular humanism, which have replaced traditional American moral values in many of our public schools, have had a profound effect on current social practice, and the tragic results are well known. As we will find in a later chapter, in 1787, when our Founding Fathers gathered in Philadelphia to write the Constitution, the Continental Congress (of which several of the Founders were members) passed a law regarding new territorial lands to the west. In it they clearly stated that religion, morality, and education should be taught throughout the territories. Today we feature secularism, amorality, and education without historic religion, values, or moral principle—at the expense of our children.

A reporter who was preparing for a prime-time TV program called from one of the major networks to ask my opinion about "a new documentary on teaching values." He said, "The mood of the country is changing; people realize that we must go back to teaching moral values." He had talked to NEA officials, who had indicated they were "deeply concerned." He had also spoken with federal education department officials, politicians (both national and local), and, of course, parents.

"What was their primary concern?" I asked.

He replied, "How we can return to teaching traditional values without violating the first amendment that separates religion and politics?" Before I responded to his basic question, I had to inquire, "Why this sudden concern? After all, these are the same people who have inundated the minds of our school children with the ridiculous notion that there are no rights and wrongs— whatever answer you give is 'a right answer' for you."

He replied, "Many things are causing this concern—the lack of patriotism in our Marines, their inability to withstand sexual temptation and subsequent betrayal of their country, stock market scandals with insider trading, one million unwed teens getting pregnant, the teen suicide epidemic, the herpes and AIDS plagues. . . ."

He was simply affirming the Biblical maxim that we reap what we sow. As a nation, we are reaping fifty years of secularist teachings on morals in our schools—and we don't like it.

He really called me to ask, "Is it possible to teach the moral values necessary to sustain life in a democracy and still not teach religion?" That question must be resolved or there will be no United States in the twenty-first century, at least as we know it today. If moral principles are not disseminated, this nation will revert to the jungle. Admittedly, it will be a modern jungle, but uncivilized nonetheless. I responded, "All moral values are rooted in someone's religious teachings. In this country, those values were originally and traditionally rooted in the Judeo-Christian religions, and that encompasses close to 94 percent of the population according to the Gallup poll."

Our present dilemma finds the secularizers—that six percent who don't believe in anyone's God or religion—maintaining a virtual stranglehold on public education. In addition, they control most of our television and radio networks, dominate 65-75 percent of our government, and until very recently held a 5-4 majority on the Supreme Court. While some of them are concerned with the tragic results of producing a whole generation of young people without moral values and character traits, they are still reluctant to resort to the teaching of "moral absolutes" for fear that it will open the door to religious teaching in our schools, public places and culture. Alarm over the moral sickness of the present day, which could develop into a virtual plague, may nonetheless force them to agree to moral teaching in a secular society in order to preserve democracy.

America, A Religious Nation—Justice Douglas

America *is* a religious nation. In 1952, one of the most atheistic, antireligious Supreme Court justices clearly admitted that fact. In *Zorach v. Clausen* (343 U.S. 306) Justice William O. Douglas penned this astonishing acknowledgment:

The First Amendment . . . does not say that in every and all respects there shall be a separation of Church and State. Rather, it studiously defines the manner, the specific ways, in which there shall be no concert or union or dependency one on the other. That is the *common sense* of the matter. Otherwise the state and religion would be aliens to each other—hostile, suspicious, and even unfriendly. . . . Municipalities would not be permitted to render police or fire protection to religious groups. Policemen who helped parishioners into their places of worship would violate the Constitution. Prayers in our legislative halls; the appeals to the Almighty in the messages of the Chief Executive; the proclamation making Thanksgiving Day a holiday; "so help me God" in our courtroom oaths—these and all other references to the Almighty that run through our laws, our public rituals, our ceremonies, would be flouting the First Amendment. A fastidious atheist or agnostic could even object to the supplication with which the Court opens each session: "God save the United States and this Honorable Court."[1]

Justice Douglas was right in pointing out that government need not be hostile to religion. Unfortunately, it *has* been these past thirty-five years—at the expense of our children. Unless we return to traditional respect for the teaching of religion and morality, which was advocated by our Founding Fathers and which is essential to maintaining moral sanity in a democracy, this country will ultimately destroy itself from within.

Teaching civic moral values is possible constitutionally without violating the first amendment. We need simply to return to the original meaning of the amendment instead of the faulty view forced on the American people by the ACLU and other secular humanists in our society. The word "church," as in "separation of church and state," doesn't even appear in our nation's Constitution! That document says nothing about the separation of church and state. When the church is robbed or on fire, it is perfectly legal and right to call the government—fire department or police officials. The first amendment merely stipulates that government make no laws that would intrude upon the church.

The true meaning of the first amendment has been turned

on its head during the past fifty years: In this decade, those who practice the religion of secular humanism are able to use the power of the federal government to impose their religion on the vast majority of the population. One such incident occurred in 1983, when a humanist educator utilized the local police to imprison Mrs. Vicky Frost, a mother who refused to let her daughter read a textbook that she felt advocated the religion of humanism and ridiculed traditional religion. Ultimately, this gross violation of the first amendment was overturned by the courts, and the school board was fined $70,000, but it shows how far we have come in the loss of religious freedom in just 200 years. It also demonstrates why we need to study the religious base, particularly that from the evangelical Protestant church, of our Constitution.

I explained to the NBC reporter, "No, it is *not* possible to teach moral values without teaching religion — if you mean by 'religion' any belief system that recognizes God." Remember, all morality has its roots in someone's religion. In fact, even amorality or antimorality has its roots in the nontheistic religion of secular humanism. But if you mean nonsectarian religion, yes! It is possible to teach basic moral values that are held by most of the religious people of our day.

As evidence of that, ask yourself, "What traditional moral values violate anyone's religion?" Ask a Roman Catholic, Baptist, Jew, Muslim, Mormon, or Presbyterian, "Is it wrong to lie, cheat, steal, kill, or commit adultery?" They will usually answer with a resounding *yes*. But ask a secular humanist, atheist, communist, or socialist, and he'll respond, "Not always," "In some circumstances," or "There are no absolute rights and wrongs." Both answers are based on religion; in fact, both rely on "Scripture." The religious answer from the Judeo-Christian Scriptures, the secularists from Humanist Manifestos I and II.

Another Possibility: Real Pluralism

In my debate with Dr. Paul Kurtz, the writer of Humanist Manifesto II and leader of the secular humanist movement, I challenged him concerning the need to restructure education in America for both the academic and moral good of our youth. Since this is a pluralistic nation, respecting the religious views of all citizens, why can't we establish a pluralistic educational system? That is, some schools would teach from the traditional Judeo-Christian base, others from the secular base, as they do at present. Parents could choose the institutions their children would attend. Or both points of view could respectfully and objectively be included in the classroom, allowing the student to choose for himself which to believe. After all, secular humanists claim that they believe in "free inquiry." So, why not let the student hear both sides and make up his own mind? Anything less than that is nothing short of brainwashing. For example, a pluralistic school system would not be hostile to the teaching of scientific creationism but would admit that many credible scientists hold that view. Similarly, evolution could be taught as a theory and then the student could make up his own mind which theory to adopt.

Early in 1987, the American Bar Association took a poll of its very liberal membership to see if lawyers felt that such teaching would violate the first amendment. To everyone's amazement, they discovered that 62 percent believed it would not violate the Constitution. Why, then, won't the secular humanists who control education permit creation science to be taught as a theory? Because it is contrary to their religiously held belief in evolution. Notice I said "belief," for evolution is merely a belief that cannot be proved. That is why Judge Hand in Mobile, Alabama, in a 1987 decision, identified secular humanism as a "non-theistic religion." In fact, it seems the only way to return pluralism to our public schools is to resort to the courts. As we'll see in the next chapter, the secularizers drove religion out of our schools through the courts, and that seems to be the only way we will drive it back in.

What Religious Freedom?

Historically, America was built on more religious freedom than any nation in the history of the world. Even secular humanists, if they were honest, would have to admit to the religious (particularly the Christian) origins of this nation. According to Dr. Paul Vitz, the new textbooks only admit that "Pilgrims are people who go on long journeys in large ships." In reality, the Pilgrims and many other religious people came here in search of religious freedom. And as I will show later in this book, it wasn't atheists who founded this nation but fifty-five men, who for the most part had an abiding faith in God, the Bible, and His church.

Historian A. James Reichley explained in *Religion in American Public Life*,

> The single most influential cultural force at work in the new nation was the combination of religious beliefs and social attitudes known as Puritanism. At the time of the Revolution, at least 75 percent of American citizens had grown up in families espousing some form of Puritanism. Among the remainder, more than half had roots in related traditions of European Calvinism. Puritanism was the creed of the Congregational church, officially established in three of the four New England colonies, and also exerted strong influence both in the South, where the Anglican church was established, and in the somewhat more cosmopolitan middle colonies. . . . The great idea of Puritanism, as of the entire Reformation, was the total sovereignty and awesome otherness of God, separated from all things human, including the institutional church, by a vast spiritual and moral gulf, crossable only by the infinitude of God's grace and love. . . . Mainline Puritanism regarded human society as tainted by sin but nevertheless potentially useful to religion. The biblical model of a "city on a hill" was the relevant goal for political action. Puritan divines called for establishment of a "Holy Community," governed according to standards derived from Christian principles of morality and justice.[2]

Religious Freedom is Being Jeopardized

James Madison would turn over in his grave if he could observe the government-inspired religious persecution that is going on in America today in the name of the first amendment. Thomas Jefferson, the closet Unitarian who had nothing to do with the founding of our nation (he was in France being humanized by the French skeptics of the Enlightenment at the time), was no friend of faith. But even he would be appalled at the religious oppression that has erupted during the past decade.

Seven Christian fathers in Nebraska spent ninety-three days in jail because they refused to testify against themselves, instead invoking the fifth amendment. And, they were refused that fifth amendment right by the court! Their crime? They sent their children to a Christian school that had been ordered closed because the teachers had not taken three secular-humanist-filled courses in education. Admitted communists have been allowed to invoke the fifth amendment—but not these Christian fathers. That may be the most anti-Christian attack on religious freedom in American history.

A close second, and perhaps an even more flagrant illustration of secular-humanist-totalitarian abuse of raw power, also occurred in Nebraska. The Faith Baptist Church was padlocked by the state after sixty-six ministers of the gospel were forcibly dragged out of a prayer meeting by eighteen carloads of highway patrolmen. This act was later called illegal by a judge, and a hearing has been scheduled to set damages. But the power of government was leveled against a church at secular humanist instigation in direct violation of the first amendment. Jefferson's so-called wall of separation has been broken down by government, not the church. Obviously, the separation of government from state and the wall to separate religious citizens from the power of government does not apply when the secular humanists have the guns and control the courts.

You may be asking, "Why Nebraska?" The answer is crucial. In Nebraska's case in 1983, the board was controlled by secularists who were determined to expand their control over public education to include all private and religious schools. The Faith Baptist Church decided to wrap itself in the first amendment and refused to let them violate its religious freedom. So much for religious freedom when the secular humanists are in control!

Are these isolated incidents, exceptions to the rule? Most Americans tend to believe that such flagrant use of government power to harass Christians or other religious people *is* an exception. They don't realize that such attacks on religious freedom are increasing at an alarming rate, not only against those who run church schools, but also against parents who choose to "home school" their children. I have before me the report of the Rev. T. N. Taylor, an Assembly of God pastor who spent thirty days in an Iowa jail for refusing to send his children to a certified school and instead teaching them at home.

In speaking with Michael Ferris, the lead counsel for the Home School Legal Defense Foundation, I found that the increase in such attacks around the country is growing "at a frightening pace." To put it in perspective, during the first twenty years that I was a pastor in Southern California, I heard of almost no attacks on churches over religious freedom issues. Gradually that began to change; in the mid '70s a total of eighty-four such intrusions into religious matters were reported. Today, one of the organizations in Washington, D.C. that keeps track of such issues has tabulated 10,000 current cases.

At this rate of increase, unless Christians rise up and defend their religious freedoms, they will lose them. Certain people in this country believe that teaching religion to children is the worst thing that could happen to them. Others of us believe, as did our Founding Fathers, that such instruction is among "the chief duties of man," and that America is one nation in which religious freedom is guaranteed by the Constitution.

If we sit back and let the secularizers continue to dominate the government, the courts, the media, and education, those guarantees will be lost. Fortunately, a groundswell of concerned citizens is getting involved. They are becoming so informed that they will wrest control of this nation from the hands of the secularizers and place it back into the hands of those who founded this nation, citizens who had a personal and abiding faith in the God of the Bible.

T W O

WHO SECULARIZED AMERICA?

At the time America was founded (1787-89), two dominant philosophies or world views prevailed in the western world. One was religious, the other secular. There were, of course, many variations of both. But for simplicity's sake, those with a religious world view (most of whom considered themselves Christian, particularly after the Reformation that swept through northern Europe and England) began their entire philosophy with a belief in God as creator and sustainer of the universe. Everything else flowed from that premise. They believed man was a created being, responsible to God to obey the truths He revealed for humanity in the Bible (for Protestants) and in the church (for Catholics).

The secularists, including atheists, skeptics, rationalists, and others of the Enlightenment, began their philosophy without God. Usually they weren't content with disbelief but also extended hostility to those theists who held strong religious beliefs. To secularists, all of life—humanity, morals, education, science, and so on—must be considered without God. Near the end of the eighteenth century, when this nation was founded, this secular form of atheistic-based thinking was dominant among intellectuals throughout France and southern Europe. It exercised an inordinate influence throughout education, literature, the arts, theater, and other intellectual fields.

Some of these secularizers considered themselves deists rather than atheists, proclaiming belief in a supreme being who created the earth and the human race but was no longer involved in His universe. Like their atheist friends, the deists had no use for Scripture, and consequently their major conclusions differed little from those of other secularists.

Europe's Two Classes of People

In most countries of Europe, there were two classes of people, the elite ruling class, predominantly secularist in their thinking, and the masses, who were more religious. The elite were usually educated; the masses, with some exceptions, were not. As a result, the undemocratic policies of an elite ruling class prevailed, offering no elections, little freedom, and much slavery. Seldom were the masses given an opportunity to participate in leadership.

The elite went to school or were tutored, graduated from college or university, and then entered government service, education, law, business, or the press. The masses were largely the farmers, peasants, and later the factory workers, except for the clergy, who usually received a creditable education. The elitists, who read the available newspapers and books, attended their lodges, clubs, and other associations where the philosophy promoted was predominantly secular. Such groups were ideal spawning grounds for skepticism, rationalism, illuminism, Enlightenment theories, and eventually socialism and Marxism.

The masses usually attended church to receive their philosophical instruction, which, of course, was basically religious. John Calvin and Martin Luther, who saw the wisdom of educating the masses, founded schools and colleges that were religious in orientation. They also pioneered the translation of the Bible into the languages of those countries touched by the Reformation.

With many notable exceptions, the religiously based masses were not attracted to the secularistic fads that swept through the educated minority during the eighteenth century. Unfortunately, the colleges and universities that in the fifteenth and sixteenth centuries insisted that man's reason be tested by or compared with Scripture gradually reversed their position; by the seventeenth century, man's reason became the test of Scripture. This prepared the way for the rejection of the Scripture in the eighteenth century and led to open hostility toward anything religious in the nineteenth and twentieth centuries.

Today many secularists agree with Karl Marx that "religion is the opium of the people." Long before the end of the eighteenth century, the philosophy of secularism dominated all college and university instruction. Consequently, while the

American colonies, with their strong religious roots and an educational system committed to Scripture as a Christian world view, were growing in excess of 3 million people, most countries of Europe (particularly France) were being secularized.

The Tension Between Secularism and Christianity

On almost every important philosophical question, these two contrasting philosophies were in opposition, and they still are. The Christian mindset believed in law based on the Scripture and advocated moral absolutes by which to live. The secularist philosophy not only negated the God of the Bible, but also advocated "freedom, liberty, and pleasure." The Christian emphasized that freedom is not absolute but is best experienced as the result of responsibility to God and man. Secularism tended to prefer unfettered freedom. This philosophy of freedom became rampant in France and other countries where the Reformation had the least effect. Ultimately, secular thinking spawned the French Revolution, reducing France, the greatest nation in the West at that time, to a fifth-rate power.

It is difficult to realize that at the time of the American Revolution, France, eight times more populous than the United States, was the world leader in art, literature, science, and education, but was overwhelmingly secular in its world view. The French Revolution that was so antagonistic to all religion, particularly Christianity, did not burst on the scene unexpectedly. It was the logical result of more than a century of secularistic thinking. Man is either free to do his own thing, as Voltaire and Rousseau taught, or he is responsible to God and his fellow man for the way he lives his life. Revolt against all authority is the logical result of secularist (later to be called secular humanist) thinking. That is why secular philosophers are usually so hostile toward God, Christianity, and Scripture.

History professor James Hitchcock has described it in these words:

> The anti-religious sentiment of the Enlightenment was not solely a matter of ideas. Voltaire also often said about the Catholic Church, "Crush the infamous thing!" In all the Western societies, education was largely the responsibility

of the churches, and the churches, established by law, were highly influential. Thus the anti-Christian intellectuals also opposed the church as an institution and a social force. The statement "I disagree with what you say, but I will defend to the death your right to say it," though often attributed to Voltaire, did not represent his views accurately. He was willing to use coercion against his intellectual enemies.

As far back as the Reformation a few people had, for religious reasons, advocated complete religious toleration. Later, many people espoused limited religious toleration as a way of avoiding destructive civil wars. In the eighteenth century, the intellectuals began to advocate religious toleration as a matter of principle. Their motives were somewhat mixed. In part they urged religious toleration out of respect for individual conscience. In part, however, it was out of the conviction that all religious beliefs were equally false and thus all should be equally tolerated. Voltaire rejoiced that, in a society where there were many religious groups, all of them would be weak.[3]

Voltaire's hatred was not limited to the Catholic church. He also hated the Bible and Protestants. He is remembered as the French skeptic who said that although "it took twelve men to establish Christianity, I will show the world that it will take but one man to destroy it." One hundred years later, the Geneva Bible society used his former residence, the very room in which he made the statement, to store Bibles for distribution throughout Europe. While Voltaire and his Enlightenment disciples may have failed to destroy Christianity, however, their philosophy has caused untold suffering throughout the whole world. As explained by Hitchcock,

The French Revolution of 1789 accomplished many of the goals of the Enlightenment, sweeping away by violence all the social institutions to which the intellectuals objected, including the church. Most of the leading *philosophes* were dead by then; the few still alive found that their ideas did not save them from prison and even execution. If they approved of many of the goals of the Revolution, they did not approve its methods. They had believed in reason, but the Revolution seemed to be the triumph of violent passions and hatreds.[4]

Unfortunately, secular humanism, which had been codified and made dominant on the college campus by the middle of the eighteenth century in France and in other European countries, had no conception of the fallen nature of humanity. Instead, it had bought from Rousseau the false concept that man is really very good and that proper education will enable him to make right choices for himself and all mankind.

In response, however, the late Dr. Francis Schaeffer, the Christian philosopher-prophet of the twentieth century, said pointedly, "All roads from humanism lead to chaos."[5] Unfortunately, it usually takes a generation or two before the chaos becomes apparent. For instance, advocating sexual permissiveness has led to 1 million unwed teenage pregnancies each year and a high school venereal disease rate that has risen to a shocking 20 percent. The secularist insistence that "homosexuality is just as good as straight" has propelled us to the threat of an AIDS epidemic that could become the worst plague since the thirteenth century. All secular humanist theories, given enough time, will lead us to chaos.

Hitchcock reviews the social disorder that describes the ultimate secularist society of the day — *in the same year* our religious forefathers were ratifying our new Constitution.

If the Revolution was in one sense the fulfillment of the Enlightenment, it was in another sense its repudiation. It destroyed the *philosophes'* dream that, having given up religious authority, man could remake his life peacefully and tolerantly. Instead, discrediting all traditional authorities ushered in a period of near anarchy. During the so-called Reign of Terror, thousands of Frenchmen were summarily guillotined. Most of them were probably innocent of any crime, and few of them had been given even the semblance of a fair trial. The Terror, an orgy of hate and revenge, was strong disproof of the Enlightenment belief that man, left to himself, would inevitably behave in a rational and just way. The dark side of human nature asserted itself with a literal vengeance in the mid-1790s.

The Terror was the first example of a familiar modern phenomenon: a movement to remake the world in the name of humanity gives birth to a murderous and destructive fanaticism. Every modern revolution has borne the same witness. It is one of the strongest arguments against total reliance on man and his goodwill. It has also given rise, among thoughtful people, to a strong distrust of all movements which proclaim that they have the welfare of "humanity" at heart. Time and again, this has meant the crushing of individual human beings in the name of a political abstraction.

The facts of the revolutionary Terror are well-known, yet their implications have not been widely recognized. Secular Humanists have often manipulated public opinion in their favor by charging that religion has a history of bloody persecution, while Humanism has always been tolerant. When they want to invoke the specter of murderous intolerance they talk about either the Catholic Inquisition or the "witch-burnings" carried out by both Catholics and Protestants. Rarely is there reference to the "Committees of Public Safety," which implemented the Reign of Terror in the name of humanity.

Modern Secular Humanism has been stained with blood from its very birth. At first, the Revolution seemed willing to tolerate the church if the clergy would promise to be loyal to the regime. Soon the government embarked on a systematic "de-Christianizing" campaign. Churches were closed and converted to profane uses, like stables for horses. Religious symbols were destroyed. The religious press was outlawed. All religious services were forbidden. Priests and nuns were rounded up in large numbers and sent into exile, imprisoned, or executed. The aim of the government was to wipe out every remaining vestige of Christianity.

Although its full fury was found in France, similar ideas

and practices spread to other parts of Europe where the Revolution itself spread. It became, in time, a permanent feature of European life.[6]

The Enlightenment's success in eighteenth century Europe paved the way for three of the most destructive philosophies ever devised by the secularist brain: evolution, Marxism, and humanistic psychology. Charles Darwin, Karl Marx, Sigmund Freud, and others who shared their views have produced more human suffering through government-sponsored secularism than all the previous evils known to man combined.

Our Founding Fathers recognized sufficient dangers in secularism to establish on this continent "a new nation dedicated to the proposition that all men are created equal." All men should be free to worship God as they please. In fact, many of them, unlike Jefferson, had a passionate hatred for French Enlightenment thinking and were particularly antagonistic to the "Jacobins," the instituters of the Reign of Terror under Robespierre.

A strong revolutionary spirit in this country during the War for Independence and immediately thereafter caused civil law to break down in many communities. Consequently, when the Founding Fathers gathered in Philadelphia to write the Constitution, they had ample evidence that unrestrained democracy led to anarchy. Such conditions had caused the religiously minded leaders and citizens to choose delegates who had a deep commitment to the religious roots of the colonists who established this country. In the providence of God, only eight of the signers of the Declaration of Independence were among the fifty-five delegates; Jefferson, Tom Paine, and Richard Henry Lee, "three of the most forceful liberal deists, were conspicuous by their absence."[7]

Those who did attend were selected for their deep commitment to Puritan and Calvinistic doctrine, as well as for other political considerations. Their goal was not to establish a democracy in which "every man does that which is right in his own eyes." Instead, they formulated a representative form of government based on divinely inspired law. The Constitution they wrote and the government they founded upon it verified that they never intended to establish a secular nation. Instead, it was and still is "one nation under God."

How Did Secularism Come to America?

When this country was founded two hundred years ago, both the citizens at large and their principal institutions (government, education, media, and church) were controlled largely by those who believed in God or had a basic respect for the Christian faith. Today the American people still hold most of those same religious beliefs (according to the Gallup polls), but the government, the media (including print, broadcast, and the entertainment industry), and most certainly education are overwhelmingly controlled by secularists. That is why I have lamented in previous books that a minority of secularists control the lives of a predominantly religious people.

The manner in which this all came about forms a very interesting story. One strong influence originated through secularized politicians like Thomas Jefferson. They then imported that secular thinking process into this country. It is of particular interest that during Jefferson's campaign to become our third President just thirteen years later, many cries of "atheist" were raised against him by the clergy of his day.

The second force that launched the secularizing process of this country was the humanizing of our bright, young educators. During the first part of the nineteenth century, our country put a priority on education. Most of the schools founded since colonial days were started by religious groups. In fact, during the first century of the colonial period, all 126 colleges were established by some religious group or denomination. By the mid-nineteenth century, these schools were maturing and making a significant contribution to the intellectual life of the new country. School teaching was considered a worthy profession, and much attention was given to the education of our young, which enabled us to develop the highest literacy rate in the world—and not just for the rich. Our country pioneered the education of every child, whether the family could afford it or not.

Because there were so few educators in our country who held masters and doctoral degrees, we developed a false intellectual inferiority complex toward the end of the century and began to send our bright, young educators to Europe to get their advanced degrees. Unfortunately, rather than just earning degrees at the Sorbonne in Paris and Bonn University in Berlin, they brought back secularism in its many forms—skepticism, German higher criticism, and raw secular humanism.

Upon their return, these degreed teachers became the heads of colleges, particularly teachers' colleges, and leaders in state and national educational organizations. Today education is one of our nation's largest industries, which explains why the NEA is the largest union in the country. In short, the educational system was secularized from the top down. Long before the Bible was expelled from the public schools by the Supreme Court, it had been excluded from most courses by hostile administrators.

Assault On Our Seminaries

As one interesting sidelight in all this, by the turn of the twentieth century, so many of these secularists had been produced that they became professors in many seminaries and Christian colleges, leading those institutions down the secularized path as well. This is essentially where liberal Christianity came from. Had it not been for the foresight of the fundamentalists who started Bible schools, Christian colleges, and seminaries in the first two decades of this century, secularism would have prevailed. Instead, these schools have grown significantly and have produced the ministers, Christian leaders, Christian educators, and others who have been so influential in the "born again" movement that has come to prominence during the past decade.

Unfortunately, these schools, which were influenced largely by the pietistic movement, didn't train young people for the fields of law, government, media, and secular education. In fact, some even *discouraged* Christians from participating in these very important fields. Consequently, with the development of technology and television, such fields have been filled by secularists in numbers far out of proportion to the religious beliefs and yearnings of the American people. For over a century (1850-1950 and beyond), the Christian community treated the fields of law, media, and secular education as "otherworldly." This was not the opinion of our Founding Fathers, who felt that Christians who could afford it had a civic obligation to God and their fellow people to serve their community. During the past decade the church has placed a new emphasis on getting involved in all spheres of life where our religious values can have a significant influence on our culture.

The Unitarian Connection

The Unitarian church in America, particularly in Boston, also had a powerful influence on the secularizing of this country. Several of its intellectual clergy went to Europe for advanced studies and brought back enough skepticism and higher criticism, particularly with regard to the deity of Jesus Christ, to split that church. All secularizers, of course, reject Jesus as anything more than a man. Like the Unitarians, many liberal churches have experienced schism over this crucial issue, but the Unitarians were the first.

Since Harvard University is located in Boston, it became the subject of takeover fights by the Unitarians and other secularists during the closing years of the eighteenth century. They needed a university, and since liberals can't start one without government funding, they prefer to take over existing schools. For over twenty-five years, such Unitarian-secularist attempts were thwarted by the religious citizens, largely those fundamentalist ministers who had enough courage to stand up to the liberal leaders of their day. Finally, however, the Unitarians won in 1805 (twenty-seven years after the founding of the United States). Today that university, considered by many to be the most influential in the nation and originally founded for the purpose of training Bible-believing ministers of the gospel, is awesomely liberal, a citadel of secular humanist teachings.

This action should not be surprising, for the liberal branch of the Unitarian church was the American mother of secular humanism. It is no accident that 25 percent of the original signers of the Humanist Manifesto of 1933 were Unitarians, many of them ministers.

Friends of Education?

A third scenario that explains how this country was secularized was presented by former school teacher and historian Samuel Blumenfeld. In his book *Is Public Education Necessary?*, he told the story of the so-called "Friends of Education."

Just twenty years after Harvard under Unitarian leadership

became a bastion of secular humanism, Robert Owen, an atheist, known to many historians as "the father of modern socialism," made an abortive attempt to start a socialist community at New Harmony, Indiana. It lasted only two years. Its failure convinced Owen that the American people weren't ready for socialism and must be conditioned for it through the educational process. As a result of the published testimony of a former Owenite follower who had been a Universalist minister but later professed a conversion to Christianity, the following details were revealed.

Robert Owen founded "The Friends of Education," a group made up of atheists, socialists, free thinkers, unitarians, universalists, transcendentalists, and other forerunners of secular humanism. These intellectuals set out to change the educational system in this country. Using the model of European education, they established three principles as early as 1830: 1) make school attendance compulsory, 2) establish government sponsored "free" schools, and 3) form teacher training schools that they would control in order to prepare the teachers of the future.

Concentrating their efforts in and around Boston, these Friends of Education first urged like-minded legislators to pass legislation in Massachusetts calling for the establishment of the nation's first office of secretary of the state board of education. They then hired Unitarian Horace Mann, known by secularist educators as "the father of public education," as the first secretary in 1837. Holding this position evidently qualified Mann later to become the first secretary of education for the U.S. government, where he could work toward the secularizing of the nation's schools much as he did those of the state of Massachusetts.

Mann was the driving force that implemented the three principles of the Friends of Education cited above. Particularly important to him was the establishment of "normal schools," later identified as state teachers' colleges under John Dewey, Mann's twentieth century counterpart. Today the disciples of John Dewey, who was head of Columbia University's teachers' college, hold most of the key positions in these state teachers' colleges so they can mold the thinking of the nation's school teachers. (For further information about the results of the Friends of Education and their influence on public education, see the author's book *The Battle for the Public Schools*.)

As we have seen, Europe was secularized in the nineteenth century, first by the takeover of its colleges and universities, which had been until then largely religious in origin. Gradually European courts, government, media, and even clergy were secularized, which has made Europe so susceptible to socialism in one form or another.

America, however, was not secularized until the twentieth century, but the procedure was the same. First the colleges and universities were taken over, then some newspapers bought up or started by secularist graduates, then radio, and finally television. Secularists established the movie industry to influence the mind through entertainment, which is why in 1948 they were equipped to take over the new medium of television. It is no accident that all four major TV networks—NBC, ABC, CBS, and PBS—are totally owned and operated by secularists. Only within the last twenty years have Christians been playing catch-up and now enjoy about 15 percent of the viewing audience. The secularizers assumed control of the law schools and slowly changed the nation's view of the Constitution, law, morality, the first amendment, and respect for God and man.

For the past thirty years, the U.S. Supreme Court has been dominated by secularist thinkers, several of whom are atheists, and whose decisions rarely hide their hostility to religion in general and Christianity in particular. With a majority of Supreme Court members holding the secularist position, far out of proportion to the beliefs of the American people, the radical anti-Christian ACLU has had a field day, using the courts to force the secularization of our society.

Changing the Face of America

This year, a 185-year-old symbol of a Nevada city had to be changed because of its "religious significance." All over the country, religious symbols that once were an integral part of our communities have been removed by court order. This year a fire station was forced to remove a cross, a Christian symbol in remembrance of a fellow fireman who lost his life in the line of duty. And the list goes on. Any cross that is located on public land is in jeopardy; it is only a matter of time before an ACLU suit will force its removal. In the name of protecting the rights of the minority, the rights of the religious majority have been trampled under foot. This process will continue until halted by the determined efforts of the religious citizens who, until recently, have sat passively by while their civil rights have been stolen from them. Such passivity certainly does not reflect the commitment of our Founding Fathers.

The ludicrous nature of all this is apparent as I look out my window at the Washington Mall while writing these words. As the current generation of secularizers is busy destroying our nation's religious symbols, I can see the monuments of our Founding Fathers, which contain at least forty-five Bible quotations and Christian symbols or references. For example, the Jefferson Memorial has inscribed in marble the President's belief in God: "I have sworn upon the altar of God eternal hostility against every form of tyranny over the mind of man." The religious statements of Abraham Lincoln appear prominently on the walls of his memorial building. The Washington Monument contains Scripture on many of its steps and a reference to God at the top. The Capitol building has references to God, as does even the Supreme Court building. One wonders how long we have before the secularizers, whose hatred for God and things religious is endless, will erupt in a vicious attack on the religious symbols of Washington, D.C.

This is the tension that exists today between the religious and the secularizers of our society. The religious majority, which is least influential (except on election day), tends to be conservative. The secular minority, which tends to be liberal, currently controls most of government, the courts, education, and the media. The conservative majority is basically religious and would like to live in a morally sane society in the traditions of America. The liberal minority, skillfully using its power to secularize our once-religious nation, knows that its number one enemy is the church — particularly "the born again" which make up about 40 percent of the population.

Consequently, there is a growing tension in this country that will last at least one full decade. The secularizers have watched the sleeping giant of religious Americans begin to rouse herself. This giant is made up of evangelical and fundamentalist Christians, prolifers, conservative Catholics and Jews, Mormons, and other religious citizens whose theology may differ but who are discovering that where citizenship is involved, they share the same yearnings for the future of American society—the yearnings of the Founding Fathers 200 years ago. They came out of their slumber in great numbers in 1980 and 1984 to give the forces of secularism their first defeat in more than fifty years. In 1986 the secularists, who had thought themselves invincible in 1980, have returned to the fight with a vengeance. They realize that if the proreligious conservatives elect a majority in government in 1988, 1992, or 1996, the secularist stranglehold on public education and the media will eventually be broken. Were that to happen, the control of our nation would pass back to the religiously minded of our nation, and the secularists would be thwarted in their published attempt to secularize this nation by the year 2000.

Our Founding Fathers beat back the attempts of the secularizers 200 years ago. If they were living today, I know whose side they would champion. And by the time you finish this book, you will, too.

THREE

WHO FATHERED AMERICA?

In recent years, it has become popular for secular humanists, atheists, and other "free thinkers" to claim that the Fathers of our country were not Christians or religious people after all, but at most deists, atheists, or secularists. Some even go so far as to suggest that several were more addicted to French Enlightenment philosophy than they were to Christianity.

Nothing could be further from the truth! Of the fifty-five men who wrote and signed the U.S. Constitution of 1787, all but three were

> orthodox members of one of the established Christian communions: approximately twenty-nine Anglicans, sixteen to eighteen Calvinists, two Methodists, two Lutherans, two Roman Catholics, one lapsed Quaker and sometime-Anglican, and one open Deist — Dr. Franklin who attended every kind of Christian worship, called for public prayer, and contributed to all denominations.[8]

As this book will reveal, most were deeply religious, all had a great respect for the Christian traditions of the colonies, and all were significantly influenced in their thinking by the Bible, moral values, and their church.

Although religious qualifications were not primary in the selection of delegates to the Constitutional Convention, it is doubtful that any of them would have been elected had they not been members of a traditional religious denomination or at least respectful of the Christian faith. It is most unlikely that a modern secular humanist would have secured enough votes to be elected. If there was a closet "secular humanist" in the group, you can be sure he kept his true beliefs hidden from the people.

So religious was the climate in the eighteenth century that even Benjamin Franklin, one of the Founding Fathers whom the humanists love to claim as their own, indicated that atheism was little known in the colonies. In his pamphlet *Information to Those Who Would Remove to America*, written to Europeans who were considering a move to this country or intending to send their young people to seek their fortune in this land of opportunity, he wrote:

> Hence bad examples to youth are more rare in America, which must be a comfortable consideration to parents. To this may be truly added, that serious religion, under its various denominations, is not only tolerated, but respected and practised. Atheism is unknown there; Infidelity rare and secret; so that persons may live to a great age in that country without having their piety shocked by meeting with either an Atheist or an Infidel. And the Divine Being seems to have manifested his approbation of the mutual forbearance and kindness with which the different sects treat each other, by the remarkable prosperity with which he has been pleased to favor the whole country.[9]

Franklin, who didn't believe this nation to be founded or populated by infidels, atheists, or hedonists, was obviously a greater authority on conditions in early America than modern secularizers. Historically, it was established largely by immigrants from northern Europe, the area most influenced by the Reformation. Among the more than 3 million Americans at the time of the Revolutionary War and the writing of the Constitution, Protestant Christianity was the dominant philosophical force.

When the fifty-five founding fathers gathered in Philadelphia to write the U.S. Constitution, it had been 156 years since the Pilgrims first came to the colonies — in search of religious freedom. The famous English version of the Scriptures, the King James Bible, had been translated in 1611, just nine years before the Pilgrims arrived.

One of the Pilgrims' greatest passions next to religious freedom was the education of their young so they could read the
Bible for themselves. Prior to that period of history, most people
heard from God secondhand (if they heard Him at all) through
their priest, divine, or Bible teachers. Now for the first time God
could speak directly even to the common man, if he could read.
For that reason, schools committed to teaching reading sprang
up almost as fast as villages, and many of the first teachers were
ministers. As long as a town had a minister, the people had a
teacher for their young. No one suggested the Bible was not an
appropriate textbook in the community or common school, and,
of course, it was automatically found in the many church-
sponsored schools.

Typical of such schools were Harvard (1636), Princeton
(1748, originally named the College of New Jersey), and Yale
(1701). These three colleges, more than others, became the headwaters for colonial education, providing most of the colonial
schoolteachers. Originally these colleges were not founded to
provide teachers but ministers and missionaries. As stated by
the Reverend John Harvard in 1636 (when he contributed his
library and property for the founding of the first college in this
new world), it was instituted "to train a literate clergy." Gradually, however, these schools became the major training source for
America's teachers, who would go out and establish the greatest
school system in history. Such teachers incorporated Judeo-
Christian morals and values in the educating of the young, and
this had a profound influence on the thinking of the next generation. Witness the Biblical content of the curricula at that time,
designed largely by Noah Webster, known as "America's schoolmaster," a deeply devoted follower of Jesus Christ and one who
believed it was the responsibility of the school to teach children
moral values.

Christianity's Influence on Colonial Education

Another factor that influenced the thinking of the American
people was the Great Awakening revivals from 1738 to 1760. According to many historians, they provided the colonists with the
mental and moral toughness to declare their independence from
England and endure the rigors of the Revolutionary War, which

lasted for seven long years. That victory was attributed by many to "the strong hand of Providence"—hardly the reaction of a nation of deists and secularists.

As we have seen in chapter 2, atheism, secularism, and humanism were largely philosophical imports from France, Germany, and England *after* the Constitution was written and *after* the death of most of our nation's Founding Fathers. It had little effect on America until the latter part of the nineteenth century. M.I.T. (Massachusetts Institute of Technology), the first college chartered by atheists, was not founded until 1861, or seventy-two years *after* the founding of America. This was followed in the twentieth century by the humanists' gradual takeover of our teachers' colleges and the moving of the headwaters of education to the citadel of secularism, Columbia University.

It was at Columbia University that John Dewey and his disciples produced "progressive education," which has turned out to be totally secularistic and very poor education. A humanist-controlled Supreme Court, which has consistently voted ever since 1962 to force the secularization of our schools by expelling prayer, the Bible, and anything else religious, has completed the secularization of public education.

Unfortunately, with religious teaching went the moral training and character building that had long been a part of our once great educational system. That isn't to say it was evangelistic or given to proselytizing, but it taught honestly the truth about all religions, particularly those most common in this country. Now, without the moral training and character building based on the Judeo-Christian religions, we have raised a generation of permissive educators and media people who look on religion as a threat rather than a stabilizing force in society.

I do not claim that this country was founded as a Christian nation, even though many of the original states were established as Christian colonies. As I shall demonstrate in chapter 6, it was a nation so predominantly Christian that the culture evidenced what the late Dr. Francis Schaeffer called "a Christian consensus." This Christian consensus is easily verified by the fact that prior to 1789 (the year that eleven of the thirteen states ratified the Constitution), many of the states still had constitutional requirements that a man must be a Christian in order to hold public office. In some cases these laws were never repealed, they were merely superseded by the adoption of the new Constitution.

"The Union" or "the United States" was founded on more Biblical principles than any nation in history—the secret to America's greatness. Those principles originally permeated our educational system, courts, public life, religious life, and economic system, producing what President Ronald Reagan calls "traditional values." When these values prevailed, the quality of life from the family to the streets was far better than it is today. While citizens certainly did not have modern means of communication, mobility, or twenty-first century technology, neither did they endure streets that were unsafe for women after dark, a tragic rate of child molestation, 1 million teen pregnancies annually, and rampant violence and crime. We were certainly not known as "the pornography capital of the world." Whenever we point out the need to return to traditional values, the humanists remonstrate that we want to take the country "back to the dark ages." In actuality, modern technology would be far more beneficial to mankind in an environment of "traditional values" than it is in the permissive, humanistic society of today.

The Importance of the Constitution

The U.S. Constitution is the foundation stone of this republic. Written in 1787 and ratified in 1789, it is considered by many to be the greatest governmental document ever written. It has provided more freedom and prosperity for more people than any similar constitution in the history of mankind. It has established the longest period of self-government in any major country (where common citizens vote their leaders into office). It has survived a civil war, two world wars, the Industrial Revolution, depressions, an extremely liberal Supreme Court, and even a radical succession of power when both a President and Vice President (Richard Nixon and Spiro Agnew) were replaced by an appointed President and Vice President—all without violence.

The fifty-five writers of our Constitution were probably not typical of the average American, for they were selected from among the more-educated landowners to represent the citizenry in the founding of this nation. A knowledge of their religious faith, their values, and their philosophy of life will provide us with important insights into the true roots of our nation. This will stand us in good stead as we face the relentless attempts of present and future secularizers to remove every vestige of Christian or religious tradition from our culture before the twenty-first century.

Seventy-three men were elected by their states to represent them at the Constitutional Convention which met between May 27 and September 17, 1787. Rhode Island so opposed the union that it didn't elect anyone. Consequently, only twelve states provided representation. Fifty-five men convened at one time or another, most of whom made some contribution to the document, but only thirty-nine were on hand to sign the Constitution at its completion. These fifty-five men from a variety of backgrounds made up this nation's Founding Fathers.

A few of the signers were rich. Washington and Robert Morris ranked among the Nation's wealthiest men. Carroll, Jenifer, and Mifflin were also extremely well-to-do. The financial resources of the majority of the rest ranged from good to excellent. Among those with the most straitened circumstances were Baldwin, Few, Brearly, Brook, Madison, Paterson, and Sherman, though they all managed to live comfortably.

A considerable number of the men were born into leading families: Blair, Butler, Carroll, Ingersoll, Jenifer, Johnson, Livingston, Mifflin, Gouverneur Morris, both Pinckneys, Rutledge, and Washington. Others were self-made men who had risen from humble beginnings: Few, Franklin, Gorham, Hamilton, and Sherman.

Most of the group were natives of the 13 colonies. Only seven were born elsewhere: four (Butler, Fitzsimons, McHenry, and Paterson) in Ireland, one (Robert Morris) in England, one (Wilson) in Scotland, and one (Hamilton) in the West Indies. But if most of the signers were native-born, many of them had moved from one State to another. Reflecting the mobility that has always characterized American life, 13 individuals had already lived or worked in more than one State or colony. They were: Baldwin,

Bassett, Bedford, Dickinson, Few, Franklin, Ingersoll, Livingston, the two Morrises, Read, Sherman, and Williamson. Others had studied or traveled abroad.

The educational background of the Founding Fathers was diverse. Some, Franklin for example, were largely self-taught and had received scant formal training. Others had obtained instruction from private tutors or at academies. About half of the individuals had attended or graduated from college, in the present United States or abroad. Some men held advanced and honorary degrees. All in all, the signers were a well-educated group.

Most of them were in the prime of their lives during the Convention, and as a whole they were relatively youthful. The average age was about 45 years. The youngest, Dayton, at 26, was one of three men in their twenties, the others being Spaight and Charles Pinckney. Eleven were in the thirties, 13 in the forties, and 8 in the fifties. Jenifer, Livingston, and Sherman were in the sixties, and Franklin was in his eighties.[10]

The product of our Founding Fathers, was a document described by John Adams—and proved by history—as "the greatest single effort of national deliberation that the world has ever seen."[11] Many believe they were guided in their writing by the same "strong hand of Providence" that guided the Pilgrims, the settlers, the signers of the Declaration of Independence, and George Washington's armies during the traumatic days of the Revolutionary War.

FOUR

INTERESTING HISTORICAL EVENTS TO KEEP IN VIEW

The Pilgrims' arrival in 1620 marked one of the first permanent colonies in North America, and the colonial period began with them. One hundred sixty-seven years later, the colonies had grown to almost 4 million people residing in thirteen very independent states who distrusted federal governments. Most wanted a weak central government (if any) and strong state governments. Even after the Revolutionary War, they floundered for five years before founding the United States of America by the writing and ratifying of the Constitution.

THE COLONIAL PERIOD
(1620-1774)

During the 154 years of the colonial period, the Puritans, colonists, and others established thirteen independent colonies dominated by the British government. "Taxation without representation" and other abuses of monarchial powers finally led the colonists to sue for their independence. The colonial period had a profound influence on the founding of this nation. It provided most of our great American heritage.

THE FIRST CONTINENTAL CONGRESS
(1774)

The continental period began with the First Continental Congress, which convened in Philadelphia to discuss the appropriate response by the colonies to the oppressive policies of Parliament and King George III. This official step toward union was not rushed into hastily, for Benjamin Franklin had made such a recommendation, called the "Albany Plan of Union," twenty years earlier in 1754. This First Continental Congress was represented by twelve of the thirteen colonies (Georgia did not send representation), providing the colonies with their first real opportunity to discuss cooperative government above the local or colony level.

Like the First Continental Congress, the second was composed of representatives selected by the legislatures of each colony. Called to serve as a deliberative body, it soon became the

THE SECOND CONTINENTAL CONGRESS
(1775)

chief organ of government for the union of states, the body that made the traumatic decision to declare independence from England. Unfortunately, it did not have the power to tax, even in a state of emergency, a policy that crippled our pursuit of the Revolutionary War, which was declared the following year.

THE DECLARATION OF INDEPENDENCE
(JULY 4, 1776)

With little more than faith in God and a determination to be "a free people," the colonists, through the Second Continental Congress, declared war on England.

The Declaration, according to constitutional attorney Michael Farris, was "the Charter of our nation." It makes clear what most citizens of the colonies believed—that they were establishing a new nation based soundly on the laws of God. The opening paragraph of the Declaration of Independence reads:

> When in the Course of human events, it becomes necessary for one people to dissolve the political bands which have connected them with another, and to assume among the Powers of the earth, the separate and equal station to which the Laws of Nature and of Nature's God entitle them, a decent respect to the opinions of mankind requires that they declare the causes which impel them to the separation.

Commenting on the relationship of the Declaration of Independence to the Constitution, Farris stated:

> By basing our right to be a free nation upon God's law, we were also saying (by implication) that we owed obedience to the law that allowed us to be a separate country. The last paragraph of the Declaration is the most important part, for it is that part which actually declared that the United States was a separate nation.

> "We, therefore, the Representatives of the United States of America, in General Congress, assembled, appealing to the Supreme Judge of the world for the rectitude of our intentions, do, in the Name and by the authority of the good people of these colonies, solemnly publish and declare, That these United Colonies are, and of Right ought to be Free and Independent States; that they are absolved from all Allegiance to the British Crown, and that all political connection between them and the State of Great Britain, is and ought to be totally dissolved; and that as Free and Independent States, they have full power to levy war, conclude peace, contract alliances, establish Commerce, and to do all the other acts and things which Independent

States may of right do. And for the support of this Declaration, with a firm reliance on the protection of divine Providence, we mutually pledge to each other our lives, our fortunes and our sacred honor."

The Declaration of the United States is our Charter. It is the legal document that made us a nation like all the other nations of the world. It doesn't tell us how we are going to run our country—that is what our Constitution does. In a corporation, the Charter is higher than the By-laws and the By-laws must be interpreted to be in agreement with the Charter. Therefore, the Constitution of the United States must be in agreement with the Declaration of the United States (more commonly known as the Declaration of Independence). The most important statement in our Declaration is that we want to operate under the laws of God.

Why is all of this so important? Because today, when the courts are deciding what the Constitution means, they should remember our Charter—the Declaration of the United States. The Constitution doesn't specifically mention God, but then it doesn't have to because the Declaration is a higher document.

THE REVOLUTIONARY WAR
(1776-1783)

The Declaration says that we are a nation under God's laws. Therefore, all other laws of our country should be consistent with the law of God or they violate our national charter.[12]

Had the colonists realized the hardships and suffering their declaration was to cause them, it is doubtful they would have made the decision to become a free and independent nation. George Washington was appointed commander-in-chief of the colonial army, and the entire nation was embroiled. Through the power of his personal prestige, military skill, and what he termed "the strong hand of Providence," the colonial armies prevailed over incredible odds, and a new nation was born.

THE ARTICLES OF CONFEDERATION
(1777-1789)

The second Continental Congress drafted the Articles of Confederation and submitted them to the states so the thirteen colonies could have a form of government. The last state to ratify them was Maryland, on March 1, 1781. This new government was severely limited by state sovereignty and couldn't pass laws without ratification by at least nine states. It was extremely difficult for the federal government to raise enough taxes from the states even to provide the necessary funds to pursue the war.

The Articles of Confederation did little more than link the

states loosely together in a "firm league of friendship with each other." They were intended to provide the colonies with a government but they failed to give it the power to govern.

A recent article from *The Constitution* magazine pointed out that the Articles of Confederation had six serious defects: (1) they provided for no chief executive, (2) no judiciary, (3) no power of enforcement, (4) no power of taxation, (5) no power to regulate commerce, and (6) no workable amendment process.

> The inherent weaknesses of the Articles of Confederation, most notably the inability of Congress to collect taxes, resulted in tragedies such as the winter at Valley Forge and almost caused the loss of the Revolutionary War. But when the war ended in 1783 and the American people no longer faced the immediate military threat that had so long bound them together, the hardships of war were only replaced by the perils of freedom. The new nation was plagued by severe economic depression, rampant inflation (hence the expression "not worth a Continental"), a complete incapacity to pay its foreign and domestic debts, trade barriers and interstate quarrels, and even a threatened secession by the New England states. What little respect had existed for the Congress quickly deteriorated; in 1784 George Washington reflected the thoughts of all his countrymen when he described Congress as "a half-starved, limping government that appears to be always moving upon crutches and tottering at every step." Alexander Hamilton lamented that the United States had reached "almost the last stage of national humiliation. There is scarcely anything that can wound the pride or degrade the character of an independent nation which we do not experience." Essentially what had happened was that America's leaders, upon escaping the tyranny of the British crown, had ridden the pendulum too far toward the opposite extreme of the political spectrum.[13]

Congress chose diplomats who were probably the ablest the United States has ever had: Benjamin Franklin, John Adams,

THE TREATY OF PARIS
(1783)

Thomas Jefferson, and John Jay successfully forged alliances
with France, Spain, and the Netherlands: and Franklin, Adams,
and Jay brilliantly represented the United States in the peace
talks in Paris. Furthermore, as a result of the Treaty of Paris, the
United States acquired vast new territories stretching to the
Mississippi River. In three ordinances passed in 1784, 1785, and
1787, the Confederation Congress established a procedure under
which this territory was organized into states, each to be admitted into the Union on an equal footing with the original thirteen. The principle behind these ordinances was later adopted in
the Constitution.[14]

The new nation was enormous by European standards. Its
area was 880,000 square miles, or four times that of France. In
population, it was still small, but growing quickly. By the end of
the war, its population was about 3,000,000, of which 500,000
were slaves. Virginia was still the largest state, with a population
of 450,000. The scars of war were comparatively light. The
cities, by and large, had been left untouched and except for the
Tory and Indian raids there were no real atrocities. American
casualties may have been 19,000 with about 4000 listed as killed
in action. The British casualties are not known but are estimated
to have been at least twice as high as the American.

The greatest tragedy befell the Loyalists, who had fought for what they considered their country and King. Had the American rebellion been crushed, they would have been heroes; as it was, they were traitors. The best thing they could do was leave a country that was now actively hostile to them. On April 26, 1783, seven thousand Loyalists left New York City as what we would today call refugees. Some went to Great Britain, some to Canada. There were many others, for estimates place the total number of Loyalist refugees who left the United States or were driven out at 100,000.[15]

Near Anarchy
(1783-1787)

Forces of disintegration were at work from 1783 to 1787. A situation of general anarchy obtained. Credit was gone. Congress made recommendations to the different States concerning the raising of revenue, and the States treated the recommendations with contempt. Congress issued paper money, and citizens in derision plastered the walls of their houses with it. The army demanded pay, and Congress was unable to pay. The army was without discipline, and one detachment of disgruntled soldiers actually besieged the State House in Philadelphia, where the Congress itself was meeting. Congress thereupon fled to Princeton, New Jersey, and then to the city of New York, where it remained until after the Constitutional Convention. Now that the

Redcoats were gone the former colonies, more than anything else, feared each other. Incipient rebellions were breaking out. Wise Americans like Washington and Franklin could foresee nothing but more disorder. Anarchy shook the land. Lawlessness was rampant. Business was paralyzed. Nothing was more certain and apparent than the disunity among the States.[16]

THE MOUNT VERNON CONFERENCE
(1785)

What began as a meeting between representatives of two states set a model for an even broader conference that blossomed eventually into the Constitutional Convention. The initial meeting came about in 1785, when Maryland and Virginia agreed to settle a long-standing dispute over jurisdictional and navigational rights in coastal waters shared by both states. Commissioners appointed by each of them were scheduled to assemble in Alexandria, Virginia, in March of that year, but George Washington offered the hospitality of his home at Mount Vernon and the commissioners met there instead. The conferees quickly agreed on a compact governing not only water rights but also matters of currency exchange, bills of exchange, and import and export duties. Both states swiftly approved the compact.[17]

As a result of the success of what became known as the Mount Vernon Conference, Virginia proposed a larger conference on commercial measures that would include all thirteen

THE TRADE CONFERENCE AT ANNAPOLIS
(1786)

states, to be held at Annapolis, Maryland, in 1786. This meeting proved a mixed bag. Delegates from only five states — Delaware, New Jersey, New York, Pennsylvania, and Virginia — arrived in time. Those from Massachusetts, New Hampshire, North Carolina, and Rhode Island showed up after the conference had already dissolved. And four states — Connecticut, Georgia, South Carolina, and even Maryland — never sent any representatives. Nevertheless, the conferees who were there adopted a resolution, drafted by Alexander Hamilton of New York, calling for a general convention of all states to meet in May 1787, this time in Philadelphia. And, unlike the Annapolis Convention, this meeting would have the authority to discuss all issues having to do with "render[ing] the constitution of the Federal Government adequate to the exigencies of the Union." The resolution was subsequently backed on February 21, 1787, by the Confederation Congress, which officially called upon all the states to send delegates to Philadelphia.[18]

More important than formulating decisions on trade and commerce, the Annapolis conference was significant because it called for the Constitutional Convention.

And because our Constitution has been so successful, many Americans, particularly conservatives, oppose tampering with it. They don't even favor a new constitutional convention to force the government to balance the budget and forbid future governments from practicing deficit spending. They reason that if the Constitutional Convention of 1787 exceeded its charter and wrote the document that produced the United States, what is to keep a modern convention from exceeding its charter and harming the Constitution that has preserved this republic for 200 years?

It is said that James Russell Lowell was asked by the French historian Francois Guizot, "How long will the American republic endure?"

He sagely replied, "As long as the ideas of the men who founded it continue dominant."[19]

The vision of destiny for this nation is best described by the oldest member of the convention, the revered Benjamin Franklin, who said, "I have . . . often, in the course of the session, . . . looked at that [sun] behind the president without being able to tell whether it was rising or setting. But now at length I have the happiness to know that it is a rising and not a setting sun."[20]

THE WRITING OF
THE CONSTITUTION

Said Thomas Jefferson, "The example of changing a constitution, by assembling the wise men of the State, instead of assembling armies, will be worth as much to the world as former examples we have given them. The Constitution . . . is unquestionably the wisest ever yet presented to men."

The United States Constitution is often called "a miracle document" because it has proved so enduring while so many other attempts at self-government have failed. In reality, it was a miracle of sorts that the Constitutional Convention ever materialized in the first place.

Benjamin Franklin, "the father of the Confederation," had been calling for a confederation of some kind among the disjointed colonies for over twenty years without success. The spirit of rivalry, suspicion, and jealousy among the individual states was intense (so much so that little Rhode Island even refused to send delegates to the Constitutional Convention).

Not only were there tariff wars and boundary disputes, but there was also disagreement on the amount of debt each owed for the Revolutionary War. The large states like Virginia, Massachusetts, and New York wanted a strong national, or central, government that could represent all the colonies to foreign nations and, if necessary, wage war to protect their fragile independence so dearly won. The smaller states, because of their negative experience with the mother country, were suspicious of putting themselves under any other authority, even that of their fellow colonists. Some of them preferred the maintenance of thirteen independent, sovereign states. This disunity had produced near anarchical conditions. The economy was in a shambles, business was all but paralyzed, and rising lawlessness made many of the best leaders in the states realize they must do something or the revolution would be lost and the young nation would become easy prey to foreign invaders.

As we have seen, the Articles of Confederation were totally inadequate, and for that reason a Constitutional Convention was called in order to strengthen that document — to provide a stronger federal government without weakening the power of each state. It is doubtful that any of the states, or even the distinguished delegates that would gather, realized that before they were through they would have designed a whole new system of government under a completely new and unique Constitution.

The Convention was scheduled to convene on May 14, 1787. No limit was set on the number of delegates each state could send, but when it came to voting, each state was allowed to cast only one vote. For economic reasons, the small states sent the smallest delegations.

Seventy-three delegates were appointed by the twelve states; fifty-five arrived in Philadelphia. A few (George Mason and Governor Edmund Randolph of Virginia, and Elbridge Gerry of Massachusetts) stayed through the entire proceedings but refused to sign (primarily because of the lack of a bill of rights). Some had to leave early for personal, family, or health reasons, and one returned to run for governor of his state.

> Taken together, the assemblage was rich in political experience, legal training, and worldly wisdom and accomplishment. The social and economic backgrounds varied, but the men were predominantly of established-family origins and comfortable or affluent circumstances, fairly representative of the educated planter-merchant-lawyer elites that had furnished America with most of its provincial leaders. All in all it was quite a group, and Thomas Jefferson's enthusiastic comment from Paris — "an assembly of demigods" — was the kind of exaggeration the cumulative historical verdict of nearly two centuries has pronounced both pardonable and mild.

> The men of Philadelphia had even more going for them than a high median level of talent and community stand-

ing. They had a political and constitutional heritage that went back through Great Britain's Glorious Revolution and Puritan Revolution to the earliest parliaments and the barons at Runnymede, and they were on speaking terms with nearly all of it. They were well versed in eighteenth-century theories of natural law and natural rights; by and large they subscribed to such theories and admired what Harrington and Montesquieu and Locke had written on the subject.[21]

The writers of the Constitution were not unaware of the emerging theories of the Enlightenment, but their legal mentors, including John Locke and Charles de Montesquieu, were both Christians who wrote their philosophies of the law from a Biblical world view. It is seldom reported that John Locke produced one of the finest books of Christian evidences of his generation, entitled *The Reasonableness of Christianity*, and John Calvin had such an influence on the thinking of most colonists in that day that one scholar has called the finished draft "John Calvin's Constitution." In addition, John Adams, an avid Bible reader and committed Christian (who did not attend the Convention because he was the American minister to England), had just completed a masterful book entitled *A Defense of the Constitutions of Government of the United States*. Because of his stature as a statesman and the nature of the subject, it is assumed that the book was widely read by the delegates to the Convention.

There were other intellectuals and patriot leaders who could not attend. John Jay, who later contributed through the *Federalist Papers* to the ratifying of the Constitution, was busy with the foreign relations of the country; Thomas Jefferson was serving as the American minister to France; John Hancock had just been elected governor of New Jersey; and Patrick Henry, though he had been appointed as a delegate of Virginia and was the greatest orator in the colonies, refused to attend because he opposed a strong federal government.

The distinguished gentlemen who gathered in Philadelphia clearly represented the thinking, aspirations, and religious values of the citizens in 1787. Although this was not a religious conclave, the overwhelming number of the delegates were of such religious belief and character as to preserve this document from including any principle that was contrary to the Bible—which nearly all held in high esteem. Besides, they knew they must have it ratified by the states, all of which were strongly Christian, eight of which still required church membership and commitment to Christ of their elected officials. It wasn't popular in 1787 to be an infidel in America.

If the delegates expected to frame a Constitution that would provide a model for the freedom-loving people of the world, it wasn't reflected in their attendance. Only Virginia and Pennsylvania achieved quorums in Philadelphia on May 14. Not until May 25 were there enough states represented so that deliberations could begin.

James Madison, the brilliant lawyer from Virginia, has often been called "the Father of the Constitution." This may not be far from the truth, for of all the delegates he was probably the one most mentally prepared for the Convention. Thomas Jefferson, a dear friend and frequent correspondent with Madison, sent him one hundred carefully selected books that he had gathered in Europe on constitutional law and related subjects.

While awaiting the arrival of the other delegates, Madison utilized the time to meet with the Virginia delegation, which drew up fifteen resolutions to present to the Convention when it began. These resolutions were called "the Virginia Plan." Of the forty-one recommendations proposed by the Virginia plan, twenty-seven were ultimately adopted by the Convention. At the first session, George Washington was elected president.

The Convention Finally Begins

Few nations have ever featured such a personage for national hero as the six-foot-two delegate from Virginia, George Washington. The esteem in which he was held appears in the fact that these dignitaries, many famous in their own right, elected him unanimously to preside over the Convention. As it turned out, this proved to be a master stroke, for as the weather and tempers increased in heat, a lesser man probably could not have kept the delegates from dissolving—possibly even in violence. *The World Book Encyclopedia* pays lofty tribute to Washington's greatness in its description of his importance as president of the convention.

Often, as the fifty-five delegates argued, it seemed that the gathering would break apart through its disagreements. At such moments, the Convention delegates would glance at the elegantly dressed, patient, dignified figure sitting in the president's chair. Then they would remember the miracle of America's victory over a great power, and go to work again. As he had in the war, George Washington served in time of peace to hold his countrymen together.[22]

Some of Washington's contemporaries believed that had he not attended, a Constitution would never have been formed; others suggested that if his name had not appeared on the final document, it is doubtful that Congress and the states would have ratified it. According to his favorite expression, however, only "the strong hand of Providence" enabled him to attend the Convention at all.

One of the surprising things connected with the convention was the fact that George Washington, who had pleaded for a convention so long, almost did not attend himself. His brother had just died, his mother and sister were seriously ill, and he was in such pain from rheumatism that he could scarcely sleep at night. Furthermore, the fraternity of military officers called the Society of the Cincinnati had wanted to honor Washington at their convention in Philadelphia during this same period. He had declined because of his personal circumstances, and now it would be embarrassing to suddenly show up for another convention. Nevertheless, the general decided to bite the bullet and go. James Madison and others pointed out that because of his position in the public mind as the most trusted leader in the nation, it would appear that he had lost confidence in the Congress and perhaps in republican principles if he did not attend. Although he had been carrying one arm in a sling because of rheumatic pain, he left Mount Vernon at sunrise on May 9 and arrived in Philadelphia the day before the delegates were to convene on May 14.[23]

Historian and constitutional authority Dr. Cleon Skousen has written a succinct description of the events that unfolded, which is quoted at length below.

The Convention Opens

A secretary by the name of Major William Jackson of South Carolina had been employed, but he was not really competent. It was James Madison who was the real secretary and historian. He sat up front and took copious notes on everything that was said. After each session Madison would work far into the night filling in details. He occasionally made himself ill from fatigue and overwork trying to capture every detail of the convention. These notes were kept secret for 30 years, but they were finally published by an act of Congress in 1843. They constitute the most authoritative record available on the Convention.

Rules Adopted

A number of interesting rules were prepared by George Wythe and his committee and were adopted by the convention.

1. The proceedings were to be conducted in secret. This was to prevent false rumors or misinformation from spreading across the country while the founders were still threshing out the formula which would solve the problems plaguing the nation. Guards were posted at the doors, and no one was admitted without signed credentials.

2. Each state was to be allowed one vote, and the majority of the delegation from a state had to be present and in agreement in order to have its vote counted.

3. Many times during the proceedings a poll was taken of the individual delegates to see how they stood, but the rule was adopted that none of these votes were to be recorded lest delegates be embarrassed if they later changed their minds as the discussion progressed.

4. Each delegate could speak only twice on each issue until after everyone else had been given the opportunity to speak. And no one could speak more than twice without special permission of the convention members.

5. Everyone was expected to pay strict attention to what was being said. There was to be no reading of papers, books, or documents while someone was speaking.

6. All remarks were to be addressed to the president of the convention and not to the members of the convention. This was to avoid heated polemics between individuals engaging in direct confrontation.

The Fifteen Resolves

It was Tuesday, May 29, after the delegations from nine states had arrived and all of the preliminaries had been arranged, that Governor Edmund Randolph of Virginia arose and introduced the "Fifteen Resolves" which had been prepared by the delegation from his state.

The convention then followed a procedure which greatly facilitated informal discussion of each issue. It resolved itself into a "committee of the whole." George Washington stepped down from the chair and Nathaniel Gorham replaced him as chairman of the Committee of the Whole. The discussion then continued on the basis of an informal "committee" instead of a formal "convention." At any time they could resolve themselves back into the "convention" and formally vote on the matter previously decided in the committee.

This was only one of several devices employed by the convention to encourage extensive discussion and numerous straw ballots to see how they were progressing. As indicated earlier, no record was officially kept of the vote, but James Madison frequently made note of how Washington voted (Washington could vote in the committee since he was not in the chair.)

Striving for Consensus

The Founders were most anxious to get general agreement whenever possible, rather than merely a majority vote. In the Anglo-Saxon meetings the freemen did not take a vote, but kept "talking it out" until everyone or practically everyone felt satisfied. This method of trying to "talk it out" until a substantial agreement could be attained was followed in the Convention.

This is illustrated by the discussion of how to choose Senators. The Virginia Resolves wanted the House of Representatives to select Senators. Apparently the Virginia delegation was finally persuaded to change its mind, because the record says the vote in favor of having Senators appointed by the state legislatures was approved "unanimously."

Three Compromises
Before the Convention was over, the members had reached general agreement on all the major issues except three. These issues included slavery, the regulation of commerce, and the apportionment of representation for each state. All three of these problems were worked out on the basis of genuine compromise, since a consensus or general agreement could not be reached.

On June 14, the proceedings were suddenly interrupted by William Paterson of New Jersey, who asked to have the day free for the preparation of a new plan which the smaller states wished to present the following day.

The New Jersey Plan
The New Jersey Plan was laid before the Convention on Friday, June 15. William Paterson said the smaller states wanted to scrap the Virginia Resolves and go back to patching up the original Articles of Confederation. He then presented the New Jersey Plan.

The following day, James Wilson of Pennsylvania compared the Virginia Plan and the New Jersey Plan point by point:

Hamilton's Plan
While those at the Convention were contemplating the two different plans, Alexander Hamilton suddenly arose and presented an entirely different plan of his own. He said it was too dangerous to tread untried waters. It would be best to go back to the British pattern. He recommended:

1. A single executive chosen for life by electors from the states. He wanted the President to have an absolute veto over any legislation, similar to the veto power of the king of England.

2. Senators were also to be chosen for life, similar to the English House of Lords.

3. The House of Representatives would be chosen by the people for a term of three years.

4. Governors of the states would be appointed by the federal government, just as the king of England did before the Revolution.

Madison noted that Hamilton's plan was "approved by all and supported by none." It was not even discussed, let alone voted upon.

Madison's Plea

On June 19, a moving speech was given by James Madison, in which he said the convention must come up with a "Constitution for the Ages" and only the Virginia Plan would stand the test of time. Immediately afterwards, the New Jersey Plan was voted down and Hamilton's plan was abandoned. Hamilton even abandoned it himself and returned to New York soon after. However, he came back before the Convention adjourned.

After June 19, the Convention tried to probe some of the more delicate questions which had previously been postponed. This is known as the crisis period and lasted clear up until July 26.[24]

Franklin's Historic Call For Prayer

During that crisis period, when the temperature and tempers threatened to go through the ceiling, eighty-one-year-old Benjamin Franklin, the second-most-respected man in the colonies, rose to make what has become a famous plea: that prayers be held in the assembly every morning before delegates proceeded with the agenda. In his address he also requested that one or more of the city's clergy be present to officiate in that service. Prayers have opened both houses of Congress ever since.[25]

Shortly thereafter the Connecticut Compromise was presented by delegate Roger Sherman (a dedicated Christian and Bible student), who called for each state to share equal representation in the Senate and allow the House of Representatives to be based on population. After much debate, this plan was adopted. It seemed to diffuse many of the differences among the delegates from the large and small states.

During the month of August, many other differences were hammered out, and on September eighth the rough draft was turned over to a special committee on style, headed by Gouverneur Morris of Pennsylvania, for a final rewrite.

Much of the credit for the final wording of the Constitution is attributed to Gouverneur Morris, an attorney and skilled penman, who completed his task in four days. Some of the delegates were surprised when they saw the words of the preamble that contained a term that may not have been used to that time but is today a national treasure. "We the People of the United States, in Order to form a more perfect Union, establish Justice, insure domestic Tranquility, provide for the common Defence, Promote the general Welfare, and secure the Blessings of Liberty to ourselves and our Posterity, do ordain and establish this Constitution, for the United States of America."

It is said that even Gouverneur Morris was at first fearful that the expression "United States" would fan the flames of antifederalism, for the people did not yet think of themselves as a united country. But in the providence of God, accept it they did, and today it is an apt description of this great nation.

Most historians agree that few if any of the delegates had any idea that they had just drafted one of the greatest documents of its kind in human history. In fact, the refusal of some to sign it suggests that they considered it an inferior document. And some may have been depressed at the results of their labors, for every man in the room had to compromise many principles he held dear in order to serve "the common good." On the last day of the Convention, Benjamin Franklin gave one of his finest speeches in pleading for its support. In it he expressed the heart of all the delegates: that the Constitution wasn't perfect, but it was the best that could be formulated, and if it should fail of adoption, the country would drift further into anarchy, chaos, and bloodshed.

"On this last day the great Washington addressed the delegates for the only time during the entire Convention: 'Should the states reject this excellent Constitution,' he said, 'the probability is that an opportunity will never again offer to cancel another in peace — the next will be drawn in blood.' "[26]

Ratifying the Constitution

No one expected ratification of the new Constitution to be easy. Although winning the approval of all thirteen states took over eighteen months, the process went surprisingly well and brought the country together at the same time. It was almost as if the divine hand of Providence, which had brought the struggling colonists through the war, was still guiding them. For in the state-by-state education process necessary to secure ratification, they were able to instruct the general population on the nature of their new laws.

It was a stroke of genius (or the result of God's providence) that the delegates decided that each state should hold a special convention to which they would elect delegates to either approve or disapprove the document. They also avoided the foolhardy path of the framers of the Articles of Confederation, who had required a unanimous vote for approving anything (which successfully puts control in the hands of one state). Instead, they called for a two-thirds vote of the states or, in this case, nine votes.

Typical of the democratic process, the Constitution was being widely discussed in pulpit, press, and state assemblies even before the delegates adjourned on September 17. Surprisingly, five states approved it quickly between December 7, 1787, and January 9, 1788. Delaware, New Jersey, and Georgia did so unanimously, probably because they received their treasured equal representation in the Senate. Connecticut ratified by a vote of 128 to 40, Pennsylvania after heated debate by a vote of 46 to 23. By June 21, 1788, Massachusetts, Maryland, South Carolina, and New Hampshire followed suit, bringing the total to nine.

Technically, that made it two-thirds, so the new government could now be formed. However, there was a problem. Virginia and New York, two of the largest and most influential states, had not yet approved it, and few people believed that the new nation would succeed without their concurrence.

Virginia experienced a long and informative debate, led in opposition by the scholarly George Mason, one of the delegates who attended but refused to sign, and the ardent oratory of Patrick Henry. On the other side were the frail but respected scholar James Madison and the highly esteemed George Washington. What finally won the 89 to 79 approval (just four days after New Hampshire ratified) was not so much the brilliance of the arguments but the announcement by Washington that he would serve as the first President if elected, along with the guarantee that a bill of rights would be added.

The Federalist Papers

New York, the great financial center of the colonies, was the last of the large states to approve. Lansing and Yates, two of New York's delegates who returned home in opposition to the new Constitution even before it was completed, joined forces with Governor Clinton to oppose it. The brilliant Alexander Hamilton led what was dubbed "the federalist charge." Assisted by John Jay and others, writing under the pseudonym "Publius," Hamilton began to publish essays as articles in the press. He invited Jay and Madison to join him in putting forth some of the ablest arguments in favor of the Constitution ever written. These articles, later were published as *The Federalist*, have provided lawyers, historians, and countless others with the nation's leading commentary on the Constitution. One historian has called them "the most important American contribution to the literature of political theory." Not until the federalists promised to agree to support amendments for a bill of rights, however, did New York approve the Constitution, and even then by only a slim margin of 30 to 27 on July 26, 1788.

North Carolina and Rhode Island were so opposed to a union that it was some time after the new government had been in operation before they joined the other states in their approval — North Carolina by a wide margin in November, 1789, Rhode Island by a narrow margin in May of 1790.

The Bill of Rights

James Madison, probably to fulfill his and other federalist promises made during the ratification process, rose early in the first Congress to propose the first ten amendments to the Constitution, which became the Constitution's Bill of Rights.

In fairness to these Founding Fathers, they didn't originally omit these because they lacked an interest in individual rights, but rather, as Roger Sherman had stated, because such provisions already existed in the different state constitutions. For this same reason they did not appear in the Articles of Confederation. Whereas the Articles had left most of the power in the hands of the states, however, under the new Constitution much of the power would pass to the federal government. For that reason the people demanded explicit guarantees that would legally protect them from a powerful central government—even their own. And history has proved that this was another evidence of "the divine hand of Providence." Can you imagine the level to which freedom in America would have sunk today without the first amendment? An overactive ACLU and seven secular-humanist Supreme Court justices, like those who voted in favor of Roe v. Wade in 1973, could have seriously injured individual rights by now.

The Bill of Rights is a distinct yet integral part of our Constitution. These ten provisions are to the Constitution what the Ten Commandments are to the Judeo-Christian religions.

The first amendment is the most important—which is why it is listed first. Every American should memorize it. "Congress shall make no law respecting an establishment of religion, or prohibiting the free exercise thereof; or abridging the freedom of speech, or of the press; or the right of the people peaceably to assemble, and to petition the Government for a redress of grievances."

What About Separation of Church and State?

Most Americans are surprised to learn that "separation of church and state" does not appear in the Constitution. In fact, the word "church" appears *nowhere* in that document.

No constitutional restriction was placed on the church. Instead, all limitations were imposed on the role of government. Eleven years after the Constitution was first adopted, it was Thomas Jefferson who brought up the "wall of separation" between church and state. Even then, however, he was referring to a wall that kept government out of the church—not church or church people out of government!

During the past fifty years or so, the ACLU and other liberal or secular-humanistic organizations have turned the meaning and intention of that statement upside down. If they could, they would remove all religious and moral values and symbols from our public life—in the name of the first amendment. The irony of this is that the amendment was written specifically to protect us from that very possibility. One hopes that the next generation of Christians and other religious citizens, unlike their fathers, will recognize that the legal profession and the political arena are worthy contexts in which to serve both God and their country. Until we have proportional representation of Christians and religious people in these important areas, we will continue to see our once-religious nation secularized under the pretense of protecting the first amendment.

THE NEW NATIONAL GOVERNMENT

It was agreed that Congress would assemble on March 4, 1789. Largely due to the long distances and arduous methods of travel in that day, it was not until March 30 that they gained the required quorum of representatives, and it was April 6 before the Senate had enough members present to examine the ballots of the presidential electors.

George Washington received sixty-nine votes and became

President. John Adams, with thirty-four votes, second in the balloting, was named Vice President. Eight years later John Adams became our second President. Again the "strong hand of Providence" selected two men who unashamedly proclaimed their faith in God and in His Son Jesus Christ, to lead the new nation through her formative stages.

> He [George Washington] reached New York in time to be inaugurated on April 30, 1789. Stepping out onto the out-door balcony of Federal Hall, in full view of the assembled multitude, he requested that a Bible be brought. Having placed his right hand on the open book, he took the oath of office. And then, embarrassed at the thunderous ovation which followed, the pealing church bells, and the roaring of artillery, the new President went inside to deliver his inaugural address to Congress. Speaking with a gravity which verged on sadness, his voice deep and tremulous, he went further than he had ever gone before in stressing the role of God in the birth of the nation: "It would be peculiarly improper to omit, in this first official act, my fervent supplication to that Almighty Being, who rules over the universe, who presides in the councils of nations, and whose providential aids can supply every

THE INAUGURATION OF GEORGE WASHINGTON
(APRIL 30, 1789)

human defect, that His benediction may consecrate to the
liberties and happiness of the people of the United States.
. . . No people, can be bound to acknowledge and adore
the invisible hand which conducts the affairs of men more
than the people of the United States. Every step by which
they have advanced to the character of an independent
nation seems to have been distinguished by some token of
providential agency. . . . We ought to be no less persuaded that the propitious smiles of Heaven can never be
expected on a nation that disregards the eternal rules of
order and right, which Heaven itself has ordained."[27]

During the next eight years the sober, prayerful judgment
of this great man established the governing foundation for the
new nation. In the providence of God and the effective administration of our first President, the United States got off to a
good start.

The Constitution, including the Bill of Rights, is the primary document that serves as our political foundation. William
Gladstone, one of Britain's greatest prime ministers, called it
"the most wonderful work ever struck off at a given time by the
brain and purpose of man."[28]

There was clearly more involved than human brain power.
For the Founding Fathers who wrote this document were not a
collection of atheists or unbelieving secularists filled with
Enlightenment thoughts. Only a few were deists, and even these
were a far cry from the atheistic humanists of today. The
eighteenth-century deists who were numbered among the delegates had a vital faith in, and an awareness of, a personal God
whom they often addressed as "divine Providence." These men
believed that within the sovereign will of God, He occasionally
intervened in the affairs of men. Most of the delegates, as I have
indicated, were committed Christians with a love for and knowledge of the Word of God, men who included God in their thinking in all affairs, particularly those of government. Even if they
weren't committed Christians, they reflected to a man the Biblical philosophy so prevalent in their day. It would have been
impossible for these men to fashion a Constitution that wasn't
based on Biblical principles, for they represented their own prin-

ciples of life as well as the convictions of those citizens who would ratify and implement the Constitution.

The late Dean Manion, former head of the Notre Dame law school has urged,

> Look closely at these self-evident truths, these imperishable articles of American Faith upon which all our government is firmly based. First and foremost is the existence of God. Next comes the truth that all men are equal in the sight of God. Third is the fact of God's great gift of unalienable rights to every person on earth. Then follows the true and single purpose of all American Government, namely, to preserve and protect these God-made rights of God-made man.[29]

America: A Miracle Nation

Whenever I study the history of America, I am conscious that we are a miracle nation. It was a miracle that Columbus found this part of the world. It was a miracle that the early colonists survived and built a nation during those first 156 years. It was a miracle that they rebelled against the motherland, and even a greater miracle that they won the Revolutionary War against overwhelming odds. It was a miracle they survived the confederacy period (1774-89), and still another that they founded "upon this continent a new nation dedicated to the proposition that all men are created equal"[30] — equal under God, and equal before the law. It is still a miracle that this nation exists today as a strong and free people.

What was the purpose of this "miracle nation" that some call "manifest destiny"? Many things, one of which would be that God would establish one nation that would do more to fulfill His basic objective for this age, to "preach the gospel to the ends of the earth," than any other nation in history. By guaranteeing religious freedom to all, this nation has enabled more people to go to the uttermost parts of the world than all the other western nations put together. And now, at the time of the world's greatest population and the world's greatest technological explosion, it is no accident that millions of Christians are willing to send billions of dollars with their sons and daughters to proclaim God's message of love to the ends of the earth. Perhaps that is the main purpose for the existence of this miracle nation.

At the conclusion of the Constitutional Convention, George Washington declared, "We have raised a standard to which the good and wise can repair; the event is in the hands of God."[31]

And it still is!

THE CHRISTIAN CONSENSUS OF AMERICA IN 1787

Edmund Burke, the outstanding orator and a leader in Great Britain during the time of the Revolutionary War, understood clearly the relationship between Christianity and the hunger for freedom of the American colonists. Said he to Parliament in 1770:

> *The people are Protestants*; and of that kind which is the most adverse to all implicit submission of mind and opinion. . . . This is a persuasion not only favorable to Liberty, but built upon it. . . . All Protestantism, even the most cold and passive, is a sort of dissent. But the religion most prevalent in our northern colonies is a refinement on the principle of resistance; it is the dissidence of dissent, and the protestantism of the Protestant religion.

America's Constitution is a magnificent document, worthy of five years of bicentennial celebration. This wouldn't be the case, however, if our predominantly Christian Founding Fathers hadn't rejected the enlightenment theories of Europe, with their ideas of unrestrained democracy. Instead, the accurate view of a fallen and unreliable human nature provided by the Bible caused them to establish a limited government, with a system of checks and balances and the guarantee of a bill of rights. All together, this guaranteed freedom with responsibility. The reason these wise men understood what the secularists of the Enlightenment could not, was the permeating influence of the Christian consensus of their day. This consensus, as stated earlier, had developed during the preceding 167 years of the colonial period and was the dominant philosophy at the time of the Founding Fathers.

What is a Christian Consensus?

Christianity is not a passive faith that occupies only a person's theological speculations. It involves everything he does. The early Christians were called "followers of the way" before they were ever called Christians, because Christianity is a way of life. And that way of life had so permeated this nation by 1787 that it extended its influence to every area, including the fields of law, government, morality, marriage, and business.

Although many different denominations are included within the spectrum of Christianity, non-Christians often fail to realize that in spite of theological differences, there is a great deal of consensus or agreement on basic doctrines, and almost universal agreement on appropriate cultural-moral values. That cultural consensus is apparent to anyone who will examine the historical facts. America is often labelled "a Christian nation" not because it was founded as such, but because its Founding Fathers were either Christians or had been influenced throughout their entire lives by the Christian consensus that surrounded them. In the next two chapters, we shall examine a number of areas, and we shall see that in these areas Christian influence was so much a part of national life that it couldn't help but affect the thinking of the Founding Fathers as they laid the foundation for this nation.

The Predominantly Christian Population of 1787

Christians have been criticized for referring to this country as a Christian nation. While it wasn't technically established for the advancement of the kingdom of God, many of the original colonies were. The more than four million citizens who shared in the founding of this republic were not only Christian, but also overwhelmingly Protestant. Even the state of Maryland, which was founded in part as a refuge for persecuted Catholics, welcomed very few Catholic immigrants prior to the Revolutionary War. It was another seventy years before Catholic immigration became pronounced. The Jewish community, settling mainly in

New York and Rhode Island, made up less than one-tenth of one percent of the colonial population.

The diversity in the makeup of the Protestant population appears in this analysis:

> At the outbreak of the Revolution some 20 per cent of the colonial churches were Congregational and another 20 per cent were Presbyterian. Anglicans and Baptists each claimed about 15 per cent of the total; the Society of Friends, about 10 per cent. Perhaps 5 per cent were German Reformed and another 5 per cent were Lutheran. Smaller groups included the Dutch Reformed, the Methodists, and German Pietist sects like the Moravians, Dunkers, and Mennonites. Not all the larger bodies were firmly united; Congregationalists and Presbyterians had split into New Light and Old Light factions, and there were already several varieties of Baptist[s].[32]

As one historian of that period wrote,

> It is significant that most of the Founding Fathers grew up in a strong religious atmosphere; many had Calvinist family backgrounds. . . . Not all the founders acknowledged a formal faith, but it was significant that their view of man had a deeply religious foundation. Rights were "God-given"; man was "endowed by his Creator"; there were "natural laws" and "natural rights"; freedom was related to the "sacredness" of man. The development of a free man was not divorced from the idea of moral man. There was also strong spiritual content in the confidence of the American founders in the capacity of man to govern his own affairs, to hold the ultimate power in the operation of his society, and to be able to decide correctly when given access to vital information.[33]

In few places of the world have religious convictions been so fiercely maintained as they were in America during the period of her founding. The reason? The most common motive for coming to this land among the original settlers was their quest for religious freedom. Most of them originated from countries having a state-approved religion, where all other religions were outlawed, and thus adherents were persecuted. Originally, most of the colonies were founded by a particular sect (denomination). During the sixteen-decade colonial period, however, "dissenters," or Christians of other persuasions became so numerous that they often outnumbered the established church in a given state. At least seven states had officially established religions or denominations at the time the Constitution was adopted, and only in the previous year had Virginia discontinued its policy of providing tax support to the Anglican church.

At the risk of being accused of not recognizing that America today is a religiously pluralistic nation, I must point out that this country was not only an overwhelmingly Protestant nation when it was founded in 1787, but it remained so until the mid-1800s. Two centuries later, as a result of the immigration of millions of European and Hispanic Catholics, millions of European Jews, plus many others, including some from Eastern and Oriental cults, we are indeed a religiously diverse nation of almost 240 million people.

Yet Christianity still prevails. A 1986 Gallup poll on religion indicates that eighty-one percent of the American people (including the unchurched) identify themselves as Christian. And, while they would differ greatly in some of their theological views, there is considerable agreement in their position on traditional social values. Evidence for this can be seen in a recent poll indicating that seventy-two percent of the American people would like to see a "return to what President Ronald Reagan calls 'traditional values.'" Let there be no misunderstanding; while these "traditional values" would not be as strictly enforced by today's Americans, they are still the Judeo-Christian values upon which this country was founded. (For a detailed description of the powerful influence the Christian religion exerted on the colonies in 1787, see Appendix C.)

The Puritan Influence on Our Check and Balance System

Authorities agree that the most ingenious part of our Constitution is the check and balance system. What they don't realize is that we owe that primarily to the influence of the Puritans and

John Calvin. According to one historian, before Americans can understand themselves, they must recognize the enormous contributions made by the Puritans to their life and society two hundred years ago.

We have already seen that the new nation was religiously diverse. But the overwhelming number of adherents, particularly those who took their religious life seriously, were Puritan Calvinists. Puritan theology wasn't limited to the New England churches, but was also prominent in the Congregational, Presbyterian, Dutch Reformed, and Lutheran churches, as well as to some extent in many of the dissident groups, including the Baptists.

To this new land Puritans brought not only their obsession for religious freedom and a commitment to hard work, but an equal commitment to family life and morals as well. They also had a deep passion for teaching the younger generation to read so they could understand the Word of God. In addition, they were committed to the need for self-government, in contrast to the theory of the "divine right of kings." They demanded leaders responsible to the people who respected God's laws for society as laid down in the Bible. In fact, it was the ministers of Puritan and Calvinistic theology who did the most to justify the colonists' revolt from the tyranny of King George III. Many historians have noted that without the support of the colonial ministry, there wouldn't have been a Revolutionary War.

At the time our nation was founded, however, the most significant doctrine brought to the Constitutional Convention by the Founding Fathers was the Calvinistic belief regarding the total depravity of man and his innate tendency to sinfulness. This translates into the realization that human beings cannot be trusted — particularly those with power, like government leaders.

If our Founding Fathers had been smitten with the idealism of the Enlightenment, the check and balance system would never have been written into our Constitution, and we would have established the same unstable form of government experienced by France, which has endured seven different governmental systems during the two hundred years that America has enjoyed only one.

This country was the first major nation to incorporate into

its official documents the principle that no leader, be he President, king, Supreme Court justice, or other official, is above the law. That is why the Founders created three distinct and independent branches of government, each checking on the other.

1. *The Executive* (a President elected by the people). This individual administers the government within the guidelines laid out in the Constitution and affirmed by Congress.

2. *The Legislative* (made up of senators and congressmen elected by the people). The legislative branch makes our laws, approves the budget, and establishes guidelines for defense policies.

3. *The Judicial* (nine Supreme Court justices appointed for life). The judicial branch determines what is legal according to the Constitution.

This check and balance system has kept tyrants from assuming totalitarian control over our people, and we owe that blessing to the Calvinistic theology that had permeated the colonies at the time the Constitution was written. James Madison's copious notes on the Constitutional Convention reveal that the desire for such a "check and balance" was never in question. Our Founding Fathers were not naive about the untrustworthiness of human nature.

A constitutional attorney friend of mine may be only slightly exaggerating when he calls our Constitution "John Calvin's Constitution," for as he says, it was influenced more by Calvin than any other single individual.

The Lingering Effects of the Great Awakening

Just fifty years before the founding of this nation, a spiritual revival that swept through the colonies had a profound effect on its people. Some historians claim that it sparked a fire providing the moral courage and spiritual faith in God that enabled them to fight for freedom while facing overwhelming odds in 1776. In addition, it generated the staying power that gave the freedom fighters strength to endure the hardships of seven years of war and deprivation.

Prior to 1737, the established church had become complacent. Children were not as responsive to the reality of religious experience that was enjoyed by their parents, and worldliness had crept into the day-to-day experiences of many. Gradually that changed under the fiery preaching of the revivalists, beginning with Jonathan Edwards's celebrated sermon in New England and then fueled by the preaching of George Whitefield and the Wesleys. The spontaneous moving of the Spirit of God in response to the faithful preaching of the Word has left a mark on the religious life of this nation that can still be felt today.

Thousands of people flocked to the preaching of "dissident" or "illegal" preachers — ministers who were not of the "approved," or state, churches. Christianity became a real and intensely personal experience. The movement spread to independent churches such as Methodists and Baptists, which have become the predominant force in Protestantism today. The Great Awakening not only affected the church life of the colonists, but had a profound effect on the moral and social life of the country as well.

State-Approved and Tax-Supported Churches and Election Laws That Required Legislators to Be Christians in 1787

One point overlooked by modern secularizers of our religious heritage is that most of the Convention's delegates came from states having established churches. Some even required voting tests that eliminated citizens who did not believe in Jesus Christ and the Holy Scriptures from being considered for election to public office. We realize, of course, that such tests would be considered both illegal and harmful to the nation today, but they do highlight the religious nature of the country at the time of its founding. If these men had really been atheists and unbelievers, they would not have been elected to represent their states.

At the time of the ratification of the First Amendment in 1791, many of the colonies were supporting a single church or religion. As Supreme Court Justice Hugo Black grudgingly acknowledged in the Supreme Court's 1962 decision banning devotional prayer from the public schools: "indeed, as late as the time of the Revolutionary War, there were established churches in at least eight of the thirteen former colonies and established religions in at least four of the other five." Moreover, this trend in some form continued in the individual states throughout the

early part of the nineteenth century. For example, Massachusetts paid the salaries of the Congregational ministers
in that state until 1833.[34]

The state of Maryland, hardly considered a hotbed of New
England Puritanism, nevertheless passed a Declaration of
Rights on August 14, 1776, after the Declaration of Independence was signed. The Declaration included the following test for
state officials:

> XXXV. That no other test or qualification ought to be
> required, on admission to any office of trust or profit,
> than such oath of support and fidelity to this State, and
> such oath of office, as shall be directed by this Conven-
> tion, or the Legislature of this State, and a declaration of
> a belief in the Christian religion.

> XXXVI. That the manner of administering an oath to
> any person, ought to be such, as those of the religious per-
> suasion, profession, or denomination, of which such per-
> son is one, generally esteem the most effectual confirma-
> tion, by the attestation of the Divine Being.[35]

This was adopted only eleven years before the Founding
Fathers gathered in Philadelphia. Maryland was not alone, however, for the majority of the states had similar laws. The writers
of the Constitution did not address the religious test requirements already on the books of most states. They made no such
requirements of the federal officers in the Constitution, leaving
such matters to state law. As it turned out, several states continued making such requirements long after the Constitution
was ratified.

The Christian Education System of that Day
One of the most abiding concerns of the earliest Christian
settlers in this country was education—not just the education of
the children of the elite, as was customary in Europe, but everyone's child. These Christians brought us our first printing press,
and as we have seen, our country's first 126 colleges, including

the very first, Harvard. While visiting Harvard University several years ago, I was impressed by the following inscription, which remains to this day on the wall by the old iron gate at the main entrance to the campus.

> After God had carried us safe to New England and we had builded our houses, provided necessaries for our livelihood, reared convenient places for God's worship and settled the civil government, one of the next things we longed for and looked after was to advance learning and perpetuate it to posterity, dreading to leave an illiterate ministry to the churches when our present ministers lie in the dust.

As mentioned earlier, it was not uncommon for ministers to serve as local school teachers, particularly in small cities. Even so, the graduates of Harvard, Princeton, and Yale, very evangelical colleges at the time, produced a majority of the nation's school teachers, who were very familiar with and taught Biblical truth and Judeo-Christian moral absolutes in the classroom.

Textbooks During that Period
The New England Primer (1737) was a common book in schools throughout the colonies. It was filled with religious teachings like the following, which were used to illustrate the letters when introducing children to the alphabet:

> A: In Adam's fall
> we sinned all;
>
> Z: Zacchaeus he
> Did climb a tree
> His Lord to see.

The children imbibed Calvinist religious principles from A to Z. . . . *Thomas Dilworth's New Guide to the English Tongue*, first published in London in 1740, had attained by 1765 a universal adoption in New England schools. This book contained a series of spelling and reading lessons, and a short grammar. Ten fables, "adorned with proper Sculptures," that is, wood engravings, served as incentives for students to reach the end of the book. Like the *New-England Primer* Dilworth's textbook was a handmaid to religion, its first reading lesson, consisting of words not exceeding three letters, being,

> "No Man may put off the Law of God.
> The Way of God is no ill Way.
> My Joy is in God all the Day.
> A bad Man is a Foe to God."

Nearly all the sentences, and the fables as well, turn upon religious duties, and the words, God and Lord, recur hundreds of times. Dilworth wanted to rescue "poor creatures from the Slavery of Sin and Satan" by setting "the word of God for a Lantern to our Feet and a Light to our Paths." The Psalter or Bible was the only other Book used in Webster's earliest school.[36]

The most influential man in the United States in the field of education at the founding of our country was Noah Webster. A brilliant scholar and dedicated Christian, he produced the nation's official spellers, dictionaries (which still bear his name), and books on learning and government, books used for more than one hundred years. He was known as "the schoolmaster of the Nation." The following passages will give you a sense of Webster's philosophy of learning, a philosophy that characterized the American educational system attended by many of the Founding Fathers and prevailing long after they were dead.

> Along with good habits of work, Webster wished students to acquire "good principles," a predisposition for a virtuous life. "For this reason society requires that the education of youth should be watched with the most scrupulous attention. Education, in a great measure, forms the moral characters of men, and morals are the basis of government. Education should therefore be the first care of a legislature; not merely the institution of schools, but the

furnishing of them with the best men for teachers. A good system of education should be the first article in the code of political regulations; for it is much easier to introduce and establish an effectual system for preserving morals, than to correct by penal statutes the ill effects of a bad system." On this point Webster was emphatic; he asserted: "The goodness of a heart is of infinitely more consequence to society than an elegance of manners; nor will any superficial accomplishments repair the want of principle in the mind. It is always better to be *vulgarly* right than *politely* wrong. . . . The education of youth [is] an employment of more consequence than making laws and preaching the gospel, because it lays the foundation on which both law and gospel rest for success."[37]

Verna Hall described Webster's contribution to education as follows:

Noah Webster established no system of education but rather provided tools for the individual's self-education. The first tool, the American Spelling Book, became the most popular book in American Education. The famous "blue-backed speller" set a publishing record of a million copies a year for one hundred years. These little books were worn out by Americans as they learned their "letters," their morality and their patriotism, from north to south, from east to west.

Noah Webster's Speller was compatible with the hearthside of a log cabin in the wilderness, or a city classroom. It travelled on the flatboats of the Ohio River, churned down the Mississippi and creaked across the prairies of the far west as pioneer mothers taught their children from covered wagons. Wherever the individual wished to challenge his own ignorance or quench his thirst for knowledge, there, along with the Holy Bible and Shakespeare, were Noah Webster's slim and inexpensive Spellers, Grammars, Readers and his *Elements of Useful Knowledge* containing the history and geography of the United States.

Webster's books were unlike texts seen today, for they openly presented Biblical admonitions, as well as principles of American government. In one of his early editions of the "blue-backed speller" appeared a *Moral Catechism*—rules upon which to base moral conduct. Webster stated unequivocally, "God's Word, contained in the Bible, has furnished all necessary rules to direct our conduct."[38]

The Christian consensus of our nation's school system and textbooks is further evidenced by the widespread acceptance of Reverend William H. McGuffey's readers, which became a mainstay in public education fifty years *after* the Constitution was ratified. They attest to the fact that the educated citizenry, of which all the Founding Fathers were members, were very familiar with Christian truth. While in some classrooms an occasional college might import old world "Enlightenment" theories hostile to traditional Christian teachings, there is no evidence that they were widespread at the time. Even Harvard College, one of the first to adopt such theories, did not hire its first Unitarian-humanist president until twenty-seven years later.

As we shall see when we examine them individually, most of the Constitutional Convention delegates were graduates of colleges founded by or sponsored by religious groups. All of these men, by education, church instruction, and personal commitment, were thoroughly conversant with Christian teachings and when they spoke of morality, values, or tradition, they meant the prevailing Judeo-Christian concepts of morals, not only for individuals but also for government and society. James Madison, referred to as "the father of the Constitution," was one of at least three Convention delegates who had studied for the ministry before he took up the study of law. His definition of religion probably represented the thinking of ninety-five percent of the Founding Fathers when he said that religion is "the duty we owe our creator."[39]

Summary

This is only part of the convincing evidence that the culture of America two hundred years ago was overwhelmingly Christian. When they spoke of religion they meant the Christian religion. When they mentioned morality it was what we know as the Judeo-Christian moral code. When they referred to education they meant learning from a God-centered base that made ample use of the Bible. Christianity was welcome in the schools and textbooks in 1787 and for one hundred years thereafter. The Christian consensus was so strong when this nation was founded that it is no wonder that many erroneously call this "a Christian nation." Nowhere is that Christian consensus more prevalent than in the field of law. This is evidenced by the major legal documents in use at the time the fifty-five delegates founded this nation. We will see the extent of that influence in our next chapter.

SEVEN

THE CHRISTIAN UNDERSTANDING OF CIVIL LAW

All law is based on something, either man's principles or God's. English law was a combination of Roman-Biblical law that had little Enlightenment influence. Colonial law was far more Biblical and, in some cases, even theocratic. Usually it was conceived with the desire for self-rule based on humanity's moral responsibility to God. It would be impossible to overestimate the influence of the Bible on the Founding Fathers before and after they wrote the Constitution. The following evidences of the influence of both the Bible and Christianity on law, government, and society will help put it in perspective.

The Influence of the Bible

The Framers of the Constitution were not unaware that they were preparing a document for a citizenry that overwhelmingly revered the Bible as ultimate authority. At that time, it was referred to as the higher law, or common law. The colonists believed that the Bible was relevant to every important aspect of life. From the Bible they derived their obsession with individual freedom. This "Christian world view," as the late Dr. Francis Schaeffer referred to it, has been described by one historian in these words:

A Christian world and life view furnished the basis for this early political thought which guided the American people for nearly two centuries and whose crowning lay in the writing of the Constitution of 1787. This Christian theism had so permeated the colonial mind that it continued to guide even those who had come to regard the Gospel with indifference or even hostility. The currents of this orthodoxy were too strong to be easily set aside by those who in their own thinking had come to a different conception of religion and hence of government also.[40]

Attorney John Whitehead described it well in saying,

The first type of law is the *fundamental law* upon which the culture and society are established. This fundamental law may be equated with the "higher law," which should be "the Laws of Nature and of Nature's God." The higher law is clearly expressed in God's revelation as ultimately found in the Bible. In this the higher law has its sustenance.

The second type of law, *constitutional law*, provides the form of civil government to protect the God-given rights of the people. The people can base their institutions upon constitutional law, in conjunction with the higher or fundamental law. Although the Constitution is undergirded by an absolute value system, it is not a source of ultimate values.[41]

The bottom line is that man's law must have its origin in God's revelation. Any law that contradicts biblical revelation is illegitimate. Illegitimate law, as the colonists protested to King George, was "of none effect." After all, it is the Creator who endows man with rights, which the law is to protect. Succinctly put, there is a law, a system of absolutes, derived from biblical principles that transcends man and his institutions. It existed before man and will exist after him.[42]

The Founding Fathers believed that God is the ultimate source of law. This was also the belief of the people whom these delegates represented in 1787, as demonstrated by the fact that seventy years later, when the issue of slavery came into obvious conflict with their Biblical beliefs (that "all men were created equal" before God and the law), the Constitution was interpreted in light of Biblical principles.

The Common Law and the Ten Commandments

John Whitehead writes further:

> Essentially common law is an age-old doctrine that developed by way of court decisions that applied the principles of the Bible to everyday situations. Judges simply decided their cases, often by making explicit reference to the Bible but virtually always within a framework of biblical values. Out of these cases, rules were established that governed future cases.

> The common law was important in the constitutional sense in that it was incorporated into the Constitution by direct reference in the Seventh Amendment. This amendment reads: "In suits at common law, where the value in controversy shall exceed twenty dollars, the right of trial by jury, shall be preserved; and no fact tried by jury, shall be otherwise re-examined in any court of the United States than according to the rules of common law." By implication this means that the framers intended to be governed in practice as well as in principle by the higher law. . . .

> Episcopalian theologian T. R. Ingram has observed that the reference point for the common law was in the Ten Commandments: "Christian men have always known that what we might call political liberty as part of all Christian liberty is a consequence of upholding the common law . . . the Ten Commandments."[43]

> Americans, who have been fed the false political dictum of the absolute separation of church and state, will probably be surprised to discover that even the first four of the Ten Commandments, those having to do with man's "religious" duty toward God, were once included without question in the law of America. They were not perceived as creating an unconstitutional "establishment of religion." In many states there were laws against blasphemy.

Although we may not agree with such laws, they were originally designed not only to honor God but also to uphold the authority of the state to act with the Bible as its reference point.[44]

Whitehead points out that after the Constitution was completed, most of the Ten Commandments were written into the law without violating the Constitution. For instance, the observance of Sunday as a day of worship, a carryover of the Christian custom based on the Fourth Commandment, was a legal weekly holiday for 175 years after the drafting of the Constitution. Not until 1961, when a secularized Supreme Court voted to strike down "blue laws," was Sunday designated a secular day of rest. But in the process, these laws were acknowledged as Christian in origin.[45]

The Awesome Influence of Four Devout Christians on the Colonial Understanding of Law

As we have already seen, most of the Framers of the Constitution were lawyers or men who had studied law either formally or personally. Consequently, they were all familiar with, and to some extent influenced by, the same four brilliant minds: Samuel Rutherford, John Witherspoon, John Locke, and William Blackstone. Two of these men were ministers of the gospel; the other two were dedicated Christian laymen. All four were frequent Bible readers whose minds were saturated with Biblical, or higher, law.

This influence had a profound effect on the writing of the Constitution. With his permission, I'll let Attorney John Whitehead tell the story.

Christian theism teaches that man is held accountable to his Creator. Absolute standards exist by which all moral judgments of life are to be measured. With the Bible, there is a standard of right and wrong. These fundamental principles made up the Reformation world view. They were passed on in substance and without significant alteration to the American colonies through the influence of a book written by Samuel Rutherford, *Lex, Rex or, the Law and the Prince (1644)*.

Government under Biblical Law

Lex, Rex challenged the fundamental principle of seven-teenth-century political government in Europe: the divine right of kings. This doctrine held that the king or state ruled as God's appointed regent. Therefore, the king's word was law. (Although Scripture was seen as normative, it was the king alone who interpreted and embodied that norm.)

Counterbalanced against this position was Rutherford's assertion that the basic premise of government and, therefore, of law must be the Bible, the Word of God rather than the word of man. All men, even the king, Rutherford argued, were *under* the law and not above it. This religious concept was considered both heresy and treason and punishable as such.

Lex, Rex created an immediate controversy. It was banned in Scotland and was publicly burned in England. Ruther-ford, a Presbyterian minister who was one of the Scottish commissioners at Westminster Abbey in London and rec-tor of St. Andrew's Church in Scotland, was placed under house arrest and summoned to appear before the Parlia-ment at Edinburgh where probable execution awaited him. He died shortly before he could be made to comply with the order.

But Rutherford's ideas lived on to influence later genera-tions. His basic presupposition of government based upon the absolutes of the Bible was finally realized in colonial America through the influence of two sources: John Witherspoon and John Locke.

Witherspoon, a Presbyterian minister who had been edu-cated at Edinburgh University, brought the principles of *Lex, Rex* into the writing of the Constitution. The only clergyman to sign the Declaration of Independence, Witherspoon was a member of the Continental Congress from 1776 to 1779 and from 1780 to 1782. He played a key role on a number of the committees of the first Congress. Witherspoon's students, profoundly influenced by him, also reached positions of eminence in the Constitutional Convention and in early United States history. They included a president, James Madison; a vice president, Aaron Burr; ten cabinet officers; twenty-one senators; thirty-nine congressmen; and twelve governors, as well as other public figures.

James Madison was particularly influenced by Witherspoon. Columbia University professor Richard B. Morris writes in *Seven Who Shaped Our Destiny*: "Most influential in shaping Madison's . . . outlook was Princeton's president, John Witherspoon, a leading empiricist of his day . . . whose expositions of the doctrines of resistance and liberty quickly established him throughout the Continent as an imposing intellectual." The Witherspoon influence later played a major role in the drafting of the Constitution. In fact, Madison has been labeled "The Father of the Constitution" for his contribution in writing the founding document.

Two principles enunciated in *Lex, Rex* were drawn upon by the colonists in declaring their independence from Great Britain in 1776. First, there was the concept of the covenant or constitution between the ruler and God and the people. This covenant, Rutherford argued, could not grant the state absolute or unlimited power without violating God's law. Taking the cue from Rutherford the colonists asserted that King George had violated his covenant with God by transgressing their God-given rights.

Rutherford's second principle declared that all men are created equal. Since all men are born sinners, Rutherford reasoned that no man is superior to any other man. He established the principle of equality and liberty among men, which was later written into the Declaration of Independence.

Although John Locke secularized the Reformed tradition, he nevertheless drew heavily from it. He elaborated fundamental concepts such as unalienable rights, government by consent, the social compact (a constitution between the people and the government), separation of powers, and the right to resist unlawful authority. The biblical base for these concepts is set forth in Rutherford's

Lex, Rex. As Francis Schaeffer has noted, many "of the men who laid the foundation of the United States Constitution were not Christians in the [full] sense, and yet they built upon the basis of the Reformation either directly through the *Lex, Rex* tradition or indirectly through Locke."[46]

John Locke is frequently referred to as the legal mind that first secularized the field of law, but this often leads researchers to assume that he was a forerunner of modern humanists. Nothing could be further from the truth. Locke wrote a seldom-mentioned book entitled *A Vindication of the Reasonableness of Christianity*, and he also penned paraphrases of the books of Romans, First and Second Corinthians, Galatians, and Ephesians. Were he living today, I believe this man, regarded as one of the geniuses in his era, would employ his gifts in the defense and spread of the gospel.

John Locke must be understood in the light of his times. He had seen the travesties of injustice when the church and civil government were one and the same. He was writing against this merging of powers in favor of two distinct areas of responsibility, religion and government. For he knew, as history records, that when religious leaders can act with the power of government, they will abuse that power. His emphasis on the division of powers and the right of individuals to resist unlawful tyrants was based on his belief in a law above the king or the Constitution.

The fourth Christian legal authority who had a profound influence on colonial legal minds was William Blackstone.

The renowned, eighteenth-century English jurist William Blackstone also played a leading role in forming a Christian presuppositional base to early American law. Because the American colonists and Blackstone shared the same background of Reformation thinking, Blackstone's ideas on law were readily accepted in the colonies.

Blackstone, who was a lecturer at law at Oxford, embodied the tenets of Judeo-Christian theism in his *Commentaries on the Laws of England*, published between 1765 and 1770. The *Commentaries* were popular in Great Britain, but by 1775, more copies of the *Commentaries* had been sold in America than in all England. So influential were the *Commentaries* that historian Daniel Boorstin writes: "In the first century of American independence, the Commentaries were not merely an approach to the study of the law; for most lawyers they constituted all there was of the law."

Blackstone, a Christian, believed that the fear of the Lord was the beginning of wisdom. Thus he opened his *Commentaries* with a careful analysis of the law of God as revealed in the Bible. He defined law as a rule of action, which is prescribed by some superior, and which the inferior is bound to obey. To illustrate this definition Blackstone expressed the presuppositional base for law as he saw it:

"The doctrines thus delivered we call the revealed or divine law, and they are to be found only in the holy scriptures. Upon these two foundations, the law of nature and the law of revelation, depend all human laws; that is to say, no human laws should be suffered to contradict these."

Blackstone took it as self-evident that God is the source of all laws, whether they were found in the Holy Scriptures or were observable in nature. His presuppositions were thoroughly Christian, founded upon the belief that there existed a personal, omnipotent God who worked in and governed the affairs of men. In consequence, man was bound by those laws, which were in turn a system of absolutes. Why? Because man is a derivative being. Blackstone wrote:

"Man, considered as a creature, must necessarily be subject to the laws of his Creator, for he is entirely a dependent being. . . . And, consequently, as man depends absolutely upon his Maker for everything, it is necessary that he should in all points conform to his Maker's will."

Blackstone argued that the cultural mandate given to Adam and Eve in Genesis 1 is the basis for the right to hold private property or, for that matter, any right. In Blackstone's view, and in the eyes of those who founded the United States, every right or law comes from God, and the very words *rights, laws, freedoms*, and so on are meaningless without their divine origin.

Blackstone's influence is clearly expressed in the Declaration of Independence. The colonists argued that it is "the Laws of Nature and of Nature's God" that entitled them to independence and to an equal station among nations. Blackstone had some years earlier written that the "will of Maker is called the law of nature." And in echoing *Lex, Rex* the colonists proclaimed that "all men are created equal."

In seeking independence from Great Britain the colonists declared to the world their belief in a personal, infinite God — "their Creator" — who endowed them with "certain unalienable" or absolute rights. To the men of that time, it was self-evident that if there were no God there could be no absolute rights. Unlike the French revolutionaries a few years later, the American colonists knew very well that if the unalienable rights they were urging for were not seen in the context of Judeo-Christian theism, they were without content.

The Declaration of Independence, therefore, is structured upon a Judeo-Christian base in two fundamental ways. First, it professes faith in a "Creator" who works in and governs the affairs of men in establishing absolute standards to which men are held accountable. Second — and even more fundamentally, since all Western nations of that era professed a belief in the Creator — there is the idea that man is a fallen creature and, hence, cannot be his own lawgiver and judge. In the end it is God to whom the appeal must be made. In this sense, the law cannot be simply what a judge or a fuhrer says it is. It is what God says it is.[47]

Not only did these four legal experts have a profound effect on the thinking of our Founding Fathers, but they also influenced several generations of lawyers after them in the implementing of the Biblical principles of government that directly shaped the ideology of the Constitution.

The Influence of John Adams

Modern historians customarily mention that John Adams, our second President, had one of the keenest legal minds in America at that time. They usually omit, however, that both he and his wife were dedicated Christians and that he recommended to his son a lifetime habit of reading five chapters of the Bible each morning, which he said only took him about one hour.

One of the committee of three who were assigned the task of writing The Declaration of Independence, Adams was a careful student of law who considered government to be a "divine science." Historian Cleon Skousen writes,

> John Adams agreed with John Locke. He believed there is a "divine science" of sound government for human happiness if finite human beings could just find the pieces and put them all together. In a letter written on June 17, 1782, from Holland, Adams mentioned twice the "divine science" of politics, and this gave meaning to an earlier letter to his wife in which he said:

> "The science of government is my duty to study, more than all other sciences; the arts of legislation and administration and negotiation ought to take place of, indeed to exclude in a manner, all other arts. [Under present war conditions] I must study politics and war, that my sons may have liberty to study mathematics and philosophy. My sons ought to study mathematics and philosophy, geography, natural history and naval architecture, navigation, commerce, and agriculture [during times of peace] in order to give their children a right to study painting, poetry, music, architecture, statuary, tapestry, and porcelain."

> After the United States became a free and independent people, Adams wrote to an English friend on February 3, 1786, that he hoped "to see rising in America an empire of liberty, and a prospect of two or three hundred millions of freemen, without one noble or one king among them."

> Adams stated that as of 1776 the Founders did not know precisely what form a government of free people

should assume, but he said they did know that "happiness of society is the end of government" and happiness of the individual is the end of man. It was in this context that Jefferson said in the Declaration of Independence that every human being has an unalienable right to "life, liberty, and the pursuit of happiness."[48]

Although Adams did not attend the Constitutional Convention, he did have a profound effect upon it through his book *A Defense of the Constitutions of Government of the United States*, which was published before the Convention was convened.

It is assumed by many that Adams's book on constitutions was read by all the delegates arriving in Philadelphia, as research material for the great task that lay before them. Like all his writings and actions, Adams's book was written from his Christian world view. It is unthinkable that it didn't have a strong effect on the thinking of our Founding Fathers.

John Adams distinguished himself by serving his country well for over fifty years. He was brilliant, loyal, and deeply committed to Jesus Christ and the use of Biblical principles in governing this nation. The extent of his personal faith is evident in a letter he sent to his son John Quincy Adams (who became our sixth President) when he was the young ambassador to Russia.

"My custom is, to read four to five chapters every morning immediately after rising from my bed. It employs about an hour of my time." He urged his son to form and adopt Biblical principles of government for individual self-government: "It is essential, my son, in order that you may go through life with comfort to yourself, and usefulness to your fellow-creatures, that you should form and adopt certain rules or principles, for the government of your own conduct and temper. . . . It is in the Bible, you must learn them, and from the Bible how to practice them. Those duties are to God, to your fellow-creatures, and to your self. 'Thou shalt love the Lord thy God, with all thy heart, and with all thy soul, and with all thy mind, and with all thy strength, and thy neighbour as thyself.' On these two commandments, Jesus Christ expressly says, 'hang all the law and the prophets'; that is to say, the whole purpose of Divine Revelation is to inculcate them efficaciously upon the minds of men."[49]

The young country could hardly have found a better candidate to succeed the godly George Washington than John Adams, who served from 1798 to 1802.

The Evidence in Early American Documents

One interesting way to identify the Christian consensus that had a profound influence on the proceedings at Philadelphia in 1787 is to examine some of the official documents in those days and for some years thereafter. We'll look at only three types of such documents: many more, however, could be given.

The Northwest Ordinance of 1787

The importance attached to the role of religion by the founding fathers and other leaders appears in Article III of the Northwest Ordinance as it was passed by the Continental Congress the same year the Founding Fathers wrote the Constitution. It states, "Religion, morality, and knowledge, being necessary to good government and the happiness of mankind, schools and the means of education shall forever be encouraged."[50]

The significance of this congressionally approved statement should not escape our attention. In opening new territory to American settlers, the federal government wanted to establish the same practices that were common or desirable in the other thirteen colonies. They recognized what modern educators often ignore—that the teaching of religion is essential in producing good citizenship and moral values.

To demonstrate that such a statement reflected the popular thinking of that day, we have only to summon the testimony of President George Washington in his farewell address, which was delivered more than ten years later. He said, "Of all the dispositions and habits which lead to political prosperity, religion and morality are indispensable supports. . . . Let us with caution indulge the supposition that morality can be maintained without religion. . . . Reason and experience both forbid us to expect that National morality can prevail in exclusion of religious principle."[51]

As we shall see, a similar statement was made by Benjamin Franklin. Such were not the affirmations of secularizing atheists, but men who were Christians or at least respectful of the Christian faith and its necessary role in their society.

All Fifty State Constitutions Appeal to Almighty God

Another evidence of the strong religious consensus of America's founders appears in the fact that all thirteen of the original state constitutions refer to Almighty God as the author of liberty or mention their dependence on His providence to sustain them as a free people.

I secured copies of each of these documents from the Library of Congress. Consider some of these inspiring preambles:

North Carolina, 1868
We the people of the State of North Carolina, grateful to Almighty God, the sovereign ruler of nations, for the preservation of the American Union and the existence of our civil, political, and religious liberties, and acknowledging our dependence upon Him for the continuance of those blessings to us and our posterity, do, for the more certain security thereof and for the better government of this State, ordain and establish this constitution.[52]

New Jersey, 1844
We, the people of the State of New Jersey, grateful to Almighty God for the civil and religious liberty which He hath so long permitted us to enjoy, and looking to Him for a blessing upon our endeavors to secure and transmit the same unimpaired to succeeding generations, do ordain and establish this Constitution.[53]

Rhode Island, 1842
We, the people of the State of Rhode Island and Providence Plantations, grateful to Almighty God for the civil and religious liberty which He hath so long permitted us to enjoy, and looking to Him for a blessing upon our endeavors to secure and to transmit the same unimpaired to succeeding generations, do ordain and establish this constitution of government.[54]

New York, 1846
We, the people of the State of New York, grateful to
Almighty God for our freedom: in order to secure its
blessings, do establish this Constitution.[55]

In addition to their universal acknowledgment of God as
protector, provider, and guide, these examples were all updated
after the Founding Fathers were dead, indicating clearly that the
consensus of reliance on God, so common at the founding of the
nation, was still very much alive more than fifty years later.

Even more interesting is a fact brought to light by the well
known Presbyterian pastor and television preacher, Dr. D. James
Kennedy, in a sermon on the subject of church and state:

In reading over the Constitutions of all fifty of our states,
I discovered something which some of you may not know:
there is *in all fifty, without exception*, an appeal or a prayer to
the Almighty God of this universe. . . . Through all fifty
state Constitutions, without exception, there runs this
same appeal and reference to God who is the Creator of
our liberties and the preserver of our freedoms.[56]

The Declaration of Independence: Recognition of God
Since the Declaration of Independence was adopted by the
Continental Congress, which was made up of delegates elected
by the people of their states, it would represent the consensus of
the people who elected them. We should keep in mind that this
declaration was prepared only eleven years before the writing of
the Constitution and that eight of those who signed it were
among the Founding Fathers who produced the Constitution.[57]

Although the following references to God are probably
known to you, I will repeat them before mentioning an interesting fact of history that you may not have heard before.

". . . the laws of nature and of nature's God entitle
them. . . ."

"We hold these truths to be self-evident, that all men are
created equal. . . ."

". . . they are endowed by their Creator with certain unalienable rights. . . ."

". . . with a firm reliance on the protection of divine
Providence. . . ."

Obviously, those who signed this document, pledging their
"lives, their fortunes and their sacred honor," were not atheists,
but men with a deep reliance on God.

That these references to their dependence on God were not
inserted idly, particularly in the last sentence, may be seen in
that they do not appear in the original draft by Thomas Jefferson. Instead, they were inserted deliberately by John Adams
and approved by the Congress. In their book, *The Light and the
Glory*, the authors make these cryptic comments:

> Jefferson did most of the final composing, borrowing
> heavily from the phraseology of popular sermons of the
> day — except for the two phrases, "appealing to the
> Supreme Judge of the World for the Rectitude of our In-
> tentions" and "with a Firm Reliance on the Protection of
> divine Providence." These Congress insisted upon in-
> cluding, over Jefferson's strenuous objection, for he was
> a confirmed "enlightened rationalist," soon to become
> privately a Unitarian. So resentful was Jefferson at their
> tampering with his prose that he sent copies of his origi-
> nal draft to his personal friends, that they might better
> appreciate his unedited effort.[58]

These documents, the Northwest Ordinance of 1787, all fifty
state constitutions, and the Declaration of Independence, provide clear and compelling evidence that the Christian consensus
was real and pervasive at the time the Founding Fathers set
about the task of writing this nation's Constitution. Benjamin
Franklin was right when he said, "Atheism is unknown [here]
and infidelity rare and secret."[59]

The National Anthem
The story of the writing of our national anthem, "The Star
Spangled Banner," is probably well known to you. It was com-

posed by Francis Scott Key, an attorney from Washington, D.C., and a dedicated Christian who devoted several hours each week to writing poetry and studying theology.

During a diplomatic mission to win the freedom of a popular American doctor (held captive aboard the flagship of the British fleet, which was sailing in the Chesapeake Bay), Key's ship was commandeered by a British crew, and he was forced to watch the British attack on Fort McHenry in September of 1814. As he waited throughout the night and into the early morning light, he spied Old Glory still waving over Fort McHenry after an unmerciful bombardment. Incidentally, that flag, which can still be seen in the Smithsonian museum, measured a full thirty by forty-two feet. So inspired was he that Key penned the moving lines of our anthem. Shortly thereafter he added the music borrowed from an old hymn, "To Anacreon in Heaven."

While "The Star Spangled Banner" didn't become our official national anthem until 1916, it was the nation's anthem and song of victory within weeks of the battle in the hearts of most Americans.

Read the following and see if you think such a national anthem could possibly be adopted by a people with an atheistic or secularistic consensus.

O! say can you see by the dawn's early light,
What so proudly we hail'd at the twilight's last gleaming?
Whose broad stripes and bright stars, thro' the perilous fight,
O'er the ramparts we watched were so gallantly streaming?
And the rocket's red glare, the bombs bursting in air,
Gave proof thro' the night that our flag was still there;
O! say does that star spangled banner yet wave
O'er the land of the free and the home of the brave!

O! thus be it ever when free men shall stand
Between their loved home and the war's desolation;
Blest with vict'ry and peace, may the Heav'n-rescued land
Praise the Pow'r that hath made and preserved us a nation!
Then conquer we must, when our cause it is just;
And this be our motto, "In God is our trust!"
And the star spangled banner in triumph shall wave
O'er the land of the free and the home of the brave!

Because the melody line of our national anthem goes so high, some find it difficult to sing. Consequently, there have been periodical efforts to find something more singable. Not until 1920 was a serious attempt made to replace it with something equally as inspiring and easier to sing. The suggested replacement? "America the Beautiful," with its references to "God shed his grace on thee, and crown thy good with brotherhood, from sea to shining sea." That is hardly a text that the Soviet Union or other secularist states would select.

Music, particularly that of a patriotic nature, usually gives insight into the religious beliefs of a nation. Our country heralds several nationally loved patriotic songs. "The Battle Hymn of the Republic" ("Mine eyes have seen the glory of the coming of the Lord"), so loved by Abraham Lincoln at the close of the Civil War, and the much more recent "God Bless America," by Irving Berlin, written during World War II, do not reflect the sympathies of atheists. If these songs, written long after our nation was founded, mirror the religious consensus of our people today, what do they say about the citizenry of 1789? As Justice Story noted, "We are a religious people."

The Printing of Bibles by the First Congress

The Bible, the greatest book ever written, is indispensable to the preservation of Christianity. That fact was clear in the first act of Congress, authorizing the printing of twenty thousand Bibles for the Indians.[60] In order to unify our people, our leaders sought for universal acceptance of and access to the Word of God.

Today the ACLU and others would scream "separation of church and state." Our Founding Fathers had no reluctance to favor Christianity, the commonly practiced religion of their day. Evidently, they didn't see this act as imposing a religion on people but as a necessary ingredient to make all citizens of the same basic moral commitment.

A Frenchman's Appraisal of Religion in America
Fifty Years after the Constitution Was Written

In 1831, a French scholar and historian, Alexis de Tocqueville, visited America. He was so impressed with our culture and constitutional system that he published an exhaustive, two-volume description of our nation that is still popular and available today. Here are some of his observations on the religious life of the nation.

> On my arrival in the United States the religious aspect of the country was the first thing that struck my attention; and the longer I stayed there, the more I perceived the great political consequences resulting from this new state of things. In France I had almost always seen the spirit of religion and the spirit of freedom marching in opposite directions. But in America I found they were intimately united and that they reigned in common over the same country.[61]

> Religion in America takes no direct part in the government of society, but it must be regarded as the first of their political institutions; for if it does not impart a taste for freedom, it facilitates the use of it. Indeed, it is in this same point of view that the inhabitants of the United States themselves look upon religious belief. I do not know whether all Americans have a sincere faith in their religion—for who can search the human heart?—But I am certain that they hold it to be indispensable to the maintenance of republican institutions. This opinion is not peculiar to a class of citizens or a party, but it belongs to the whole nation and to every rank of society.[62]

> The sects that exist in the United States are innumerable. . . . Moreover, all the sects of the United States are comprised within the great unity of Christianity, and Christian morality is everywhere the same.

> In the United States the sovereign authority is religious, and consequently hypocrisy must be common: but there is no country in the world where the Christian religion retains a greater influence over the souls of men than in America; and there can be no greater proof of its utility and of its conformity to human nature than that its influence is powerfully felt over the most enlightened and free nation of the earth.

I do not question that the great austerity of manners that is observable in the United States arises, in the first instance, from religious faith. Religion is often unable to restrain man from the numberless temptations which chance offers; nor can it check that passion for gain which everything contributes to arouse; but its influence over the mind of woman is supreme, and women are the protectors of morals. There is certainly no country in the world where the tie of marriage is more respected than in America or where conjugal happiness is more highly or worthily appreciated. . . .

In the United States the influence of religion is not confined to the manners, but it extends to the intelligence of the people. Among the Anglo-Americans some profess the doctrines of Christianity from a sincere belief in them, and others do the same because they fear to be suspected of unbelief. Christianity, therefore, reigns without obstacle, by universal consent; the consequence is, as I have before observed, that every principle of the moral world is fixed and determinate, although the political world is abandoned to the debates and the experiments of men. Thus the human mind is never left to wander over a boundless field.[63]

As we read the evaluation of this French scholar (himself a Roman Catholic), we are forced to notice that evangelical Protestants are not much different today from what they were in 1787 — at least in lifestyle. The reason? They observe the Christian way of life that was the American consensus 200 years ago. Secular humanists and moral liberals would not have been comfortable back then.

It is impossible to exaggerate the influence of the Bible, Christian tradition, the Protestant churches of the eighteenth century, and the early American Christian's emphasis on learning and literary achievement in the writing of the amazing document we call the Constitution of the United States. It could never have been provided by an amoral, Bibleless people.

EIGHT

THE TWO
MOST-HONORED
FOUNDING FATHERS

GEORGE WASHINGTON
(1732-1799)

BENJAMIN FRANKLIN
(1706-1790)

There is no disagreement among historians that George Washington and Benjamin Franklin were the most respected of all the fifty-five delegates at the Constitutional Convention.

Franklin, eighty-one years old at the time of the Convention, had just returned to Philadelphia in 1785 following ten years of very distinguished service for his country as our envoy to France, where he was accorded many honors. Washington, as we shall see, was held in such awe that had he not so strongly

99

supported a republican form of government, he could easily have been pronounced king of the colonies.

Considering their equal greatness in selfless service to their country, two more physically different men could scarcely be found. Franklin, short and portly with a slightly stooped frame, was rarely found without his ready wit and penetrating humor. In spite of his age, he had a clear mind, and his contributions to the deliberations were significant. Lauded in both America and Europe as an intellectual, this inventor, philosopher, and wise statesman was widely recognized for his literary skills. Franklin well deserved the description given him in his day as "the illustrious and benevolent citizen of the world."

Though he was the oldest member of the Convention and often had to be carried in as the result of severe pain from gout and a large bladder stone, Franklin attended deliberations daily and even grew stronger as the sessions progressed. He was elected president of Pennsylvania almost immediately upon his return from France, which, as one historian said, restored harmony to a community on the verge of civil war. It was as a leader of the Pennsylvania delegation that he attended the Constitutional Convention.

Washington, a towering man in his day at six feet two inches tall, and weighing about two hundred pounds, was in his fifty-fifth year at the time of the Convention. In spite of a body that often ached from the pain of arthritis, this great man walked erect and stately. In addition to Washington's impressive physical bearing, he had the mind and composure of a statesman. Like Franklin, he was the leader of his delegation, and typical of his life, he arrived the day before the delegates were scheduled to meet in Philadelphia. Harry Lee ("Light Horse Harry") uttered the fitting and now famous tribute to Washington, "First in war, first in peace, first in the hearts of his countrymen."

Franklin, one of only six signers of the Declaration of Independence who also signed the Constitution, at first tended to favor a limited federal government. Washington, on the other hand (no doubt due to his experiences as commander-in-chief of the Continental Army under the weak Continental government), leaned toward a strong central government. Yet, while both men freely entered into the debate, neither tried to impose his viewpoints, and both were content with the consensus conclusions of the delegates.

These two men were so highly esteemed that it is doubtful that a majority of the fifty-five delegates could have finally agreed on the Constitution without their endorsement. It is all but certain that it would never have been ratified by the states without their enthusiastic approval. Though living in an age of heroes, these statesmen and patriots were in a category all by themselves. Of the two, Washington's faith is the easiest to document, largely from his own writings. Even Franklin, however, an admitted deist, was never hostile to the Christian faith or to religion in general. In fact, as we shall see, he believed that religion and morality were indispensable to the preservation of a self-governing society of free people.

While these two great patriots may have reflected mental and physical differences, they were identical in their one great passion — a love for America.

GEORGE WASHINGTON
(1732-1799)
VIRGINIA, EPISCOPALIAN: SURVEYOR; PLANTER; STATESMAN; SOLDIER; WAR HERO; COMMANDING GENERAL OF THE CONTINENTAL ARMY IN THE REVOLUTIONARY WAR; CHAIRMAN OF THE CONSTITUTIONAL CONVENTION; THE FIRST PRESIDENT OF THE UNITED STATES (1789-1796); "THE MOST POPULAR MAN IN THE COLONIES."

Said John Marshall, chief justice of the Supreme Court, about Washington, "Without making ostentatious professions of religion, he was a sincere believer in the Christian faith, and a truly devout man."[64]

Said the Reverend J. T. Kirkland after Washington's death in 1799,

> The virtues of our departed friend were crowned by piety. He is known to have been habitually devout. To Christian institutions he gave the countenance of his example; and no one could express, more fully, his sense of the Providence of God, and the dependence of man.[65]

By almost every contemporary account, George Washington was the greatest man in the colonies — and he was acknowledged so by almost all Americans. In fact, his work and leadership for our country were such that *World Book Encyclopedia* has stated in opening remarks about Washington that "in the history of the world, no man has done more to help any country than Washington did to help the United States."[66] Yet, it has been all but omitted from modern history texts that he was an extremely dedicated Christian.

The oldest of Augustine and Mary Washington's six children (George had two older half-brothers and one half-sister from his father's first wife, who died very young), he was raised primarily by his deeply devout mother, who had a profound effect on his faith. Her letters and spiritual advice are preserved for us today in the Library of Congress.

George was born February 22, 1732, into a Christian family living along the Potomac River in what is now known as Westmorland County, Virginia, about seventy-five miles down the river from modern-day Washington D.C. His father died when George was just eleven years old, and he was therefore not able to finish his formal education. He learned surveying in his teens and joined the Virginia militia as a young man, distinguishing himself as a junior officer in the French and Indian Wars. In one battle alone, four bullets passed through his coat and two horses were shot out from under him, yet he was miraculously protected. In describing that event, he began a series of references to "the miraculous care of Providence,"[67] which certainly indicate he was no deist. He believed in and prayed to a personal God almost every day of his adult life. This man, who persisted through overwhelming odds and led the Continental Army to victory in the Revolutionary War, always acknowledged the hand of God at work.

As the nation's first President, he steered our young country in the proper direction by establishing it along the lines designed in the new Constitution. He then transferred the leadership of the country to John Adams and retired to his beloved home at Mount Vernon in 1797, where he remained (except for a brief period in 1798, when he answered the call of President Adams to put on the uniform once again as commander of the American forces during a threatened attack by the French) until his death on December 14, 1799.

It was providential that our first President was a godly man of humble character and sterling commitment to God. William White reports of his sincere piety in *Washington's Writings:*

> It seems proper to subjoin to this letter what was told to me by Mr. Robert Lewis, at Fredricksburg, in the year 1827. Being a nephew of Washington, and his private secretary during the first part of his presidency, Mr. Lewis lived with him on terms of intimacy, and had the best opportunity for observing his habits. Mr. Lewis said that he had accidentally witnessed his private devotions in his library both morning and evening; that on those occasions he had seen him in a kneeling posture with a Bible open before him, and that he believed such to have been his daily practice.[68]

Raised in the Anglican church, Washington remained a member throughout his life. He had a deep appreciation for all religions that produced good character, but he expressed a special appreciation for all Christian denominations. During his presidency, he used his influence to assure religious freedom in order to protect the dissident sects (from which our many current evangelicals find their roots) that were springing up at that time.

Although he was a very private man who never forced his

faith on others, neither did Washington shy away from freely displaying his faith in his writings and speeches. In fact, those who would have us believe he was a deist or addicted to the Enlightenment theories are hard pressed to account for his many acknowledgments of "the strong hand of Providence" in his own handwriting, to which he attributed his victory in the Revolutionary War.

The best way to become familiar with Washington's faith is to examine his own writings. Consider the following excerpts.

The Existence of a Supreme Being

It is impossible to account for the creation of the universe, without the agency of a Supreme Being. It is impossible to govern the universe without the aid of a Supreme Being. It is impossible to reason without arriving at a Supreme Being. Religion is as necessary to reason, as reason is to religion. The one cannot exist without the other. A reasoning being would lose his reason, in attempting to account for the great phenomena of nature, had he not a Supreme Being to refer to; and well has it been said, that if there had been no God, mankind would have been obliged to imagine one.[69]

The Author of All Good

. . . that great and glorious Being, who is the beneficent Author of all the good that was, that is, or that will be.[70]

The Source of All Blessings

. . . The sentiments we have mutually expressed of profound gratitude to the source of those numerous blessings—the author of all good obligations to unite our sincere and zealous endeavours, as the instruments of divine providence, to preserve and perpetuate them.[71]

Divine Protection

. . . by the miraculous care of Providence, that protected me beyond all human expectation; I had four Bullets through my Coat, and two Horses shot under me, and yet escaped unhurt.[72]

Providence has heretofore taken us up when all other means and hope seemed to be departing from us, in this I will confide.

I consider it an indispensable duty to close this last solemn act of my Official life, by commending the Interest of our dearest Country to the protection of Almighty God, and those who have the superintendence of them, to his holy keeping.

The Supreme Ruler of the Universe

The situation in which I now stand, for the last time, in the midst of the Representatives of the People of the United States, naturally recalls the period when the Administration of the present form of Government commenced; and I cannot omit the occasion, to congratulate you and my Country, on the success of the experiment; nor to repeat my fervent supplications to the Supreme Ruler of the Universe, and Sovereign Arbiter of Nations, that his Providential care may still be extended to the United States; that the virtue and happiness of the People, may be preserved; and that the Government, which they have instituted, for the protection of their liberties, may be perpetual.[73]

The Ruler of Nations

Let us unite, therefore, in imploring the Supreme Ruler of nations, to spread his holy protection over these United States: to turn the machinations of the wicked to the confirming of our constitution: to enable us at all times to root out internal sedition, and put invasion to flight: to perpetuate to our country that prosperity, which his goodness has already conferred, and to verify the anticipation of this government being a safeguard to human rights.[74]

. . . we may then unite in most humbly offering our prayers and supplications to the great Lord and Ruler of Nations and beseech him to pardon our national and other transgressions, to enable us all, whether in public or private stations, to perform our several and relative duties properly and punctually, to render our national government a blessing to all the People, by constantly being a government of wise, just and constitutional laws, discreetly and faithfully executed and obeyed, to protect and guide all Sovereigns and Nations (especially such as have shown kindness unto us) and to bless them with good government, peace, and concord. To promote the knowledge and practice of true religion and virtue, and the increase of science among them and Us, and generally to grant unto all Mankind such a degree of temporal prosperity as he alone knows to be best.

Religion, Distinguished from Morality
Let us with caution indulge the supposition, that morality can be maintained without religion. Whatever may be conceded to the influence of refined education on minds of peculiar structure, reason and experience both forbid us to expect that National morality can prevail in exclusion of religious principle.[75]

Religious Duties of Nations
It is the duty of all Nations to acknowledge the providence of Almighty God, to obey his will, to be grateful for his benefits, and humbly to implore his protection and favor.[76]

Religion and Morality, the Pillars of Human Happiness
Of all the dispositions and habits which lead to political prosperity, Religion and morality are indispensable supports. In vain would that man claim the tribute of Patriotism, who should labour to subvert these great Pillars of human happiness, these firmest props of the duties of Men and citizens. The mere Politician, equally with the pious man ought to respect and to cherish them. A volume could not trace all their connections with private and public felicity. Let it simply be asked where is the security for property, for reputation, for life, if the sense of religious obligation desert the oaths, which are the instruments of investigation in Courts of Justice?[77]

National Homage To God

It would be peculiarly improper to omit in this official Act, my fervent supplications to that Almighty Being who rules over the Universe, who presides in the Councils of Nations, and whose providential aids can supply every human defect, that his benediction may consecrate to the liberties and happiness of the People of the United States, a Government instituted by themselves for these essential purposes: and may enable every instrument employed in its administration to execute with success, the functions allotted to his charge. In tendering this homage to the Great Author of every public and private good, I assure myself that it expresses your sentiments not less than my own; nor those of my fellow-citizens at large, less than either. No people can be bound to acknowledge and adore the invisible hand, which conducts the Affairs of men more than the People of the United States. *Every step, by which they have advanced to the character of an independent nation, seems to have been distinguished by some token of providential agency.* And in the important revolution just accomplished in the system of their United government, the tranquil deliberations and voluntary consent of so many distinct communities, from which the event has resulted, cannot be compared with the means by which most Governments have been established, without some return of pious gratitude along with an humble anticipation of the future blessings which the past seems to presage. These reflections, arising out of the present crisis, have forced themselves too strongly on my mind to be suppressed. You will join with me I trust in thinking, that there are none under the influence of which the proceedings of a new and free Government can more auspiciously commence.[78]

Example of Its Divine Author

I now make it my earnest prayer, that God would have you, and the State over which you preside, in his holy protection, that he would incline the hearts of the Citizens to cultivate a spirit of subordination and obedience to Government, to entertain a brotherly affection and love for one another, for their fellow Citizens of the United States at large, and particularly for their brethren who have served in the Field, and finally, that he would most graciously be pleased to dispose us all, to do Justice, to love mercy, *and to demean ourselves with that Charity, humility and pacific temper of mind, which were the Characteristicks of the Divine Author of our blessed Religion, and without an humble imitation of whose example in these things, we can never hope to be a happy Nation.*

Christian Morals
The General hopes and trusts, that every officer and man, will endeavor so to live, and act, as becomes a Christian Soldier defending the dearest Rights and Liberties of his country.[80]

Civil and Religious Liberty
It shall still be my endeavor to manifest, by overt acts, the purity of my inclination for promoting the happiness of mankind, as well as the sincerity of my desires to contribute whatever may be in my power towards the preservation of the civil and religious liberties of the American People.[81]

The liberty enjoyed by the People of these States of worshipping Almighty God agreeable to their consciences is not only among the choicest of their blessings but also of their *rights*.

While men perform their social duties faithfully, they do all that society or the state can with propriety demand or expect; and remain responsible only to their Maker for the religion, or modes of faith, which they may prefer or profess.

Religious Freedom
As the contempt of the religion of a country by ridiculing any of its ceremonies, or affronting its ministers or votaries, has ever been deeply resented, you are to be

particularly careful to restrain every officer and soldier from such imprudence and folly, and to punish every instance of it. On the other hand, as far as lies in your power, you are to protect and support the free exercise of the religion of the country, and the undisturbed enjoyment of the rights of conscience in religious matters, with your utmost influence and authority.

Every man conducting himself as a good citizen, and being accountable to God alone for his religious opinions, ought to be protected in worshipping the Deity according to the dictates of his own conscience. . . . If I could have entertained the slightest apprehension that the Constitution framed in the Convention, where I had the honor to preside, might possibly endanger the religious rights of any ecclesiastical Society, certainly I would never have placed my signature to it; if I could now conceive that the general Government might ever be so administered as to render liberty of conscience insecure, I beg you will be persuaded that no one would be more zealous than myself to establish effectual barriers against the horrors of spiritual tyranny, and every species of religious persecution. . . . Be assured, Gentlemen, that I entertain a proper sense of your fervent supplications to God for my temporal and eternal happiness.[82]

Toleration of the Jews
May the same wonder-working Deity, who long since delivering the Hebrews from their Egyptian Oppressors planted them in the promised land — whose providential agency has lately been conspicuous in establishing these United States as an independent Nation — still continue to water them with the dews of Heaven and to make the inhabitants of every denomination participate in the temporal and spiritual blessings of that people whose God is Jehovah.

Regard To Conscientious Scruples
In my opinion the conscientious scruples of all men should be treated with great delicacy and tenderness, and

it is my wish and desire that the laws may always be as extensively accommodated to them, as a due regard to the Protection and essential interests of the nation may justify and permit.[83]

Religious Tenets and Civil Rights

We have abundant reason to rejoice that in this Land the light of truth and reason has triumphed over the power of bigotry and superstition, and that every person may here worship God according to the dictates of his own heart. In this enlightened Age and in this Land of equal liberty it is our boast, that a man's religious tenets will not forfeit the protection of the Laws, nor deprive him of the right of attaining and holding the highest offices that are known in the United States.[84]

George Washinton's Private Prayers

That President George Washington was a devout believer in Jesus Christ and had accepted Him as His Lord and Savior is easily demonstrated by a reading of his personal prayer book (written in his own handwriting), which was discovered in 1891 among a collection of his papers. To date no historian has questioned its authenticity. It consists of twenty-four pages of his morning and evening prayers, revealing many of his theological beliefs about God, Jesus Christ, sin, salvation, eternal life, and himself as a humble servant of Christ. Consider the following selections.

(1) Sunday Morning

Almighty God, and most merciful Father, who didst command the children of Israel to offer a daily sacrifice to Thee, that thereby they might glorify and praise Thee for Thy protection both night and day; receive, O Lord, my morning sacrifice which I now offer up to Thee. . . . I beseech Thee, my sins, remove them from Thy presence, as far as the east is from the west, and accept of me for the merits of Thy Son, Jesus Christ, that when I come into Thy temple, and compass Thine altar, my prayers may come before Thee as incense; and as Thou wouldst hear me calling upon Thee in my prayers, so give me grace to hear Thee calling on me in Thy word, that it may be wisdom, righteousness, reconciliation and peace to the saving of my soul in the day of the Lord Jesus.

(2) Sunday Evening

O most Glorious God, in Jesus Christ my merciful and loving Father, I acknowledge and confess my guilt, in the weak and imperfect performance of the duties of this day. I have called on Thee for pardon and forgiveness of sins. . . . Let me live according to those holy rules which Thou hast this day prescribed in Thy holy word; make me to know what is acceptable in Thy sight, and therein to delight, open the eyes of my understanding, and help me thoroughly to examine myself concerning my knowledge, faith and repentance, increase my faith, and direct me to the true object, Jesus Christ the Way, the Truth and the Life, bless, O Lord, all the people of this land, from the highest to the lowest, particularly those whom Thou hast appointed to rule over us in church & state. Continue Thy goodness to me this night. These weak petitions, I humbly implore Thee to hear, accept and answer for the sake of Thy Dear Son, Jesus Christ our Lord, Amen.

(3) Monday Morning

O eternal and everlasting God, I presume to present myself this morning before Thy Divine Majesty, beseeching Thee to accept of my humble and hearty thanks. . . .

Daily frame me more and more into the likeness of Thy
Son, Jesus Christ, that living in Thy fear, and dying in
Thy favor, I may in Thy appointed time attain the resurrection of the just unto eternal life. Bless my family,
friends and kindred, and unite us all in praising and glo-
rifying Thee in all our works.

(4) Monday Evening

Most Gracious Lord God, from whom proceedeth every
good and perfect gift, I offer to Thy Divine Majesty my
unfeigned praise and thanksgiving for all Thy mercies
towards me. . . . I have sinned and done very wickedly,
be merciful to me, O God, and pardon me for Jesus
Christ sake. . . . Bless O Lord the whole race of mankind, and let the world be filled with the knowledge of
Thee and Thy Son, Jesus Christ. . . . I beseech Thee to
defend me this night from all evil, and do more for me
than I can think or ask, for Jesus Christ sake, in whose
most holy Name and Words, I continue to pray, Our
Father, who art in heaven, hallowed be Thy Name. . . .

(5) Tuesday Morning

O Lord our God, most mighty and merciful Father, I,
thine unworthy creature and servant, do once more approach Thy presence. Though not worthy to appear before Thee, because of my natural corruptions, and the
many sins and transgressions which I have committed
against Thy Divine Majesty; yet I beseech Thee, for the
sake of Him in whom Thou art well pleased, the Lord
Jesus Christ, to admit me to render Thee deserved thanks
and praises for Thy manifold mercies extended toward
me. . . . Bless the people of this land, be a Father to the
fatherless, a Comforter to the comfortless, a Deliverer to
the captives, and a Physician to the sick. Let Thy blessings be upon our friends, kindred and families. Be our
Guide this day and forever through Jesus Christ in
whose blessed form of prayer I conclude my weak petitions — Our Father, who art in heaven, hallowed be Thy
Name. . . .

(6) Tuesday Evening

Most gracious God and heavenly Father, we cannot cease, but must cry unto Thee for mercy, because my sins cry against me for justice. . . . That I may know my sins are forgiven by His death and passion. Embrace me in the arms of Thy mercy; vouchsafe to receive me unto the bosom of Thy love, shadow me with Thy wings, that I may safely rest under Thy protection this night; and so into Thy hands I commend myself, both soul and body, in the name of Thy Son, Jesus Christ, beseeching Thee, when this life shall end, I may take my everlasting rest with Thee in Thy heavenly kingdom. Bless all in authority over us, be merciful to all those afflicted with Thy cross or calamity, bless all my friends, forgive my enemies and accept my thanksgiving this evening for all the mercies and favors afforded me; hear and graciously answer these my requests, and whatever else thou see'st needful grant us, for the sake of Jesus Christ in whose blessed Name and Words I continue to pray, Our Father, who art in heaven. . . .

(7) A Prayer for Wednesday Morning

Almighty and eternal Lord God, the great Creator of heaven and earth, and the God and Father of our Lord Jesus Christ; look down from heaven, in pity and compassion upon me Thy servant, who humbly prostrate myself before Thee, sensible of Thy mercy and my own misery. . . . Help all in affliction or adversity — give them patience and a sanctified use of their affliction, and in Thy good time, deliverance from them; forgive my enemies, take me unto Thy protection this day, keep me in perfect peace, which I ask in the name and for the sake of Jesus. Amen.[85]

An objective reading of these beautiful prayers verifies that were George Washington living today, he would freely identify with the Bible-believing branch of evangelical Christianity that is having such a positive influence on our nation.

BENJAMIN FRANKLIN
(1706-1790)

PENNSYLVANIA, DEIST (OR "SECULARIZED PURITAN"): PRINTER; PHILOSOPHER; SCIENTIST; HONORED INTELLECTUAL; DIPLOMAT TO FRANCE AND ENGLAND; STATESMAN; "FATHER OF THE CONFEDERATION"; SIGNER OF THE ARTICLES OF CONFEDERATION AND THE DECLARATION OF INDEPENDENCE; PRESIDENT OF PENNSYLVANIA; FOUNDER OF THE UNIVERSITY OF PENNSYLVANIA; CONSIDERED THE MOST RESPECTED MAN IN THE COLONIES.

Benjamin Franklin was easily one of the most renowned men of the colonies, and certainly the most outstanding personality in Pennsylvania. He was the fifteenth child in a family of seventeen children. His godly parents hoped he would become a minister, but they lacked the funds from their candle-making business to pay for his formal education.

Franklin became a printer early in life, having begun his apprenticeship at age twelve, and moved from his home in Boston to Philadelphia. There, despite his youth, he distinguished himself as a literary genius with a rare, practical outlook on life. He received wide acclaim from his annual writing and publication of *Poor Richard's Almanac* (from 1732 through 1757), second in popularity only to the Bible throughout the colonies.

His intellectual gifts are obvious in that while he had only two years of formal schooling at best, he taught himself five languages and became a great inventor and scientist, which earned him the reputation as "the Newton of his age." His practical, philosophical, and scientific writings were translated and used in many languages, granting him worldwide acclaim. Several foreign universities awarded him honorary degrees, earning him the title "Doctor Franklin." He was famous for the stove that bears his name, the discovery of electricity through his famous kite experiment, and his subsequent invention of the lightning rod—which has no doubt spared many families from tragedy.

Such fame was not enough for this gifted and likable man. Franklin also invested his life in public service as a member of the Pennsylvania assembly, deputy postmaster of the colonies, for five years the U.S. representative in England, and until the Revolutionary War the spokesman for Americans to the British. In 1776, after the Declaration of Independence was signed, he was sent to negotiate France's military aid and to secure loans from that government. While there he became very popular and succeeded in bringing the French into the war on the side of our new nation. Subsequently, he was sent to Paris in August 1781, where he negotiated a peace treaty with the British to end the war on September 3, 1783. The terms of this Treaty of Paris "were so advantageous to the Colonies that it has been called the greatest achievement in the history of American diplomacy."[86]

When Franklin returned to Pennsylvania in 1785, he was immediately elected president of the executive council of Pennsylvania (i.e., governor), which entitled him to the honor of hosting the fifty-five delegates attending the convention meeting in his home city to draft a constitution for the people of the thirteen colonies. At eighty-one years of age, he was easily the oldest delegate to attend, yet not even poor health kept him from being present at nearly every session. Of his many distinctions, he is the only man who signed all four of our founding documents—the Declaration of Independence, the Treaty of Alliance with France, the Treaty of Paris with England, and the United States Constitution.

There is no evidence that Franklin ever became a Christian, but he was extremely respectful of Christianity and never hostile to it. For instance, after listening to Great Awakening evangelist George Whitefield preach from Philadelphia's courthouse steps,

Franklin, then in his thirties became very interested in White-field's ministry and the two soon became fast friends. He was involved in printing many of Whitefield's sermons and journals. Franklin's respect for Christianity is evident from his description of Whitefield's ministry and influence on city life in the colonies. In his autobiography Franklin wrote,

> It was wonderful to see the change soon made in the manners of our inhabitants. From being thoughtless or indifferent about religion, it seemed as if all the world were growing religious, so that one could not walk thro' the town in an evening without hearing psalms sung in different families of every street.[87]

Many modern secularizers try to claim Franklin as one of their own. I am confident, however, that Franklin would not identify with them were he alive today. He had a definite belief in a sovereign and personal God, gave credence to Bible reading and prayer, and held a deep commitment to the traditional civil and moral values of the churches of his day. Franklin was a strong advocate of religious freedom. The following statements by Franklin verify that he would not find himself at home with today's secular humanists.

In a letter to Ezra Skyles, president of Yale University, Franklin defined his religious creed:

> Here is my creed. I believe in one God, the Creator of the universe. That He governs it by His Providence. That He ought to be worshipped. That the most acceptable service we render to Him is in doing good to His other children. That the soul of man is immortal, and will be treated with justice in another life respecting its conduct in this. These I take to be the fundamental points in all sound religion.[88]

Commenting on Franklin's creed, modern historian, Cleon Skousen writes:

> The five points of fundamental religious belief which are

to be found in all of the principal religions of the world are those expressed or implied in Franklin's statement:

1. Recognition and worship of a Creator who made all things.

2. That the Creator has revealed a moral code of behavior for happy living which distinguishes right from wrong.

3. That the Creator holds mankind responsible for the way they treat each other.

4. That all mankind live beyond this life.

5. That in the next life individuals are judged for their conduct in this one.

All five of these tenets run through practically all of the Founders' writings. These are the beliefs which the Founders sometimes referred to as the "religion of America," and they felt these fundamentals were so important in providing "good government and the happiness of mankind" that they wanted them taught in the public schools along with morality and knowledge.[89]

[Statements of the Founders Concerning These Principles]

Samuel Adams said these basic beliefs which constitute "the religion of America [are] the religion of mankind." In other words, these fundamental beliefs belong to all world faiths and could therefore be taught without being offensive to any "sect or denomination," as indicated in the Virginia bill establishing elementary schools.

John Adams called these tenets the "general principles" on which the American civilization had been founded.

Thomas Jefferson called these basic beliefs the principles "in which God has united us all."

From these statements it is obvious how significantly the Founders looked upon the fundamental precepts of relig-

ion and morality as the cornerstones of a free government. This gives additional importance to the warning of
Washington, previously mentioned, when he said: "Of all
the dispositions and habits which lead to political prosperity, religion and morality are indispensable supports. . . .
Who that is a sincere friend to it can look with indifference upon attempts to shake the foundation of the fabric?"

Washington issued this solemn warning because in
France, shortly before he wrote his Farewell Address
(1796), the promoters of atheism and amorality had seized
control and turned the French Revolution into a shocking
bloodbath of wild excesses and violence. Washington
never wanted anything like that to happen in the United
States. Therefore he had said: "In vain would that man
claim the tribute of patriotism who should labor to subvert these great pillars of human happiness [religion and
morality]."[90]

Proof that Benjamin Franklin was no Atheist

There is abundant evidence that Franklin was not an atheist.
At the age of twenty-two, he drafted his *Articles of Belief and Acts of
Religion*. I quote selections here for your consideration.

> It is that particular wise and good God, who is the Author
> and Owner of our system, that I propose for the Object of
> my praise and adoration.

> For I conceive that He has in Himself some of those pas-
> sions He has planted in us, and that, since He has given
> us reason whereby we are capable of observing His
> Wisdom in the Creation, He is not above caring for us,
> being pleas'd with our praise, and offended when we
> slight Him, or neglect His Glory.

> I conceive for many reasons that He is a good Being, and
> as I should be happy to have so wise, good and powerful a
> Being my Friend, let me consider in what Manner I shall
> make myself most acceptable to Him.[91]

(1)

O Creator, O Father, I believe that Thou art Good, and Thou art pleas'd with the pleasure of Thy children.

> Praised be Thy Name forever.

(2)

By Thy Power hast thou made the glorious Sun, with his attending worlds; from the energy of Thy mighty Will they first received [their prodigious][92] motion, and by Thy Wisdom hast Thou prescribed the wondrous laws by which they move.

> Praised by Thy Name forever.

(3)

By Thy Wisdom hast Thou formed all things, Thou hast created man, bestowing life and reason, and plac'd him in dignity superior to Thy other earthly Creatures.

> Praised be Thy Name forever.

(4)

Thy Wisdom, Thy Power, and Thy GOODNESS are every where clearly seen; in the air and in the water, in the heavens and on the earth; Thou providest for the various winged fowl, and the innumerable inhabitants of the water; Thou givest cold and heat, rain and sunshine in their season, and to the fruits of the earth increase.

> Praised be Thy Name forever.

(5)

I believe Thou hast given life to Thy creatures that they might live, and art not delighted with violent death and bloody sacrifices.

> Praised be Thy Name forever.

(6)

Thou abhorrest in Thy creatures treachery and deceit, malice, revenge, [Intemperance][93] and every other hurtful Vice; but Thou art a Lover of justice and sincerity, of friendship, benevolence and every virtue. Thou art my Friend, my Father, and my Benefactor. Praised be Thy
> Name, O God, forever. Amen.[94]

Franklin's Petitions to God

That I may be preserved from atheism and infidelity, impiety and profaneness, and in my addresses to Thee carefully avoid irreverence and ostentation, formality and odious hypocrisy,

Help me, O Father.[95]

And forasmuch as ingratitude is one of the most odious of vices, let me not be unmindful gratefully to acknowledge the favours I receive from heaven. . . . For all Thy innumerable benefits; For life and reason, and the use of speech, for health and joy and every pleasant hour, my Good God, I thank Thee.[96]

Franklin's Statements on Doctrines to Be Preached

Doctrines to be preached:

That there is one God Father of the Universe.

That He [is] infinitely good, powerful and wise.

That He is omnipresent.

That He ought to be worshipped, by adoration prayer and thanksgiving both in publick and private.

That He loves such of His creatures as love and do good to others: and will reward them either in this world or hereafter.

That men's minds do not die with their bodies, but are made more happy or miserable after this life according to their actions.

That virtuous men ought to league together to strengthen the interest of virtue, in the world: and so strengthen themselves in Virtue.

That knowledge and learning is to be cultivated, and Ignorance dissipated. That none but the virtuous are wise, That man's perfection is in virtue.[97]

Franklin's Epitaph

Franklin's epitaph, which he wrote himself, gives further evidence that he was not an atheist:

THE BODY
of
BENJAMIN FRANKLIN,
Printer
Like the cover of an old book,
Its contents torn out,
And stripped of its lettering and gilding
Lies here, food for worms;
Yet the work itself shall not be lost,
For it will (as he believed) appear once more,
In a new,
And more beautiful edition,
Corrected and amended
By The AUTHOR[98]

In his book on Benjamin Franklin, Carl Becker summarized Franklin's beliefs by saying:

> The substance of the creed which he held throughout his life was that the one God, who made all things and governs the world through his providence, ought to be worshipped by adoration, prayer, and thanksgiving; that the most acceptable service of God is doing good to men; that the soul is immortal, and that God will certainly reward virtue and punish vice, either here or hereafter. Aiming at "moral perfection," he made a list of the useful virtues, which turned out to be thirteen — Temperance, Silence, Order, Resolution, Frugality, Industry, Sincerity, Justice, Moderation, Cleanliness, Tranquillity, Chastity, and Humility. To each of these in turn he gave "a week's strict attention, marking down in a book the measure of daily success achieved in the practice of each." Thus he went through "a course complete in thirteen weeks, and four courses a year."[99]

Amplifying his beliefs in God, Franklin wrote,

> Next to the praise resulting from and due to His wisdom, I believe He is pleased and delights in the happiness of those He has created; and since without virtue man can

have no happiness in this world, I firmly believe He delights to see me virtuous, because He is pleased when He sees me happy. And since He has created many things which seem purely designed for the delight of man, I believe He is not offended when He sees his children solace themselves in any manner of pleasant exercises and innocent delights; and I think no pleasure innocent that is to man hurtful. I love Him therefore for His Goodness, and I adore Him for His Wisdom.[100]

Franklin on Prayer

Being mindful that before I address the Deity my soul ought to be calm and serene, free from passion and perturbation, or otherwise elevated with rational joy and pleasure, I ought to use a countenance that expresses a filial respect, mixed with a kind of smiling that signifies inward joy and satisfaction and admiration. . . . O Creator, O Father! I believe that Thou art good and that Thou art pleased with the pleasure of Thy children. — Praised be Thy name for ever. By Thy power has Thou made the glorious sun, with his attending worlds; from the energy of Thy mighty will they first received their prodigious motion, and by Thy wisdom hast Thou prescribed the wondrous laws by which they move. — Praised be Thy name for ever. Thou abhorrest in Thy creatures treachery, deceit, malice, revenge, intemperance, and every other hurtful vice; but thou art a lover of justice and sincerity, of friendship and benevolence, and every virtue. Thou art my friend, my father, and my benefactor. — Praised be Thy name, O God, for ever! Amen![101]

Did Benjamin Franklin believe prayer to be a practical and profitable use of one's time? In short, did he believe in a God who hears and answers our prayers? In answer to this question, I direct your attention to a climactic session of debate at the Constitutional Convention on Thursday, June 28, 1787.

The debate on the floor over representation and voting had reached a hopeless deadlock, and tempers were heating up. Some of the New York delegation had already left, and others were on the verge of following suit. At this dismal and unpromising point of debate, the eighty-one-year-old philosopher, scientist, and statesman rose to address the president (George Washington) and delegates. As recorded by the convention's secretary, James Madison, here is what Franklin said:

Mr. President,

The small progress we have made after four or five weeks close attendance & continual reasonings with each other—our different sentiments on almost every question, several of the last producing as many noes as ays, is methinks a melancholy proof of the imperfection of the human understanding. We indeed seem to feel our own want of political wisdom, since we have been running about in search of it. We have gone back to ancient history for models of government, and examined the different forms of those Republics which having been formed with the seeds of their own dissolution now no longer exist. And we have viewed modern states all round Europe, but find none of their Constitutions suitable to our circumstances.

In this situation of this Assembly, groping as it were in the dark to find political truth, and scarce able to distinguish it when presented to us, how has it happened, Sir, that we have not hitherto once thought of humbly applying to the Father of lights to illuminate our understanding! In the beginning of the contest with Great Britain, when we were sensible of danger, we had daily prayer in this room for the Divine protection. —Our prayers, Sir, were heard, and they were graciously answered. All of us who were engaged in the struggle must have observed frequent instances of a superintending Providence in our favor. To that kind Providence, we owe this happy opportunity of consulting in peace on the means of establishing our future national felicity. And have we now forgotten this powerful Friend? Or do we imagine we no longer need His assistance? I have lived, Sir, a long time, and the longer I live, the more convincing proofs I see of this truth—*that God governs in the affairs of men.* And if a sparrow cannot fall to the ground without His notice, is it probable that an empire can rise without His aid? We have been assured, Sir, in the Sacred Writings, that "except the Lord build the house, they labor in vain that build it." I firmly believe this; and I also believe that without His concurring aid, we shall succeed in this political building no better, than the builders of Babel: We shall be divided by our little partial local interests; our projects will be confounded; and we ourselves shall become a reproach and bye word down to future ages. And what is worse, mankind may hereafter from this unfortunate instance, despair of establishing governments by human wisdom and leave it to chance, war, and conquest.

I therefore beg leave to move — that henceforth prayers imploring the assistance of Heaven, and its blessings on our deliberations, be held in this Assembly every morning before we proceed to business, and that one or more of the clergy of this city be requested to officiate in that service.[102]

Further indication of Franklin's love and respect for a personal God appears in his rewriting of the Lord's Prayer:

Heavenly Father,

May all revere Thee,

And become Thy dutiful children and faithful subjects.

May Thy Laws be obeyed on earth as perfectly as they are in Heaven.

Provide for us this day as Thou hast hitherto daily done.

Forgive us our trespasses, and enable us likewise to forgive those that offend us.

Keep us out of temptation and deliver us from Evil.[103]

All the evidence points to Benjamin Franklin's believing in the personal, omnipotent God of the Bible who has made clear His expectations of how people should live — and how governments should function. While Franklin's view of Jesus Christ as just a good man and moral teacher was not adequate to classify him as a Christian, he was a deeply religious man whose Biblical beliefs influenced the monumental contributions he made to the founding of this nation.

THE FIVE MOST INFLUENTIAL FOUNDING FATHERS

In addition to the two Founding Fathers already discussed, five other men had a significant influence on the writing of the U.S. Constitution: James Madison, who later became our fourth President; Gouverneur Morris, who actually wrote the final draft; George Mason, who like Madison was considered a Virginia intellectual and whose handwritten copy of the bill of rights to the Virginia Constitution formed the basis for our present Bill of Rights; Roger Sherman, the devout Christian from Connecticut who served as the leader of "The Peacemakers" and who successfully resolved the thorny problem of representation between the large and small states that at one time threatened to destroy the convention; and the gifted Alexander Hamilton, whose Federalist Papers and tireless efforts helped win ratification of the Constitution once it was written.

These early Americans were patriotic to the core. Although they represented differing positions on government, all expressed themselves freely and were willing to compromise for the common good.

When assessing their religious persuasion, one must keep the times in view. The Founding Fathers were residents of colonies, some of which imposed the Church of England on them as a part of the land grants of the mother country. The colonies had also experienced the Great Awakening, however, and there had been a proliferation of "dissident sects" that appealed far more to the common people—and even to many intellectuals. The state churches had become decadent since they were paid for by taxes — always a hindrance to Christian growth. The moral conduct of the clergy of those churches had sunk so low that people seeking God went to hear the preaching of the "dissidents," even if they were "illegals" and had to hold their services out in the woods. Such "sects," or, as we would call them, denominations, outnumbered the state church in attendance by several times.

As we have seen, the cultural Christian consensus was so strong that it influenced all these men and their thinking. For example, when Benjamin Franklin made his famous appeal for prayer for divine guidance, Madison made the motion that it be enacted, and it was seconded by Roger Sherman.[104]

While it is true that all fifty-five delegates made some contribution to the Constitution, the five we'll consider in this chapter, particularly Madison, had more influence on its outcome than the others.

JAMES MADISON
(1751-1836)

EPISCOPALIAN (WITH PRESBYTERIAN INFLUENCE): "FATHER OF THE CONSTITUTION"; LAWYER; PLANTER; VIRGINIA LEGISLATOR WHO HELPED WRITE THE STATE CONSTITUTION; MEMBER OF THE HOUSE OF DELEGATES; MEMBER OF THE CONTINENTAL CONGRESS; RECORD KEEPER OF THE CONSTITUTIONAL CONVENTION; AUTHOR OF TWENTY-NINE OF THE EIGHTY-FIVE FEDERALIST PAPERS; MEMBER OF THE FIRST U.S. CONGRESS, WHERE HE FATHERED THE BILL OF RIGHTS; U.S. SECRETARY OF STATE; FOURTH U.S. PRESIDENT (1809-1817); OUT-LIVED ALL FIFTY-FOUR OF THE OTHER FOUNDING FATHERS.

"If men were angels," said Madison, "no government would be necessary."

He defined religion this way:

> Religion, or the duty we owe to our Creator, and the manner of discharging it, can be directed only by reason and conviction, not by force or violence; and, therefore, that all men should enjoy the fullest toleration in the exercise of religion according to the dictates of conscience, unpunished and unrestrained by the magistrate, unless under color of religion any man disturb the peace, the happiness, or safety of society, and that it is the mutual duty of all to practice Christian forbearance, love, and charity toward each other.[105]

James Madison is referred to by most historians as "the Father of the Constitution." No man was better prepared to be one of the Founding Fathers in temperament, intellect, background, education, and commitment.

On March 16, 1751, he was born into the devout home of James and Molly Conway Madison in Port Conway, Virginia. His father was a wealthy plantation owner and member of the Episcopal, or state church, in which he was baptized on the twenty-first day of his life. He was homeschooled by his godly mother and grandmother, and two tutors came to his residence to give instruction, one of whom was an Episcopalian minister. These men taught him Latin, Greek, arithmetic, literature, French, and Spanish. They also established a broad and diverse reading schedule.

Due to what his parents considered heretical views, which they felt had crept into the local college of William and Mary (probably the early waves of French skepticism), they sent him to Princeton, where he studied for the ministry. Here he fell under the influence of the Reverend John Witherspoon, one of the nation's leading theologians and legal scholars. This helped to establish a theological base for Madison's thinking, and it never left him. He also developed lifetime friends, some of whom went into the ministry. Chief among them were William Bradford, who after his divinity studies went into law, and

Samuel Stanhope Smith, who became a Presbyterian minister and was later Witherspoon's successor at Princeton.

> During his stay at Princeton a great revival took place, and it was believed that he partook of its spirit. On his return home he conducted worship in his father's house. He soon after offered for the Legislature, and it was objected to him, by his opponents, that he was better suited to the pulpit than to the legislative hall.[106]

Long after he returned to Virginia, young Madison continued to pursue his theological studies. It may have been at this period in his life, while out walking with his father one day, that he entered into a life-molding experience. We don't know exactly when it took place, but an incident in his youth that made a deep impression on him was his standing with his father outside the jail in the village of Orange and listening to several Baptists preach from the window of the cell in which they were confined because of their religious opinions.[107]

Something must have been stirred in young Madison's heart that day, for he, like Patrick Henry, became a fierce champion of religious freedom. He had seen the excesses that can be perpetrated when one religion acts with the power of government.

This experience so moved him that after he went into law and politics, he became a major defender of religious liberty. While Henry served as the volunteer legal defender of the "dissident sects," whose only crime was as he described it, "preaching the Gospel of the Son of God,"[108] Madison gave his attention to changing the laws. Primarily as the result of his efforts, Jefferson's religious freedom guarantees (which had been previously rejected) were approved in the Virginia constitution.

Later, as a member of the first Congress, Madison made religious freedom the first item in his Bill of Rights. He placed it first because he considered it of primary importance. He knew that when citizens lose their religious freedoms, all other freedoms are in jeopardy. Some of his best arguments on religious freedom and separation of church and state are particularly appropriate today, when secularists seem to have no aversion to using the awesome power of government to advance the religious beliefs of humanism, particularly in our government-controlled public schools.

It would be difficult to imagine a Founding Father who exercised greater influence on America. During his long career — he lived to be eighty-five in spite of a frail body — he served in the Virginia Convention, which drafted a new constitution. He was a delegate to the Continental Congress and the Constitutional Convention. He served in the first U.S. Congress, where in keeping with his earlier promises, he wrote and pushed through the Bill of Rights. He was appointed by Thomas Jefferson to the post of secretary of state, from which he engineered the Louisiana Purchase in 1803, and he succeeded Jefferson to the presidency, serving from 1809-17 and acting as commander-in-chief during the War of 1812. He and his wife had to flee the White House for safety when it was captured and burned by the British.

Madison's most lasting contribution to America was probably his service to the Continental Congress, where for practical purposes he served as secretary. Except for Gouverneur Morris, Madison spoke more than any other delegate (161 times), served on the committee on postponed matters and the committee on style, and was a prime mover in the drafting, ratification, and passage of the Bill of Rights.

The Religious Views Of James Madison

Our fourth President lived and served in public life so long and wrote so much during those years that the nature of his religious views has provoked considerable speculation. Because he was personally a very private man and did not believe that government should provide a platform for religious discourse, his early life provides us with the best evidence of his Christian faith. His later comments are best understood in the light of these early affirmations.

Madison's Personal Notes

One historian had this to say about Madison as a Bible student:

After the manner of the Bereans he seems to have searched the Scriptures daily and diligently. . . . He explored the whole history and evidences of Christianity on every side, through clouds of witnesses and champions for and against, from the Fathers and schoolmen down to the infidel philosophers of the eighteenth century. No one not a professed theologian, and but few even of those who are, have ever gone through more laborious and extensive inquiries to arrive at the truth.[109]

This is clearly reflected in the publication of the notes found in his personal Bible, some of which have been lost.

Acts Chapter 19

Believers who are in a State of Grace, have need of the word of God for their Edification and Building up therefore implies a possibility of falling v. 32.

Grace, it is the free gift of God. Luke. 12. 32-v.32

Giver more blessed than the Receiver. v. 35

To neglect the means for our own preservation is to Tempt God: and to trust to them is to neglect him v.3 & Ch. 27. v. 31

Humility, the better any man is, the lower thoughts he has of himself v. 19

Ministers to take heed to themselves & their flock. v. 28[110]

Madison evidently believed in the miracles of Jesus:

The apostles did greater Miracles than Christ, in the matter, not manner, of them v. 11.[111]

Madison's belief in eternal life and salvation are clear in a personal letter to his close college friend William Bradford. Writing on November 9, 1772, Madison said,

A watchful eye must be kept on ourselves lest while we are building ideal monuments of Renown and Bliss here we neglect to have our names enrolled in the Annals of Heaven. [Bad health has] intimated to me not to expect a long or healthy life, yet it may be better with me after some time tho I hardly dare expect it and therefore have little spirit and alacrity to set about any thing that is difficult in acquiring and useless in possessing after one has exchanged Time for Eternity.[112]

Madison on God

Many years later, Madison wrote "Memorial and Remonstrance," in which he said,

"Whilst we assert for ourselves a freedom to embrace, to profess, and to observe the Religion which we believe to be of divine origin, we cannot deny an equal freedom to those whose minds have not yet yielded to the evidence which has convinced us. If this freedom be abused, it is an offence against God, not against man: To God, therefore, not to man, must an account of it be rendered."[113]

In light of the fact that he was addressing a predominantly Christian audience, it is clear that he was referring to the God of the Bible as the divine originator of the Christian religion. The God he alluded to was obviously personal.

In agreement with John Adams and others who believed that our Constitution was written for a religious people, Madison stated,

The belief in a God All Powerful, wise and good, is so essential to the moral order of the World and to the happiness of man, that arguments which enforce it cannot be drawn from too many sources nor adapted with too much solicitude to the different characters and capacities to be impressed with it.[114]

Even though he was reluctant to bring God into his public statements, he did so in his inaugural address of March 4, 1809. In it he expressed his confidence in God "in the guardianship and guidance of that almighty Being, whose power regulates the destiny of nations."[115]

When we take into consideration that this statement was made twenty-two years after the Constitution was written, it is apparent that Madison was not hostile to Christianity and showed evidence that the faith of his divinity school days was not dead, even after serving in the legal profession and public life for many years.

One writer summed up his comments on Madison's religious life as follows:

> If Madison ever rejected the fundamental doctrines of the Christian faith, he never said so in writing that has survived to date. And throughout his life he remained friendly and respectful toward Christianity and toward the Church.

> Was Madison a believer in Jesus Christ? Did he remember, in the phrase he used to his youthful friend in 1772, to have his name "enrolled in the Annals of Heaven?" We must leave that question to God, and to Madison himself.

> But this much is very clear: The Christian religion, and particularly Rev. Witherspoon's Calvinism, strongly influenced Madison's view of law and government.[116]

GOUVERNEUR MORRIS
(1752-1816)

PENNSYLVANIA, EPISCOPALIAN: MERCHANT; LAWYER; PLANTER; FINANCIER; DELEGATE TO THE CONSTITUTIONAL CONVENTION; HELPED WRITE THE NEW YORK CONSTITUTION; MEMBER OF CONTINENTAL CONGRESS; WROTE THE FINAL DRAFT OF THE U.S. CONSTITUTION; FIRST U.S. MINISTER TO FRANCE; U.S. SENATOR; ACTIVELY PROMOTED THE ERIE CANAL.

Gouverneur Morris will always be remembered in American history for two reasons: first, as the man who spoke the greatest number of times during the Convention debates—173 times!—and second, as the author of the final draft of the Constitution.

It is assumed by many that to Morris we owe the symmetry, grace, and elegance of our Constitution. The fifty-five delegates hammered out the substance of the document, but it was Gouverneur Morris, only thirty-five years old at the time, who gave it the final touch. And it is said that he was the first to use (in writing) the expression, "We the people of the United States." So divided were the colonies at the time, that many doubted it would be acceptable. Fortunately for all of us, it was.

Born in New York, this delegate from Pennsylvania (where he had moved for business reasons) was both a brilliant and a personable man. He was possibly the most well-liked delegate, popular with almost everyone, a charming conversationalist and second only to Benjamin Franklin for his ready wit.

Morris was born into wealth, graduated with honors from King's College, became a lawyer and a very successful merchant, was the new nation's first minister to France, later became a U.S. senator from New York, and was a pioneer promoter of the Erie Canal.

Little is known of the religious life of this warm, personable, and very gifted man. A member of the Episcopal church, he evidenced in his speeches and writings a familiarity with the Bible. At the end of his life he acknowledged that he would "descend towards the grave full of gratitude to the Giver of all good." One can only speculate about the impact that the religious atmosphere of King's College had on his thinking.

Morris was sufficiently indoctrinated with the "Christian consensus" that he believed strongly in the depravity of human nature and totally rejected the Enlightenment-inspired "fanatical ideology of the Jacobin French republic."[117]

His patriotic spirit is evident in this prediction of his beloved homeland written in 1801:

> The proudest empire in Europe is but a bauble compared
> to what America will be, must be, in the course of two
> centuries, perhaps of one! If, with a calm retrospect to the

progress made within forty years, we stand on the firm
ground of calculation, warranted by experience, and
look forward to the end of a similar period, imagination
shrinks from the magnitude of rational deduction.[118]

ROGER SHERMAN
(1721-1793)

CONNECTICUT, CONGREGATIONALIST: SHOE COBBLER; SURVEYOR;
MERCHANT; SELF-TAUGHT LAWYER; JUDGE; LAY THEOLOGIAN;
STATE SENATOR; MEMBER OF CONTINENTAL CONGRESS; SERVED ON
THE COMMITTEE TO DRAFT THE DECLARATION OF INDEPENDENCE; A
SIGNER OF THE DECLARATION OF INDEPENDENCE AND THE ARTICLES
OF CONFEDERATION; A U.S. CONGRESSMAN; ELECTED TO THE U.S.
SENATE AT SEVENTY YEARS OF AGE.

John Adams, our second President, described Sherman as
". . . an old Puritan, as honest as an angel and as firm in the
cause of American Independence as Mount Atlas."[119]
The inscription on Sherman's tomb reads:

IN MEMORY OF
THE HON. ROGER SHERMAN, ESQ.
MAYOR OF THE CITY OF NEW HAVEN,
AND SENATOR OF THE UNITED STATES.
HE WAS BORN AT NEWTOWN, IN MASSACHUSETTS,
APRIL 19th, 1721

AND DIED IN NEW HAVEN, JULY 23rd, A.D. 1793,
AGED LXXII.

. . . He ever adorned
the profession of Christianity
which he made in youth;
and, distinguished through life
for public usefulness,
died in the prospect
of a blessed immortality.

"Roger Sherman was . . . in many respects the most remarkable man in the Convention," wrote one historian.[120]

In addition to signing the U.S. Constitution, Sherman also
signed the Articles of Association in 1774, the Declaration of
Independence, and the Articles of Confederation. Once the
Constitution was completed, he was instrumental in getting
Connecticut to ratify it.

During his long public life (forty-eight years) he served as
surveyor, self-taught lawyer, state legislator, judge, superior
court judge, delegate to the Continental Congress and Constitutional Convention, and later in the new nation he became both a
congressman and a U.S. senator.

Another historian says of Sherman:

His greatest public service . . . was performed in the
Federal Constitutional Convention. In the bitter conflict
between the large state party and the small state party he
and his colleagues, Oliver Ellsworth and William Samuel
Johnson, acted as peacemakers. Their share in bringing
about the final settlement, which provided for equal representation in one house and proportional representation
in the other, was so important that the settlement itself
has come to be called the "Connecticut Compromise."[121]

Spiritually speaking, Roger Sherman was undoubtedly one
of the most devout men at the Convention. He joined the Congregational church in 1742 and served as deacon, clerk, and
treasurer. Of his pastor, the Reverend Jonathan Edwards, the
younger, he said,

I esteem him one of the best of preachers that I am acquainted with, sound in faith, and pious and diligent in
his studies and attention to the duties of his office.[122]

Sherman's religious writings,

. . . display the same acuteness and good sense which
characterize his political writings and speeches. They also
show great familiarity with the Bible, of which he was a
constant student. It was his custom to purchase a Bible at
the commencement of every session of Congress, to
peruse it daily, and to present it to one of his children on
his return home.[123]

In 1788, Mr. Sherman was a member of the White Haven
Congregational Church and participated in the revision of its
creed. The following confession of faith, *in Mr. Sherman's own
handwriting*, succinctly describes his fundamental beliefs.

I believe that there is one only living and true God, existing in three persons, the Father, the Son, and the Holy
Ghost, the same in substance equal in power and glory.
That the scriptures of the old and new testaments are a
revelation from God, and a complete rule to direct us
how we may glorify and enjoy him. That God has fore-
ordained whatsoever comes to pass, so as thereby he is
not the author or approver of sin. That he creates all
things, and preserves and governs all creatures and all
their actions, in a manner perfectly consistent with the
freedom of will in moral agents, and the usefulness of
means. That he made man at first perfectly holy, that the
first man sinned, and as he was the public head of his posterity, they all became sinners in consequence of his first
transgression, are wholly indisposed to that which is good
and inclined to evil, and on account of sin are liable to all
the miseries of this life, to death, and to the pains of hell
forever. I believe that God having elected some of man-

great deal of canting speculation has been indulged in by
rious persons as to Hamilton's religious faith, for it was
eged that he died without belief. Bishop Moore's account
his death, on the contrary, shows that he was a man of
rnest, simple faith, quite unemotional in this respect, so
as display was concerned, but his belief was very strong.

e who had all his life made his way by more or less mili-
nt methods, or by appeals to reason, by careful and
btle argument, and diplomatic manoeuvres, conceived,
his fear for the future welfare of his country, the estab-
hment of a vast religious body to be called "The Chris-
n Constitutional Society." With his keen insight he
ew that even the mob could be swayed by such an or-
nization, and that the mental epidemic that was caused
the poisonous French Doctrines" might be replaced,
rhaps, by a movement of a healthy and uplifting kind.[129]

s friend Bayard he wrote,

my opinion, the present constitution is the standard to
hich we are to cling. Under its banners *bona fide* must we
mbat our political foes, rejecting all changes but
rough the channel itself provided for amendments. By
ese general views of the subject have my reflections
en guided. I now offer you the outline of the plan they
ave suggested. Let an association be formed to be
enominated "The Christian Constitutional Society," its
bject to be 1st: The support of the Christian religion. 2d:
he support of the United States.[130]

nterestingly, Hamilton turned on Thomas Jefferson because
s "Jacobin" influence from France. Many believe that Jeffer-
who was accused of being an atheist by ministers of the gos-
during the election of 1800, had been "humanized" by the
cal instigators of the French Revolution. At best we would
im a "humanized Anglican" or "closet Unitarian." Hamilton
ved that Jefferson's European ideas would corrupt the United
es. "He fought the spread of Jacobinism on these shores with
f his energy. Particularly with his pen did he thunder that
ocracy' and 'Christian civilization' were incompatible."[131]

kind to eternal life, did send his own son to become man, die in the room and stead of sinners, and thus to lay a foundation for the offer of pardon and salvation to all mankind, so as all may be saved who are willing to accept the gospel offer: Also by his special grace and spirit, to regenerate, sanctify and enable to persevere in holiness, all who shall be saved; and to procure in consequence of their repentance and faith in himself their justification by virtue of his atonement as the only meritorious cause. I believe a visible church to be a congregation of those who make a credible profession of their faith in Christ, and obedience to him, joined by the bond of the covenant. . . . I believe that the souls of believers are at their death made perfectly holy, and immediately taken to glory: that at the end of this world there will be a resurrection of the dead, and a final judgment of all mankind, when the righteous shall be publicly acquitted by Christ the Judge and admitted to everlasting life and glory, and the wicked be sentenced to everlasting punishment.[124]

If this man who had such a profound effect on the U.S. Constitution were living today, it is reasonable to conclude from the above statements that Roger Sherman would be quite comfortable in our Bible-believing churches—particularly among Presbyterians.

He is also to be remembered for his opposition to what became our first amendment, which originally was to have read,

No religion should be established by law, nor shall the equal rights of conscience be infringed. Mr. Sherman thought the amendment altogether unnecessary, inasmuch as *Congress had no authority whatever* delegated to them by the Constitution *to make religious establishments*.[125]

He also worked successfully to have President Washington officially establish Thanksgiving Day as a national holiday. Roger Sherman was a public leader of whom every Christian can be proud.

ALEXANDER HAMILTON
(1757-1804)

NEW YORK, EPISCOPALIAN: SOLDIER; LAWYER; WRITER; POLITICAL PHILOSOPHER; STATESMAN; ECONOMIST; AUTHOR OF FIFTY-ONE OF THE EIGHTY-FIVE FEDERALIST PAPERS; SECRETARY OF THE TREASURY; BANKER; FOUNDER OF THE NEW YORK POST; CONSIDERED "THE RATIFIER OF THE CONSTITUTION."

One historian described Hamilton this way:

> A man of extraordinary gifts, almost a prodigy, but possessed of a certain confidence, with a touch of swagger and hyperbole, that earned him enemies throughout his career. Born on the island of Nevis, one of the Leeward chain in the West Indies. Natural son of James Hamilton of Ayshire, Scotland, fourth son of Alexander Hamilton, the laird of Grange; and of Rachel Fawcett, the daughter of a French planter and physician. The union of his parents, perhaps sanctioned by some kind of ceremony, but illegal, and, by reason of certain irregularities, at best a common law marriage. Marked throughout his life by the stigma of his origins. Without a father from an early age and all but an orphan at eleven. Educated privately on St. Croix, in apprenticeship to the island firm of Nicholas Cruger; at Francis Barber's school in Elizabethtown, New Jersey; and at King's College [now Columbia] in New York, where he was enrolled in 1773. A superb and sys-

tematic student and at seventeen, with th
pute between the American colonies and tl
George III, a fledgling orator and politica
Left school without a degree for military
in the American army in the spring of 177

Alexander Hamilton was one of those b
patriots without whose help it is doubtful the C
have been completed, and it is probable that
port, it would not have been ratified—particul
tant state of New York, for all its other delegat
tion in disgust before it was completed.[127]

Hamilton, a prolific writer, inspired the *F*
were circulated throughout the colonies, fifty
wrote. While Madison is termed "the Father of
it isn't an exaggeration to call Hamilton "the R
stitution." It was his tireless and brilliant energ
tification from more than the required two-th
most of which passed it on the first vote.

During the Revolutionary War, the young
guished himself in battle and with the pen, v
the attention of General George Washingto
him his aide-de-camp and staff lawyer. He serv
for four years and was promoted to Lieutenant
tary of the treasury, he distinguished himself i
called "Hamiltonianism." After the Constituti
founded the *New York Post* and one of the sta

Hamilton the Christian

Little is known of the Christian faith of 1
obviously not raised in a devoutly Christian hc
He did, however, attend King's College, whi
founded to honor "The King of Kings."[128] One

> He believed in the moral decay of the Uni
> loss of religious principle in consequence
> of Paine, and those of irresponsible fanatic
> so much to unsettle the simple faith of the
> The future to him was threatening, and
> means of regeneration.

As is well known, Hamilton was killed by Aaron Burr in a duel on July 12, 1804. It is said that he

> accepted Burr's challenge, but refused to fire upon his adversary. On the heights of Weehawken, Burr was less scrupulous, and gave to Hamilton a wound which, on July 12, 1804, at two o'clock in the afternoon, proved mortal. (Though Presbyterian by upbringing, Hamilton was an Episcopalian, and a few hours before his death received the last rites from New York Bishop Benjamin Moore.) There was a nationwide interval of shock when these events were reported. A revulsion set in against Burr which, ironically, made of Hamilton's death his final public service.[132]

While only God knows the degree of reality in Hamilton's faith, it is safe to say that Hamilton was favorable to the Christian faith, was influenced by the prevailing Christian consensus, and did nothing in his public life that would secularize this nation.

GEORGE MASON
(1725-1792)
VIRGINIA, EPISCOPALIAN: LAWYER; PLANTER; POLITICAL PHILOSO-
PHER; JUDGE; MEMBER OF VIRGINIA HOUSE OF BURGESSES; HELPED
WRITE VIRGINIA CONSTITUTION; AUTHOR OF THE "VIRGINIA BILL OF
RIGHTS."

One historian said this about George Mason's contribution to the Constitutional Convention:

> At sixty-one, Mason was older than most members at the Great Convention. He was an old-school gentleman, majestic in size and of princely bearing, austere, courtly, self-willed, his face browned with sun and wind, and his hair flecked with the snows of sixty-one well rounded years. He was a man of profound learning and took a leading part in the debates, proposing many curious schemes. He advocated the election of President directly from the people, and for a term of seven years, with ineligibility afterward. He had a mortal hatred to paper money, and disapproved of the slave-trade.[133]

William Pierce described him as "undoubtedly one of the best politicians in America."[134] He was superbly qualified to participate in the writing of a national Constitution.

> In 1776 Mason was the leading member of the special convention which drew up a new constitution for the independent state of Virginia, and from 1776 through 1781 he sat in the Virginia legislature for Fairfax County. These were the most active political years in his career. Mason was himself the principal author of the Virginia Declaration of Rights, which laid a predicate for the Declaration of Independence adopted within the next three months. There were many competing versions of the original Virginia constitution but, according to the participants, "that proposed by George Mason swallowed up all the rest." In the view of authorities on Mason's thought, the distinguishing characteristic of this document is its almost complete similarity to the old colonial government of Virginia under the British Crown, with a limited executive, an appointed council, and stringent property qualifications for seats in both houses of the legislature. Mason's constitution is no democratic document, but it is republican in the classical sense. Its object was to restrict and distribute power, not to enforce an a priori ideological plan on Virginia society.[135]

Mason feared that a strong federal government would usurp the sovereignty of the individual states, and who can deny he was right? The longer the Convention went on, the more his fear intensified until on August 31, he announced he would oppose this Constitution, principally because it contained no bill of rights, although he had other reasons. He called unsuccessfully for "a second convention."

Much to the consternation of Washington and Madison, Mason returned to Virginia and vigorously opposed the ratification of the Constitution. He was joined by Patrick Henry, who opposed the Convention in the first place, and they did royal battle throughout the state to cause its defeat. They lost by four votes. Thanks to their efforts and those of other statesman like them who opposed the Constitution for similar reasons, however, the Bill of Rights was added by the first U.S. Congress. As one historian relates,

> in another sense, they won the day. For the issue in the convention came down finally to a choice between previous or subsequent amendments to the Constitution and to specifications concerning the proper understanding of the language of the document as it stood. Thanks to George Mason and Patrick Henry, Virginia spoke with a united voice in these regards.[136]

After the Convention, Mason refused a position in the United States Senate and retired to his palatial home.

Mason was an Anglican, with a thorough distrust for fallen human nature. He knew the Bible well and on occasions included it in his public speeches, as he did before the Virginia ratifying convention, when he quoted our Lord in referring to the work of the framers of the Constitution: "They have done what they ought not to have done, and have left undone what they ought to have done."[137]

TEN

OUTSTANDING CHRISTIANS AMONG THE FOUNDING FATHERS

While all but one of the fifty-five Founding Fathers was a member of a church and most made some kind of statement of traditional faith in order to qualify as a delegate to the Convention, not all were "evangelical Christians" as we would think of them today. Little is known about the depth of the religious commitment of several of the Founders, due partly to the fact that they were personally obscure and little is known of their lives. In addition, it was not as common in those days as it is today to speak openly of your religious faith. Many people felt their faith was an extremely personal matter. This was particularly true of political leaders, and after all, the Constitutional Convention was a political meeting, not a religious assembly.

Nevertheless, we know that many of the delegates were active churchmen who would feel very comfortable in some of our Bible-believing churches of today. This chapter contains only those not already mentioned whose religious experience has been well established in history and was obviously an integral part of their lives. That is not to suggest that some of those not included in this chapter did not have an equal commitment to our Lord and Savior, Jesus Christ. Further research, particularly in the communities where they originated, would doubtless give encouraging documentation about many of them, but such research will have to be left for others. The other delegates are, however, sketched briefly in Appendices A and B.

Several of those Christian gentlemen listed in Appendix B

could just as well be included here. They were sound, active Christians, made significant contributions to the Constitution, but for personal or political reasons were not on hand to sign the final document.

Were you an active Christian two hundred years ago, you might find many of the following sitting next to you on the pew in church on any given Sunday.

ABRAHAM BALDWIN
(1754-1807)

GEORGIA, CONGREGATIONALIST: CLERGYMAN; ARMY CHAPLAIN; LAW-YER; EDUCATOR; STATESMAN; MEMBER OF CONGRESS; U.S. SENATOR.

One of the delegates from the South who contributed most to the writing of the Constitution, Abraham Baldwin was born and raised in Connecticut. His deeply religious parents gave him a thorough Puritan training that prepared him to attend Yale Divinity School, where he studied for the ministry.

He did so well in his theological studies that after graduation in 1772, he was invited to join the faculty. During the four years he taught there, he also became a licensed Congregational minister and volunteered to serve in the Continental Army as a chaplain. Following his military career he studied law and was admitted to the bar in 1783.

Interestingly enough, Baldwin's famous career was not in his native state but in Georgia, where he had migrated in 1784.

There he was admitted to the bar in three months and elected to the state assembly the following year. "Because of his energy, prudence and application,"[138] he quickly distinguished himself in a state that was not yet advanced in the field of education. Instrumental in drawing up the bill that provided for the educational system of the state, he was one of the founders of the Georgia state college that today is well known as the University of Georgia. In fact, he served as the college's first president and wrote the college charter. One historian said of him, "He was one of the best classical and mathematical scholars of the age."[139]

Baldwin certainly was far-sighted, for he secured forty thousand acres of land for the university. One historian exclaimed, "Had he performed no public duty other than this, Mr. Baldwin's title to the gratitude of succeeding generations would have been unquestioned."[140]

Baldwin was elected as one of Georgia's eight representatives to the Constitutional Convention. He was highly respected by the other delegates, whom he formally addressed eight times.

One insight into the thinking of this devout man, called "the Puritan of Georgia" by his peers, is found in the charter of the College of Georgia, which he wrote just prior to attending the Convention in Philadelphia. His training for the ministry as well as law obviously gave him insight into the significance of the college's religious roots and the positive influence it would become on its students and the state of Georgia.

As it is the distinguishing happiness of free governments that civil order should be the result of choice and not of necessity, and the common wishes of the people become the laws of the land, their public prosperity and even existence very much depend upon suitably forming the minds and morals of their citizens. When the minds of the people in general are viciously disposed and unprincipled, and their conduct disorderly, a free government will be attended with greater confusions and evils more horrid than the wild, uncultivated state of nature. It can only be happy when the public principles and opinions are properly directed, and their manners regulated. This is an influence beyond the reach of laws and punishments, and can be claimed only by religion and education. *It should therefore be among the first objects of those who wish well to the national prosperity to encourage and support the principles of religion and morality,* and early to place the youth under the forming hand of society, that by instruction they may be moulded to *the love of virtue and good order.* Sending them abroad to other countries for their education will not answer these purposes, is too humiliating an acknowledgment of the ignorance or inferiority of our own, and will always be the cause of so great foreign attachments that upon principles of policy it is inadmissible.[141]

It is obvious from this admonition that our present university system has forsaken the principles deemed necessary by this Founding Father to educate future generations adequately. We no longer seem to consider it necessary for society's good to train our young in "the principles of religion and morality." But it was deemed essential two centuries ago.

RICHARD BASSETT
(1745-1815)
DELAWARE, METHODIST: PLANTER; LAWYER; CAPTAIN IN THE REVO-
LUTIONARY WAR; JURIST; INFLUENTIAL STATE LEADER; PARTICIPATED
IN WRITING DELAWARE'S CONSTITUTION; U.S. SENATOR; STATE CHIEF
JUSTICE; CIRCUIT COURT JUDGE; GOVERNOR; ACTIVE METHODIST
LAYMAN.

After working with Richard Bassett at the Constitutional Convention for several months, Pierce described him as "a religious enthusiast, lately turned Methodist, who serves his country because it is the will of the people that he should do so. He is a man of plain sense, and has modesty enough to hold his tongue. He is a gentlemanly man, and is in high estimation among the Methodists."[142]

Historian M. E. Bradford concurs with this description.

> Richard Bassett was one of the most devout of the Framers. He was converted to Methodism during the Revolution and became a close personal friend of Bishop Francis Asbury, who held meetings on his plantation. Bassett freed his slaves and then employed them as hired labor. But he was no egalitarian or champion of radical change. Rather, he should be remembered as one of the pillars of the old order in Delaware. . . . He is best remembered for his contributions to the life of his chosen church, his generosity toward what he saw as the work of God.[143]

Although he was born of a tavern-keeper who abandoned him and his mother, Bassett was adopted by a relative named Peter Lawson, who provided him a Christian environment and training, which may account for his deep commitment to Christ and His church. It is said that he contributed half the cost for building the First Methodist Church in Dover.

Mr. Lawson willed him a six thousand acre estate, which established him en route to becoming a wealthy man. His closest political friends, like John Dickinson, shared his faith and political philosophy. He was later appointed to the U.S. circuit court by President John Adams, who also shared his faith.

After the Convention, Basset became a leading member of the Delaware ratifying convention and had no small part in seeing his state become the first to ratify the new Constitution.

Gunning Bedford of Delaware

Bedford was born in Philadelphia of parentage that originally settled in Jamestown, Virginia. He attended Princeton College, where he shared a room with James Madison and

GUNNING BEDFORD
(1747-1812)
DELAWARE, PRESBYTERIAN: LAWYER; ATTORNEY GENERAL OF STATE;
MEMBER OF CONTINENTAL CONGRESS; FEDERAL JUDGE.

where both men were influenced in their views of law and theology by the godly John Witherspoon. He was active in his attendance at the Presbyterian church, where he was buried.

During the Constitutional Convention, he distinguished himself as a speaker and "played a considerable part in the Federal Convention."[144]

In 1789, after the Convention, President Washington appointed this devout man to the First Federal District Court, an office he held for the rest of his life.

John Blair of Virginia

Born into a wealthy family, John Blair was only thirty-three when he became a member of the Virginia delegation to the Constitutional Convention.

Blair attended almost every session of the Convention but remained silent. He primarily contributed through voting with the majority of the Virginia delegation. After he returned from the Convention, he was elected to Virginia's Supreme Court of Appeals. In 1789 he was appointed to the Supreme Court bench by his friend President George Washington. He served on that

JOHN BLAIR
(1732-1800)

VIRGINIA, EPISCOPALIAN: LAWYER; POLITICAL LEADER DURING THE
REVOLUTION; JURIST; SUPREME COURT JUSTICE.

court until bad health made traveling (to hold court) too difficult.

Little is known of Blair's religious beliefs except that he remained an active worshipper at the Episcopal church in his home town of Williamsburg, where he was buried at Bruton Parish Church. A letter written to his sister at the time of her husband's death gives evidence of his belief in and understanding of Biblical principles regarding salvation, death, the life hereafter, and the sovereign will of God for individuals. Writing to his sister, he said,

> With much grief of my own and real sympathy for yours, I sit down to write you a Letter of Condolence on as great a Loss as could have befallen you . . . but an event no way contingent but absolutely certain itself *it being appointed for all men once to die.* . . .

> Let us seek for comfort where alone it may be found, let us learn a dutiful acquiescence in whatsoever proceeds from that Great Being from whom we ourselves proceeded and who being the Sole Author of all our enjoyments has an undoubted Right to withdraw them in his own good

time and whose Goodness so conspicuous in his General Providence may be as eminent for aught we know though not so plainly discerned even when He deals to us the bitter cup of Affliction. We may all profit in the School of Adversity if we will but make a proper use of its Sacred Lessons. If in this life only we had hope it would indeed be harder to acquire a due serenity of mind upon the loss of a beloved Friend. If he were absolutely extinct to forget him would be perhaps necessary to our Peace of Mind. But now as our Holy Religion teaches we may contemplate him translated to a better Life and ineffably enjoying all that variety of Bliss which Eye hath not seen nor Ear heard nor the Heart conceived. May the Celestial vision forever preserve you from the Gloominess of Grief and reconcile you to all the Dispensations of Him who cannot err. My Situation both with Respect to my Family and Fortune (all being in the Power of the Enemy and much in their possession) is bad enough. But I trust for a happy issue and for power to bear all His appointments as I ought.[145]

It should be kept in mind that just six years after writing these words, this man was selected by his peers to participate in the founding of our nation. It is obvious that the voters of Virginia did not send a deist or skeptic to Philadelphia when they sent John Blair.

David Brearly
(1745-1790)
NEW JERSEY, EPISCOPALIAN: LAWYER; COLONEL IN THE REVOLUTIONARY ARMY; CHIEF JUSTICE OF STATE SUPREME COURT; FEDERAL JUDGE.
[*portrait not available*]

Brearly attended Princeton College, from which he received an honorary M.A. degree, studied law, and was admitted to the bar in 1767. He was so outspoken for the colonial cause that he was arrested for "high treason" against the mother country. Serving in the New Jersey regiment, he rose to the rank of colonel of infantry, which he held from 1776-79. Elected chief justice of the New Jersey Supreme Court, he distinguished himself as a jurist. He was "a warden of St. Michael's Church," a "compiler of the Protestant Episcopal prayer book and a delegate to the Episcopal General Convention in 1786."[146]

During the convention, just one year later, this active Christian layman assisted in the preparation and presentation of the "New Jersey Plan," was chairman of the committee of postponed matters, and presented their reports. Bradford notes that he was "the most regular in his attendance of the Philadelphia Convention."[147]

David Brearley, Pierce recorded, was a "man of good rather than of brilliant parts. . . . As an orator he has little to boast of." As a man, however, he had "every virtue to recommend him," and was "very much in the esteem of the people."[148]

After the Convention, he was appointed by President Washington as federal judge of New Jersey, a post he held until his death.

Jacob Broom
(1752-1810)
DELAWARE, LUTHERAN: SURVEYOR; FARMER; MERCHANT; BANKER; ENTREPRENEUR; VERY ACTIVE IN DEVELOPING HIS STATE.
[portrait not available]

According to one historian, "Before and after 1765, when The Old Academy was built, and Jacob Broom was thirteen years old, he enjoyed the advantage of substantial instruction, both secular and religious, at home, in the church and in the local schools of the time."[149]

During his youthful years, Jacob Broom was influenced for Christ and His church by three godly pastors of the old Swedes Church. "The influence of Pastor Girelius on the growing boy and developing young man was extended through a score of years, and was good and wholesome and well adapted to develop courageous patriots and useful citizens."[150] The same pastor performed his wedding ceremony in 1773, the year of the Boston Tea Party.

Jacob Broom, like many individuals of his day, was raised in a Quaker background. He experienced no little tension between the Quaker pacifism of his early family years and his patriotic involvement in the Revolutionary War. This seems clear from the fact that he and his family joined the Episcopal church, in which he had his children baptized. Yet his youthful training in the Old Swedes church, where he was a vestryman for many years, made him comfortable as an interdenominational Protestant.

One insight into this man's thinking can be gleaned from a letter written by him in 1794 to his son, a senior at Princeton College, seventeen years after the Constitutional Convention. "Do not be so much flattered as to relax in your application; do not forget to be a Christian. I have said much to you on this head, and I hope an indelible impression is made."[151]

In the official papers of Delaware written in 1909, tracing the history of that state, the following appears:

As I have studied Mr. Broom's life he was, I think, a fair example of the product of a sturdy, energetic, sagacious ancestry and evangelical Swedish orthodoxy, co-operating amid the trying environments of a struggling colony in an undeveloped land. He wrought with fine material. He lived in one of the potential crises of history, in which and for which the sublime visions and words of prophets and apostles had developed and inspired a stalwart manhood.[152]

As it is an accepted fact that "the foundation of all 'permanent prosperity' is a right regard for the Divine Being," it is proper to say that Jacob Broom was a God-fearing man.[153]

Like many of the nonattorney delegates to the Constitutional Convention, he said very little. In fact, according to M. E. Bradford, "During the debates he made only one significant speech." He added that Broom was "a quiet man of moderate views, and one of the least of the Framers."[154]

While he may have made a minimal contribution to the document itself, Broom did vote regularly with the other delegates of his state and was active in his state's ratification process. Pierce described him "as a plain good man."[155]

JOHN DICKINSON
(1732-1803)

DELAWARE, QUAKER/EPISCOPALIAN: LAWYER; PLANTER; POLITICAL PHILOSOPHER; STATE LEGISLATOR; DELEGATE TO THE CONTINENTAL CONGRESS; WRITER OF THE FIRST DRAFT OF THE ARTICLES OF CONFEDERATION.

John Dickinson was "one of the most prominent members of the Convention." He was best remembered as "the Penman of the Revolution" because of his popular pamphlets that were widely circulated, and he was considered "the most learned of the Framers."[156] A contemporary said of him,

> "Famed through all America for his *Farmer's Letters*; he is a scholar, and said to be a man of very extensive information. . . . He is . . . a good writer and will be ever considered one of the most important characters in the United States."[157]

Born of Judge Samuel and Mary Dickinson, both Quakers, he was educated at home and privately. He passed the bar in 1753, then went to London to further his studies in law. Upon his return he became one of the most respected attorneys in the colonies and served in the state houses of both Delaware and Pennsylvania.

In 1771 he wrote a "Petition to the King"; in 1774, "The Declaration and Resolves of the First Continental Congress"; and in 1775, "The Declaration of the cause of taking up arms." The famous "Song of the Farmer" was one of many popular pamphlets penned by this gifted man.

Dickinson was an intellectual activist, yet he refused to sign the Declaration of Independence because no union of government was ready to take the place of the old. He did fight in the war, however, and was later recognized by both Delaware and Pennsylvania, where he served as president of the Supreme Executive Council. He founded Dickinson College in Carlisle, Pennsylvania, in 1773.

During the Constitutional Convention, he contributed most by being the first to advocate the compromise between the large and small states, granting them equal representation in the Senate and proportional representation in the House. After the Constitution was signed, he campaigned for its passage by writing letters signed "Fabius," which compare in quality to the *Federalist Papers*. It was largely due to his influence that Delaware and Pennsylvania were the first two states to ratify the Constitution.

With his roots deeply entrenched in the Pennsylvania Quaker faith, John Dickinson was anything but a sectarian or unbeliever. In fact, making the decision of going to war was for him, as it was for all Quakers, a difficult one. Arriving at the conclusion, however,

> that defensive war, at least, was permissible, he advocated and engaged in it as if he were performing a solemn duty from which there was no escape. He had nothing of the swaggering military adventurer or hero about him. He was in the finest and best sense, a man of peace, never invading the rights of others, and never suffering his own to be trodden upon, yet firmly believing, and acting all the time upon the belief, that "the pen was mightier than the sword." Wherever we meet him, from his earliest manhood, we find him always mild and amiable, disposed to be conciliatory, free from anything that looks like a quarrelsome disposition. He was beloved even by many of his political opponents.[158]

At that time in history (fifty years before state-supported public schools were established), Dickinson and his wife gave generously to the meeting of Friends in Philadelphia for their educational pursuits. He felt strongly that learning and the study of religion were compatible; as we have already seen, so did most of the Christian community of 1787.

Although the majority of his writings are of a political nature, designed with a nonsectarian appeal to the broadest possible extent (whether to declare independence or to ratify the Constitution), occasionally his Christian faith and beliefs surface. For example, here are a few extracts from his popular "Letters from a Farmer in Pennsylvania":

But while Divine Providence, that gave me existence in a land of freedom, permits my head to think, my lips to speak, and my hand to move, I shall so highly and gratefully value the blessing received as to take care that my silence and inactivity shall not give my implied assent to any act, degrading my brethren and myself from the birthright, wherewith heaven itself *"hath made us free."*[159]

I pray GOD that he may be pleased to inspire you and your posterity, to the latest ages, with a spirit of which I have an idea, that I find a difficulty to express. To express it in the best manner I can, I mean a spirit that shall so guide you that it will be impossible to determine whether an *American's* character is most distinguishable for his loyalty to his Sovereign, his duty to his mother country, his love of freedom, or his affection for his native soil.[160]

But, above all, let us implore the protection of that infinitely good and gracious being [Proverbs 8:15] "by whom kings reign, and princes decree justice."[161]

A communication of her rights in general, and particularly of that great one, the foundation of all the rest — that their property, acquired with so much pain and hazard, should be disposed of by none but themselves — or to use the beautiful and emphatic language of the sacred scriptures [Micah 4:4] "that they should sit *every man* under his vine, and under his fig-tree, and NONE SHOULD MAKE THEM AFRAID."[162]

But whatever kind of *minister he is, that attempts to innovate a single iota in the privileges of these colonies, him I hope you will undauntedly oppose; and that you will never suffer yourselves to be either cheated or frightened into any unworthy obsequiousness*. On such emergencies you may surely, without presumption, believe that ALMIGHTY GOD himself will look upon your righteous contest with gracious approbation.[163]

It is interesting to note that the conferees and delegates of the people of Pennsylvania, of which John Dickinson was a prominent member, less than two months before the Declaration of Independence was signed, met to establish suggested requirements (among other things) of each member of the proposed Convention before he could be seated. One requirement stipulated that he subscribe the following declaration of his religious faith:

"I do profess faith in God the Father, and in Jesus Christ his Eternal Son the true God, and in the Holy Spirit, one God blessed for evermore; and I do acknowledge the Holy Scriptures of the Old and New Testaments to be given by Divine inspiration."[164]

It is doubtful that this requirement was ever established, but its inclusion here clarifies that such belief was so commonly held in that day that it would not be difficult to find delegates who believed in the Trinity and the divine inspiration of the Scriptures, basic to almost all colonial religions.

In the midst of the revolutionary fervor of 1776, Mr. Dickinson reported to the Pennsylvania Assembly as the chairman of a committee appointed "by a large majority" of that assembly, bringing new instructions to the Pennsylvania delegates to the Continental Congress regarding their position on seeking independence from Britain. It is said that he courageously "bid farewell to the expiring government in these noble . . . words":

The happiness of these Colonies has been, during the whole course of this fatal controversy, our first wish; their reconciliation with Great Britain our next: ardently have we prayed for the accomplishment of both. But if we must renounce the one or the other, we humbly trust in the mercies of the Supreme Governor of the universe that we shall not stand condemned before His throne if our choice is determined by that law of self-preservation which his Divine wisdom has seen fit to implant in the hearts of His creatures.[165]

While it is true that the Whigs in the delegation boycotted the meeting, and thus a quorum of members was not present, the personal faith and patriotism of John Dickinson is clearly seen in his address to the Assembly.

WILLIAM SAMUEL JOHNSON
(1727-1819)
CONNECTICUT, ANGLICAN: SON OF WELL-KNOWN ANGLICAN MINISTER SAMUEL JOHNSON; FIRST PRESIDENT OF KING'S COLLEGE, NEW YORK; HIS GREAT GRANDFATHER, ROBERT JOHNSON, CAME TO AMERICA IN 1638 "TO ASSIST IN FOUNDING A 'GODLY COMMONWEALTH' AT NEW HAVEN."[166]

[portrait not available]

Most historians note that the Reverend Samuel Johnson was deeply disappointed that his son did not follow him into the ministry. He did, however, serve as a lay preacher, studied the Bible and theology carefully, and with great difficulty finally settled on the profession of law. He was a devout Christian and member of the Anglican church his entire life. His wife, Anne Beach, was of similar spiritual bent, the daughter of a well-known Anglican clergyman.

Once he made the decision to enter law, this intellectually gifted man became enormously successful as an attorney in both his home state and New York. A state representative between 1761 and 1765, he served as a delegate to the Stamp Act Congress, received an honorary doctorate degree of civil law from Oxford in 1766, became a Connecticut supreme court judge and a commissioner to England, was elected to the Continental Congress, and after helping to write the Constitution became a U.S. senator and the president of King's College, subsequently renamed Columbia University. Ezra Stiles, later a president of Yale, observed that Johnson "was the first Episcopalian ever brought into the Council"—according to one historian, due in part "to his pleasing personality and conciliatory temper."[167]

This same theme was echoed by Major William Pierce, delegate to the convention from Georgia.

> A character much celebrated for his legal knowledge; he is said to be one of the first classics in America, and certainly possesses a very strong and enlightened understanding.

> He is eloquent and clear, always abounding with information and instruction.[168]

As president of King's College, he made the following remarks in his address to the first graduating class:

> You this day, gentlemen, assume new characters, enter into new relations, and consequently incur new duties. You have, by the favor of Providence and the attention of friends, received a public education, the purpose whereof hath been to qualify you the better to serve your Creator and your country. . . .

> Your first great duties, you are sensible, are those you owe to Heaven, to your Creator and Redeemer. Let these be ever present to your minds, and exemplified in your lives and conduct. Imprint deep upon your minds the principles of piety towards God, and a reverence and fear of His holy name. The fear of God is the beginning of wisdom and its consummation is everlasting felicity. Possess yourselves of just and elevated notions of the Divine character, attributes, and administration, and of

the end and dignity of your own immortal nature as it stands related to Him. Reflect deeply and often upon those relations. Remember that it is in God you live and move and have your being, — that in the language of David He is about your bed and about your path and spieth out all your ways, — that there is not a thought in your hearts, nor a word upon your tongues, but lo! he knoweth them altogether, and that he will one day call you to a strict account for all your conduct in this mortal life. Remember, too, that you are the redeemed of the Lord, that you are bought with a price, even the inestimable price of the precious blood of the Son of God. Adore Jehovah, therefore, as your God and your Judge. Love, fear, and serve Him as your Creator, Redeemer, and Sanctifier. Acquaint yourselves with Him in His word and holy ordinances. Make Him your friend and protector and your felicity is secured both here and hereafter. And with respect to particular duties to Him, it is your happiness that you are well assured that he best serves his Maker, who does most good to his country and to mankind.[169]

Obviously this challenge, which would be appropriate for any current theological seminary graduating class, could never come from a Deist or secularist, but only from the soul of a dedicated Christian.

Rufus King of Massachusetts

King was described by Pierce as "a man much distinguished for his eloquence and great parliamentary talents. . . . He may, with propriety, be ranked among the luminaries of the present age."[170]

He was an advocate of strong government to enforce the law, fearing the French Enlightenment defense of "liberty" as being an excuse for anarchy. An ardent proponent of the fallen nature of mankind (which demanded a check and balance system in government), he was not surprised by the French Revolution and subsequent reign of terror. Following America's successful bid for independence, he was quick to inform his English friends

RUFUS KING
(1755-1827)

MASSACHUSETTS, EPISCOPALIAN: LAWYER; AIDE TO GENERAL SULLI-
VAN IN THE REVOLUTIONARY WAR; MEMBER OF THE CONTINENTAL
CONGRESS; UNITED STATES SENATOR FROM NEW YORK; DIPLOMAT;
MINISTER TO ENGLAND.

that "there was no likelihood of our becoming zealous in the
Propagation of Liberty and 'the Rights of Man.' "[171]

At thirty-two, he was one of the youngest delegates at the
Constitutional Convention, but his youthfulness did not deter
him from taking an active role in the debate. His notes on the
Convention have proved helpful to historians.

King was educated in the religious schools of his community
and attended Harvard during the last year the school was led
by a minister. During his college days, he shifted allegiance
from the Congregational to the Episcopalian church. His atti-
tude toward the source of true law is evident from a speech he
made in the Senate when Missouri was seeking statehood. In it
he stated, "I hold that all laws or compacts imposing any such
condition [as involuntary servitude] upon any human being are
absolutely void because contrary to the law of nature, which is
the law of God."[172]

It is clear from this statement that Rufus King acknowledged
a personal, sovereign God who demands implicit obedience

from mankind. Such a mindset usually acknowledges that the Bible contains the "law of God" and that happiness in life comes from obedience to it.

An interesting event on record from 1814, though admittedly inconclusive, involved the brother of Rufus King. Thomas Jefferson was about to give 6,487 books from his private library to help start the United States congressional library. Cyrus King, a member of the Senate and House Joint Committee, made a very perceptive motion, reflecting the suspicions of many Christians of that day concerning Jefferson. He moved, in part, that the committee give instructions

> to report a new section authorizing the Library Commit-
> tee, as soon as said library shall be received at Washing-
> ton, to select there from all books of an atheistical, irre-
> ligious, and immoral tendency, if any such there be, and
> send the same back to Mr. Jefferson without any expense
> to him.[173]

Obviously, Jefferson's personal atheistic or skeptical tendencies were well known by this time, and Congressman King represented many people of his day in believing that the federal government should not subsidize atheism by housing its books. That situation has been reversed in our day, Christian books being all but excluded from public libraries and "atheistic" books welcomed.

John Langdon of New Hampshire

At the time he was elected to the Constitutional Convention, John Langdon, a sixth-generation American, was one of the two most important men in his state and one of the most popular. He was the first citizen of significant means to put his own wealth in jeopardy during the Revolutionary War by supplying arms and money to the Continental Army.

While some talked of patriotism, John Langdon demonstrated it and earned the lifetime admiration of his peers. He served as a colonel in the militia and in 1785 became president of his state. In his communications with both the Constitutional Convention and the next session of Continental Con-

JOHN LANGDON
(1741-1819)
NEW HAMPSHIRE, CONGREGATIONALIST: MERCHANT; SOLDIER; STATE
POLITICAL LEADER AND UNITED STATES SENATOR.

gress, Langdon equated sloth with infidelity. On one occasion he gave a speech indicating that such individuals who wanted something for nothing posed a danger to his state. He said "there was evidence in New Hampshire of an 'infidel age' in which the 'indolent, extravagant and wicked may divide the blessings of life with the industrious, the prudent and the virtuous.' "[174]

During the convention, "he spoke at least twenty times during the debates and was a vigorous proponent of provisions restricting tariffs between the states. Langdon announced as his opinion that there should be no necessary hostility between state and national government."[175]

His deeply held religious convictions at the time of the Convention appear in his function as president of his state. One year prior to the Constitutional Convention, President (of New Hampshire) Langdon called for a day of prayer and fasting and a day of thanksgiving.

**A Proclamation For A Day Of Public
FASTING and PRAYER Throughout this State [1786]**
Vain is the acknowledgement of a Supreme Ruler of the Universe, unless such acknowledgements influence our

practice, and call forth those expressions of homage and adoration that are due to his character and providential government, agreeably to the light of nature, enforced by revelation, and countenanced by the practice of civilized nations, in humble and fervent application to the throne for needed mercies, and gratitude for favors received.

It having been the laudable practice of this State, at the opening of the Spring, to set apart a day for such denomination, to assemble together on said day, in their respective places of public worship; that the citizens of this State may, with one heart and voice, penitently confess their manifold sins and transgressions, and fervently implore the divine benediction, that a true spirit of repentance and humiliation may be poured out upon all orders and degrees of men, and a compleat and universal reformation take place: that he who gave wisdom and fortitude in the scenes of battle, would give prudence and direction to extricate us from succeeding embarrassments, build up, support and establish this rising Empire; particularly, that he would be pleased to bless the great Council of the United-States of America, and direct their deliberations to the wise and best determinations, succeed our embassies at foreign Courts, bless our Allies, and national Benefactors: that he would always be pleased, to keep this State under his most holy protection: that all in the legislature, executive and judicial departments, may be guided and supported by wisdom, integrity and firmness, that all the people through this State, and through the land, may be animated by a true estimation of their privileges, and taught to secure, by their patriotism and virtue, what they have acquired by their valour: that a spirit of emulation, industry, economy and frugality, may be diffused abroad, and that we may all be disposed to lead quiet and peaceable lives, in all godliness and honesty: that he would be graciously pleased to bless us in the seasons of the year, and cause the earth to yield her increase, prosper our husbandry, merchandise, navigation and fishery, and all the labour of our hands, and give us to hear the voice of health in our habitations, and enjoy plenty of our borders: that unanimity, peace and harmony, may be promoted and continue, and a spirit of universal philanthropy pervade the land: that he would be pleased to smile upon the means of education, and bless every institution of useful knowledge; and above all, that he would rain down righteousness upon the earth, revive religion, and spread abroad the knowledge of the true GOD, the Saviour of man, throughout the world.

And all servile labour and recreations are forbidden on said day.

GIVEN at the Council-Chamber in Portsmouth, this twenty-first day of February, in the year of our LORD, one thousand seven hundred and eighty-six, and in the tenth year of the Sovereignty and Independence of the UNITED STATES OF AMERICA.

A Proclamation For A General Thanksgiving
THE munificent Father of Mercies, and Sovereign Disposer of Events, having been graciously pleased to relieve the UNITED STATES of AMERICA from the Calamities of a long and dangerous war: through the whole course of which, he continued to smile on the Labours of our Husbandmen, thereby preventing Famine (the almost inseparable Companion of War) from entering our Borders; — eventually restored to us the blessings of Peace, on Terms advantageous and honourable: — And since the happy Period, when he silenced the Noise of contending Armies, has graciously smiled on the Labours of our Hands, caused the Earth to bring forth her increase in plentiful Harvests, and crowned the present Year with new and additional Marks of his unlimited Goodness: It therefore becomes our indispensable Duty, not only to acknowledge, in general with the rest of Mankind, our dependence on the Supreme Ruler of the Universe, but as a People peculiarly favoured, to testify our Gratitude to the Author of all our Mercies, in the most Solemn and public manner.

I DO therefore, agreeably to a Vote of the General Court, appointing *Thursday* the 24th Day of *November* next, to be observed and kept as a Day of GENERAL THANKS-GIVING throughout this State, by and with the Advice of Council, issue this Proclamation, recommending to the religious Societies of every Denomination, to assemble on that Day, to celebrate the Praises of our divine Benefactor; to acknowledge our own Unworthiness, confess our manifold Transgressions, implore his Forgiveness, and intreat the continuance of those Favours which he has been graciously pleaded to bestow upon us; — that he would inspire our Rulers with Wisdom, prosper our Trade and Commerce, smile upon our Husbandry, bless our Seminaries of Learning, and spread the Gospel of his Grace over all the Earth.

And all servile Labour is forbidden on said Day.

GIVEN at the Council-Chamber in Concord, this Twenty-first Day of October, in the Year of our LORD, One Thousand Seven Hundred and Eighty-five, and in the Tenth Year of the Independence of the UNITED STATES of AMERICA.

The quality of John Langdon's character and life are expressed by an historian close to his period in these words:

In private life we know he was unspotted; yet a man of the world, rich, generous, and sympathetic, indulging in splendid hospitality, polished and amiable, a man of affairs as well, versed in the phrase of commerce, owning many argosies. He loved his country. He trusted his fellow-men. He believed in God. The last days of his life were passed in the good old Portsmouth of his boyhood; a father among his children, honored, revered, remembered in the prayers of many a household, he watched with dim and thankful vision the descending of the sun.[176]

During his time in the Senate, Langdon's brother died, and as a result Langdon experienced a genuine spiritual revival. According to one biographer,

At this period, Langdon reaffirmed his strong feeling for religion. He was a "zealous" member of the North Congregational Church in Portsmouth, for which he served as a warden and gave nearly one thousand dollars for the first parish house. In August, 1805, he received an LL.D. degree from Dartmouth College.[177]

Another historian described it this way:

The loss of his brother seems to have wrought a great change in him in this respect. Religious questions began to interest him very much and he began to cultivate the acquaintance of ministers of various denominations. On April 6, 1806, he and his wife and his sister Elizabeth (Mrs. Barrell) were admitted to membership in the church. A little later he became one of the founders and the first president of the New Hampshire Bible Society, a benevolent organization that aspired — and still aspires — to place the Bible within the reach of every New Hampshire home. After his retirement in 1812 conversation with him was very apt to fall into one of two channels — politics or religion.[178]

While he served as governor of his state, one day he took the President of the United States to church with him.

In the summer of 1817 President Monroe made a tour of the New England states, and a Sunday in July found him at Portsmouth. A local newspaper recorded with pride: "While at Portsmouth, the President spent that part of the Sabbath which was not devoted to public divine service, with that eminent patriot and Christian, John Langdon. His tarry at the mansion of Gov. L. was probably longer than the time devoted to any individual in New England. It is thus that the President has evinced his partiality to our most distinguished and illustrious citizen."[179]

In their quest to make our Founding Fathers appear neutral or hostile to Christianity, modern secular historians will have to avoid any consideration of this very influential leader of the New Hampshire delegation.

WILLIAM LIVINGSTON
(1723-1790)

NEW JERSEY, PRESBYTERIAN: LAWYER; BRIGADIER GENERAL OF THE MILITIA; STATESMAN; GOVERNOR OF STATE; MEMBER OF CONTINENTAL CONGRESS; GOVERNOR OF NEW JERSEY 1776-90; MEMBER OF FIRST AND SECOND CONTINENTAL CONGRESS.

At sixty-six years of age, Livingston was one of the elder statesmen at the Constitutional Convention. He had already distinguished himself as an attorney and legislator in New York, where, prior to the war, he decided to retire from public life and thus moved to a rural area in New Jersey. The prerevolution spirit stirred him to become an early volunteer, however, and with the rank of brigadier general he commanded a brigade of militia. During that same year (1776), he was transferred from the battlefield to the governor's mansion.

Throughout the next fourteen years, until his death in 1790, William Livingston was governor of New Jersey. As much as any man, he may be credited with having created the government and institutions of a sovereign state. While the Revolution continued, New Jersey was frequently a battleground of competing armies, and there was a considerable division of loyalties among its population. Yet, with moderation and careful stewardship, Governor Livingston pulled it together and guaranteed its respectable contribution to the struggle for American liberty. In his later years, the people of his state would not let him retire, seeing in his patient and patriarchal presence a summary of what they had fought to achieve.

. . . Governor Livingston said little during the Constitutional Convention, but his name and reputation gave weight to the New Jersey delegation. . . .

He did not arrive in Philadelphia until June 5 and missed many of the debates in July, but he played a major role as chairman of the committee which drew up a compromise on slavery. Returning home, he exercised his potent influence in behalf of ratification and was responsible for the speed and unanimity of New Jersey's response.[180]

William Livingston was a godly Christian. Raised by a dedicated Christian grandmother, he lived as a youth on the frontier around Albany with missionaries among the Mohawks. Pierce, his colleague at the Convention, said of him, "A man of the first rate talents . . . equal to anything, from the extensiveness of his education and genius. His writings teem with satire and a neatness of style."[181]

He finished first in his class at Yale and studied law under the Scotch Presbyterians John Morin Scot and William Peartree Smith. While still in New York, he began writing articles for newspapers and engaged in defending the faith against what he considered the dangers of the established church of this country. As one modern historian describes it,

In a weekly, *The Independent Reflector*, Livingston, a Presbyterian, criticized the Episcopal Church for what he considered attempts to make it the established religion of the colony.[182]

In religion Livingston was true to his ancestry. "The faith of his mother Lois and his grandmother Eunice" was in him also, and he defended it stoutly by word and pen. In 1758, when the Church was the dividing line in politics, he was sent to the Assembly.[183]

An interesting sidelight of his life was noted by the same historian:

In May 1772 Livingston retired to an estate in New Jersey, and that October the 16-year-old Alexander Hamilton arrived with a letter of introduction from the Presbyterian minister who had helped finance his trip from the British West Indies. Livingston provided Hamilton the opportunity to attend school in Elizabethtown and King's College in New York.[184]

After the founding of the new nation and the election of the first President, "Livingston lived to see Washington form the first government of the new United States, with the young man he had sent to college as the new President's principal domestic adviser, the first Secretary of the Treasury."[185]

Called the "Presbyterian lawyer," William opposed Anglican control of the proposed King's College in 1751. William was baptized in the Dutch Reformed Church, but later became a Presbyterian, because of the language difficulty.[186]

James McHenry of Maryland

Born in Ireland, McHenry came to America in 1771 and urged his family to join him the next year in Philadelphia, where they established a prosperous importing business.

James McHenry was a refined gentleman who studied medicine under the famous Dr. Rush of Philadelphia (a dedicated Christian). He was an ardent patriot with a pronounced hostility toward England (quite typical of the Irish). When war broke out, he volunteered and served with distinction on the medical staff under Washington and Lafayette. Fort McHenry, birthplace of our national anthem, was named in his honor. He said little during the Constitutional Convention, but his presence

JAMES MCHENRY
(1753-1816)

MARYLAND, PRESBYTERIAN: PHYSICIAN; SOLDIER; STATE LEGISLATOR;
MEMBER OF CONTINENTAL CONGRESS AND SECRETARY OF WAR (DUR-
ING WHICH TIME HE DIRECTED THE ESTABLISHING OF WEST POINT).

made Maryland's majority vote favor the strong federal government advocated by Washington, Madison, and Randolph. After
the Convention, it was McHenry who argued in favor of adoption before the Maryland legislature. From an Ulster Presbyterian background, he deplored the libertine excesses of the French
Revolution and its American admirers, and he believed that
government's primary obligation was to protect its citizens from
the unrest and mob spirit of Enlightenment theories.

McHenry was a deeply spiritual man who spent the remaining years of his life (after his retirement from public service in
1800) serving his church and family. In 1813, he became president of the first Bible society founded in Baltimore. One measure of his deeply held evangelical faith appears in an article
soliciting funds for the Bible society.

In elevated style, McHenry drew attention to the need of
carrying out the purposes of the Society and of placing
Bibles in the hands of all the people: "Neither, in considering this subject, let it be overlooked, that public utility

pleads most forcibly for the general distribution of the Holy Scriptures. The doctrine they preach, the obligations they impose, the punishment they threaten, the rewards they promise, the stamp and image of divinity they bear, which produces a conviction of their truths, can alone secure to society, order and peace, and to our courts of justice and constitutions of government, purity, stability and usefulness. In vain, without the Bible, we increase penal laws and draw intrenchments around our institutions. Bibles are strong intrenchments. Where they abound, men cannot pursue wicked courses, and at the same time enjoy quiet conscience.

"Consider also, the rich do not possess aught more precious than their Bible, and that the poor cannot be presented by the rich with anything of greater value. Withhold it not from the poor. It is a book of councils and directions, fitted to every situation in which man can be placed. It is an oracle which reveals to mortals the secrets of heaven and the hidden will of the Almighty. . . .

It is an estate, whose title is guaranteed by Christ, whose delicious fruits ripen every season, survive the worm, and keep through eternity. It is for the purpose of distributing this divine book more effectually and extensively among the multitudes, whose circumstances render such a donation necessary, that your cooperation is most earnestly requested."[187]

William Paterson of New Jersey

At five-foot-two inches Paterson, was "the smallest of the Framers, and spokesman in their company for the special interests of the smaller states. Pre-eminently a 'man of law' and defender of the Anglo-American tradition of inherited legal rights."[188]

Paterson was a brilliant speaker and debater. His New Jersey Plan, sometimes called the "Paterson Plan," is credited with keeping the Virginia plan from either being adopted or hopelessly dividing the Convention. After the Convention, he was

WILLIAM PATERSON
(1745-1806)
NEW JERSEY, PRESBYTERIAN: LAWYER; POPULAR STATE LEADER;
MEMBER OF THE CONTINENTAL CONGRESS; STATE ATTORNEY GENERAL;
U.S. SENATOR; GOVERNOR; U.S. SUPREME COURT JUSTICE.

elected to the U.S. Senate, from which he resigned to become
the governor of New Jersey upon the death of Governor Livingston. In 1793, President Washington appointed him to the
U.S. Supreme Court, where he served until his death.

Raised in a strong, Irish Presbyterian family of the Ulster
Presbyterian tradition, he was brought to America at the age of
two. Trained in local schools with a high degree of Christian emphasis he went to Princeton College at a time when it was a hotbed of evangelicalism. Twelve of his eighteen classmates were
ministerial students and later became ministers. An item from
Paterson's journal, relating to his experiences earlier in life when
he paid a visit to the West Indies, gives us insight into his religious and moral character.

On my arrival in the West Indies in the year 1776, a new
scene was opened to me for which I was little prepared,
for I had previously lived with religious people, and my
new acquaintances, and those with whom I was to trans-
act business were the reverse of this. No one went there to

settle for life; all were in quest of fortune, to retire and spend it elsewhere; character was little thought of. Of course it required the utmost circumspection and caution to steer clear of difficulties. A kind superintending Providence, in this, as in many other concerns of my life, enabled me, however, to surmount every difficulty, young and inexperienced as I then was.[189]

Delegate Pierce said of Paterson that he was

one of those kind of men whose powers break in upon you and create wonder and astonishment. He is a man of great modesty with looks that bespeak talents of no great extent, but he is a classic, a lawyer, and an orator; and of a disposition so favorable to his advancement that every one seemed ready to exalt him with their praises. He is very happy in the choice of time and manner of engaging in a debate, and never speaks but when he understands his subject well.[190]

The esteem in which the people of his state regarded this Christian man can be seen in that they named the city of Paterson, New Jersey, after him.

Charles Cotesworth Pinckney of South Carolina

Charles C. Pinckney was not only one of the most popular men of his state, enormously influential in it and the Union, but also a deeply spiritual man with a real and abiding faith. Born of famous, aristocratic parents and grandparents, he received a private education and was then sent to Westminster School at Oxford, where he studied under Sir William Blackstone, the godly legal genius. During his stay in Europe, Pickney attended the Royal Military Academy at Caen, France, which trained him for the military career in which he found himself soon after returning to the colonies. He was active in opposing the British and was captured in the battle of Charles Town. After being held prisoner for two years, a trade was effected and Pinckney was released. He returned to the service and by his retirement had reached the rank of brigadier general. He then went home to

CHARLES COTESWORTH PINCKNEY
(1746-1825)
SOUTH CAROLINA, EPISCOPALIAN: SOLDIER; STATESMAN; LAWYER;
PLANTER; STATE OFFICE HOLDER; HELPED FORM STATE CONSTITUTION;
VICE PRESIDENTIAL CANDIDATE IN 1800; RAN FOR PRESIDENT (UNSUC-
CESSFULLY) IN 1804 AND 1808; SERVED AS MINISTER TO FRANCE.

help establish the government of his own state, helping to write
the state constitution. To catch a glimpse of this man's influence,
consider the words of historian M. E. Bradford:

> Most new legislation and a new state Constitution passed
> under his shaping hand. And in many respects his word
> *was the* authority in the Low Country—his, and that of
> the Rutledge brothers, to whom he was connected by
> marriage. After the establishment of the new national
> government, Pinckney stayed at home in Carolina, be-
> coming eventually the most famous citizen of the state.[191]

> . . . to the end of his life he functioned as patriarchal
> leader of the bar and oracle in his city and state, univer-
> sally trusted and admired. He embodied the best qualities
> of a very special civilization, and left to Carolina as his
> legacy the example of a prudent and ample spirit, a civility
> rare in any time and place.[192]

Without Charles Cotesworth Pinckney, no Constitution
could have been agreed upon in Philadelphia or approved
in the Lower South.[193]

Forty-one at the time he was elected as a delegate to the Constitutional Convention, Charles C. Pinckney commanded the
respect of his peers because of his elegant grace and charm combined with scholarship that was seasoned with practicality learned
in the military. His philosophy of government shines forth clearly
in a personal letter written to an old military friend: "the great
art of government is not to govern too much."

[He] liked the new Constitution so well when it reached
its final form that, during the Convention's last days, he
pledged publicly to fight for its approval in South
Carolina. And he kept that pledge, acting as the leading
supporter of ratification during the debates in the legislature of his state and in the special convention of January,
1788, called to pass judgment on the new law.[194]

So highly respected was this good man by President Washington that he was offered many high posts — the U.S. Supreme
Court and several cabinet offices. Finally he accepted the
diplomatic post of emissary to France.

Charles C. Pinckney fulfilled his father's prayerful dreams
for his son as carefully laid out in his will. The elder Pinckney,
who had been the chief justice of South Carolina, stipulated:

To the end that my beloved son Charles Cotesworth may
the better be enabled to become the head of his family and
prove not only of service and advantage to his country,
but also an Honour to his Stock and kindred, my order
and direction is that my said son be virtuously, religiously
and liberally brought up and Educated in the Study and
practice of the Laws of England; and from my said son I
hope, as he would have the blessings of Almighty God,
and deserve the Countenance and favour of all good men,
and answer my expectations of him, that he will employ
all his future abilities in the service of God, and his Coun-

try, in the Cause of virtuous liberty as well religious as Civil; and in support of private right and Justice between Man and Man; and that he do by no means debase the dignity of his human nature, nor the honour of his profession, by giving countenance to, or ever appearing in favour of irreligion, injustice or wrong, oppression or tyranny of any sort, public or private; but that he make the glory of God and the good of Mankind, the relief of the poor and distressed, the widow and the fatherless, and such as have none else to help them, his principal aim and study.[195]

Eyewitness accounts of someone who lived 200 years ago are scarce. Such testimony is, however, available from Pinckney's pastor, Christopher Gadsen. In the sermon preached at Pinckney's funeral in St. Phillips Church, Charleston, South Carolina, the Reverend Gadsen said of him,

He was a vestryman for several years, regularly attended and took an active part at church meetings, and zealously promoted by his efforts and his contributions every measure of utility. He was a sincere friend of your clergy, always ready to assist them with his counsel, to strengthen them by his influence, and to advance their cause and welfare.

Among the evidences of his piety, might not his moral attainments with propriety be enumerated? For let me ask in what irreligious man has the same assemblage of virtues ever been found? In whom has the like degree of uprightness been discovered separate from religious principle? The irreligious may have a love of country, but it is not of the disinterested self-denying ruling character which the Christian exercises. Their independence of conduct is founded in pride, not in conscientious motives; and it is not invincible by the power of self-interest.[196]

You beheld him enjoying with moderation a large share of prosperity, not unmindful of the divine benefactor, and of the peculiar duties to which it called him. In the day of trouble you would have found him, had you entered the private circle, meek, quiet, patient, and practicing a christian resignation. You met him in this holy temple, and kneeled with him, and those most dear to him at that altar of the Saviour on whom the great and those of low degree equally must rest their hopes; to whom all must look for present peace and everlasting safety.[197]

So deep was Charles Cotesworth Pinckney's commitment to Jesus Christ and the advancement of His kingdom that he made time in his busy life to help found and serve as the first president of the Charleston Bible Society. The Reverend A. Gibbes read the following resolutions at the time of his death, reflecting a measure of Pinckney's spiritual zeal:

The Board of Managers of the *Charleston Bible Society*, entertaining a high sense of the benefits conferred on his country and on society, by their late revered President, General CHARLES COTESWORTH PINCKNEY, in the course of a long life, steadily and honorably devoted to the service of both; and of the fidelity, zeal and ability, with which he fulfilled the duties of the important and responsible public functions, to which he was called; as well as of the virtues, which adorned his private life and character, and by which he justly earned and secured the permanent respect, veneration and affection of all his fellow citizens. . . .

That they give devout thanks to Almighty God for the invaluable services which the life, influence and example of their late revered President, have rendered to the cause of religion, virtue and good order, to his country and to mankind; and that they submit themselves to this painful dispensation of Providence, with a sorrow mitigated by the grateful remembrance of his virtue, and by a pious trust in Divine mercy. . . .

For fifteen years past he presided over our Society, and at our Board. Our meetings were held at his house. We will long remember his kindness and hospitality to us all, while the patience, industry, perseverance and zeal, which he exercised to promote the interests of our Society, merit the approbation of the cause in which we were engaged. The last time he met our Society he was so feeble that it was necessary to support him to the chair.

It was evident to all of us, that his long and useful life was drawing to a close. He seemed to come among us to show that in his last hours the cause of the Bible was nearest his heart, to give us his blessing and to bid us farewell; for from that day [I am informed] he was confined to his chamber; and after having lived nearly four-score years, an age seldom attained, he soon after fell to the ground, like as a shuck of corn cometh forth in his season.[198]

GEORGE READ
(1733-1798)
DELAWARE, EPISCOPALIAN: LAWYER; JUDGE; POLITICAL LEADER OF HIS STATE; SIGNER OF THE DECLARATION; UNITED STATES SENATOR.

Born in Maryland to wealthy parents, Read was considered "the father of Delaware" in that he wrote the state constitution and "the first edition of her laws."[199] While Read was quite young, his family moved to New Castle, Delaware, where he was educated in a school in Chester.

From there he was transferred to the seminary of the Rev. Dr. Allison, at New London, who was eminently qualified to mould the young mind for usefulness, by imparting correct principles, practical knowledge, and general intelligence, fit for every day use, combined with refined classics and polite literature. Under this accomplished teacher, Mr. Read completed his education, preparatory to his professional studies. At the age of seventeen, he commenced reading law with John Moland Esq., a distinguished member of the Philadelphia bar. His proficiency was so great that in two years he was admitted to the practical honours of his profession.[200]

His seminary training had a profound affect on George, refining his character and moral standards, for which he was distinguished during his entire life. He was active in his church and married a particularly devout young woman. As one of his biographers wrote in 1839,

> In the year 1769, Mr. Read married a daughter of the Reverend George Ross, who had been, during fifty years, pastor of Immanuel Church, in the town of Newcastle. . . .
> The understanding of Mrs. Read, naturally strong, was carefully cultivated by her father, who bestowed more attention upon her instruction than it was the common lot of females, at that period, to receive. Her person was beautiful, her manners elegant, and her piety exemplary.[201]

The Convention biographer said of him, "He is a very good man, and bears an amiable character with those who know him."[202]

George Read had a significant influence on the Constitution, for he made the motion helping to resolve the dispute between the large and small states over equal representation, granting that form of representation in the Senate. In addition to this, he spoke several times at the Convention.

One of the facts of recorded history giving clear evidence to his thorough Christian persuasion is the constitution of Delaware, which he personally wrote and signed in 1776. One of the requirements for holding office in the House of Burgess State Assembly was the taking of the following oath:

> I, A. B. do profess Faith in God the Father, and in Jesus Christ his only Son, and in the Holy Ghost, one God blessed for evermore; and I do acknowledge the Holy Scriptures of the Old and New Testament to be given by divine Inspiration.[203]

Keep in mind that these requirements were in effect when the Constitutional Convention met in 1787.

In describing Read, historian M. E. Bradford wrote:

> George Read was United States Senator from Delaware under the new Constitution from 1789 until 1793. While in Congress, he voted consistently for the Federalist program. On September 18, 1793, he resigned from the Senate to become the chief justice of his state, a position he held until his death. . . .

> Socially, he was one of the most conservative of the Framers, and the greatest single influence over the politics of his state. Quiet and composed, a lawyer's lawyer and a man of the prescription, he was a force for order in his world, a moralist of the "public virtue" in the early life of the Republic.[204]

Hugh Williamson
(1735-1819)
NORTH CAROLINA, PRESBYTERIAN: PREACHER; PHYSICIAN; SCIENTIST; LAND SPECULATOR; POLITICIAN; MEMBER OF CONTINENTAL CONGRESS; MEMBER OF U.S. HOUSE OF REPRESENTATIVES.

[portrait not available]

Dr. Williamson was a brilliant and energetic man who was raised by deeply religious parents. A frail boy, he "received a country school education near his father's home."[205]

He was sent at an early age to learn the languages at an academy established at New London Cross Roads under the direction of the Reverend Francis Alison, whose talents, learning, and discipline had gained him the honor of being entitled the *Busby* of the western hemisphere. Hugh was fitted for college there, and in the pursuit of his studies he distinguished himself by his diligence, his love of order, and his correct moral and religious behavior.

It was Williamson's intention to become a minister. Before he entered upon the study of divinity and while still a young man, he visited and prayed with the sick in the neighborhood. A little prior to his graduation, his father and family had moved to Shippensburg, Cumberland County. The year of his graduation his father died, leaving him sole executor of the estate. He now took up residence with his mother at Shippensburg and spent two years studying divinity, collecting debts, and administering the affairs of the estate. In 1759 he went to Connecticut, where he pursued his theological studies and was licensed to preach. After returning from Connecticut, he was admitted to membership in the Presbytery of Philadelphia. Although he preached nearly two years, he was never ordained or placed in charge of a congregation. One reason for his non-success in this vocation was a chronic weakness. It was questionable whether his lungs would bear the exertions of public speaking. The fears were verified, for he became much troubled with pains and strictures in his chest.[206]

Gifted in mathematics, Williamson taught his way through medical school, after which he practiced medicine in Philadelphia. Later he traveled to Europe, where he served the colonial cause, arriving in America shortly after the Declaration of Independence was signed. Moving to North Carolina, he became surgeon general and distinguished himself during the war. He was elected by the people to represent them in the Continental Congress, the Constitutional Convention, and later in the

U.S. Congress. During the Constitutional Convention he was quite outspoken. M. E. Bradford writes that "he was the most articulate of the members from North Carolina." When tempers flared, "he counseled moderation." Bradford added that from his adopted state he was "a source of great influence over our national destiny."[207]

By this time his investments and land speculations had made him wealthy, and after he left Congress, he settled in New York, the home of his wife. There he distinguished himself in the medical and literary societies, spending much of his time writing books and articles that won him literary acclaim. His early Presbyterian faith characterized him all through his life, as evidenced by his writing.

In 1811 Williamson produced a classic book entitled *Observations on the Climate in Different Parts of America*. In it he rolled back the historical record to provide a scientific explanation for the reliability of the Holy Scriptures in relation to the flood of Noah and the experiences of Moses. While it is clear that he was aware of the theories of "higher criticism" that ridiculed the accuracy of Scripture, Dr. Williamson was obviously a believer in divine inspiration.

Summary

There are many other Christians among the Founding Fathers who are not included in this chapter. Unfortunately, sufficient personal testimonies or recorded acts of their lives have not survived to warrant their inclusion. But these above provide evidence that Christians had a significant influence on the founding of this nation — just as they have had on its affairs during the past two hundred years.

ELEVEN

A CONSTITUTION
FOR THE AGES –
IF WE CAN KEEP IT

When the fifty-five representatives of the three million American colonists gathered in Philadelphia, few if any realized they were destined to create the constitutional foundation for the greatest nation in the history of the world. Contrary to the thinking of modern liberal historians, these men were not ignorant and unlearned farmers. According to Dr. Forrest McDonald, one of the nation's leading authorities on the authors of the Constitution, "1787 marks the zenith of America's golden age, the likes of which we will not see again." As a reporter who heard his Jefferson lecture described it:

> According to Mr. McDonald, no fewer than thirty-five of the Convention's delegates had attended college, which apparently was no small feat in the 18th Century.

> Just to get into college in the period, one had to be fluent in Latin and Greek and be able to translate the first 10 chapters of the Gospel of John from Greek into Latin, he told an audience of invited guests in Great Hall of the National Building Museum.

> Collegians also had to have "blameless moral character" and be "expert in arithmetic."

> While the nation's founders themselves were a highly educated group, the general populace was also quite literate,

making the colonies fertile ground for the proliferation of newspapers, Mr. McDonald said.

Nearly four times as many newspapers were published in colonial America as were published in France, notwithstanding the fact that France had six times as many people and regarded as the most literate nation in Europe, he added.

The founders cited the Bible the most often but also read widely from the Roman classics.[208]

One of their contemporaries who did not attend the convention and did all he could to keep the Constitution from being ratified, Richard Henry Lee, begrudgingly acknowledged, "America probably never will see an assembly of men of like number more respectable." Thomas Jefferson, from his vantage point in Paris, is supposed to have called them "an Assembly of demigods."

It was not, however, their native brilliance, nor was it their education that allowed them to craft the Constitution for the ages. It was "the divine hand of providence" drawing on the Christian faith of most of them that knew Him well, and the effects the Christian consensus of that time had on the others.

While James Madison is often called "the Father of the Constitution," this masterpiece of freedom was not the work of any one man, and a case could be made for many "fathers" of the Constitution. All fifty-five delegates contributed their past, prejudices, experience, learning, political stature, reputation, moral character, and religion to the final document. It took the combined efforts of the honored George Washington and Benjamin Franklin; the legal minds of Madison, Mason, Hamilton, Livingston, Sherman, Johnson, Dickinson, Davie, Charles Cotesworth Pinckney, and many others to produce the magnificent work we know today. As we have already seen, even some of those who vehemently objected to it had a profound influence on the final result. By the time they were finished, there was such a blending of thought that most of the delegates were disappointed in it and some predicted that it wouldn't last.

Two hundred years later, it has proved to be the greatest Constitution for a free people in the history of mankind. But now we must raise the crucial question, can we keep it? As this book clearly points out, it was designed by and for a religious people, most of whom were Christians. The secularization of the past fifty years, particularly during the Warren Supreme Court, has consistently chipped away at the time-honored safeguards that made our nation.

For two hundred years it has lasted, providing more religious and personal freedom than ever given to a people for as long a period. Two hundred years! To show the significance of that, we should realize there are five billion people living on this planet in 164 countries, 156 of which have written constitutions—but fifty percent of them date back only to 1974.

What These Founders Accomplished

To put their marvelous contributions to America and to freedom in perspective, read what Pat Robertson wrote:

> Every American should make a pilgrimage at least once in a lifetime to visit Independence Hall in Philadelphia. Take the guided tour or stand alone behind the green velvet rope and stare into that single room where the two greatest documents in this nation's history were created. Two hundred years later, we find it difficult to understand the unprecedented and amazing work accomplished there.
>
> Those two documents signed by our forefathers created a form of government almost entirely new upon the earth. For free people from sovereign states to enter into a compact with each other, granting power to a strong central government over their own recently won sovereignty, was a kind of miracle. This voluntary compact among "free and independent states" would forever bind them to each other, yet guarantee them certain powers of their own. It was a bold and daring idea, totally different from all other governments in the world at that time.
>
> On September 17, 1987, the day our Constitution was signed, the absolute monarch Ch'ien Lung, emperor of

the Manchu (or Ch'ing) Dynasty, reigned supreme over the people of China. To guard against revolt, Chinese officials could not hold office in their home provinces, and the emperor constantly shuffled government appointees to keep any one man from gaining power against him. Revolts were put down by ruthless military force. China's armies had penetrated Burma and Nepal; even Korea paid tribute.

In Japan the shogun (warriors) of the corrupt Tokugawa chamberlain Tanuma Okitsugu exercised corrupt and totalitarian authority over the Japanese. Japan had been ruled by the ancestors of Tokugawa Ieyasu since the beginning of the seventeenth century. The Japanese, like their Chinese neighbors, were a great people with a great cultural and religious heritage, but the notion of a voluntary contract among peoples to form a democratic government would not be introduced there for almost two centuries.

In India, Warren Hastings, the British Governor of Bengal, had successfully defeated the influence of the fragmented Mogul dynasties that ruled India since 1600. He also had effectively nullified France's claims on this huge subcontinent.

Catherine II was the enlightened despot of all the Russias. Joseph II was the emperor of Austria, Bohemia, and Hungary. For almost half a century, Frederick the Great had ruled Prussia. Louis XVI sat uneasily on his throne in France just years away from revolution, a bloody experiment in democracy, and the new tyranny of Napoleon Bonaparte. A kind of constitutional government had been created in the Netherlands in 1579 by the Protestant Union of Utrecht, but that constitution was really a loose federation of the northern provinces for defense against Catholic Spain and not a strong, legal contract upon which a lasting central government could be formed.

What was happening in America had no real precedent, even as far back as the city-states of Greece. The only real

precedent was established thousands of years before by
the tribes of Israel in the covenant with God and with
each other. Yet our forefathers moved swiftly and grace-
fully toward that goal during the tumultuous Congress of
1776 and that long, hot summer of 1787.

What model did the framers use to shape this unprece-
dented Constitution? What historic textbook guided them
in its creation? I am convinced by the documents and by
the testimony of the signers themselves that the Old Testament stories of God at work with His people, Israel,
and the New Testament stories of the Christian church
were two major influences on the creation of our Constitution. The framers and the great legal minds that influenced their deliberations — including Montesquieu,
John Locke, Hugo Grotius, William Blackstone, and
Samuel Rutherford — all confessed their debt to the Bible
and to the example of the church in the shaping of their
views of government.

Samuel Adams, the "Father of the American Revolution"
and a signer of the Declaration of Independence, wrote:
"The right to freedom being the gift of God Almighty . . .
'The Rights of the Colonists as Christians'. . . may
be best understood by reading and carefully studying
the institutes of the great Law Giver . . . which are to
be found clearly written and promulgated in the New
Testament."[209]

Now, as a result, we are a republic, ruled by representatives chosen in free elections by the people. We are not a
theocracy, ruled outright by God. Nor are we a theocracy
ruled by godly prophets, priests, or elders in His name.
The framers did not intend that we strive to be a theocracy in any form. Our government is made by men and
women. To protect our God-given rights, the people have
voluntarily entered into a contract creating a general government charged with the power to do for all of us
together what we cannot do for ourselves alone.[210]

Government is of Divine Origin

Somehow many fine Christian people have gotten the impression that God is against government. That is not true. God originated government; look at Genesis 8-9; the nation of Israel; Romans 13:1-6, where rulers are called "ministers of God"; and 1 Timothy 2:1-5, where the Bible says that He has the power to raise up whom He wishes and put down whom He wills. In Scripture we find that the only nations that He is against are those that are against Him, or who defy His laws and persecute people. Unfortunately, that is most of the governments of the world today. Without God and His principles, governments traditionally have been either too totalitarian and harsh or too permissive and anarchical, either of which extreme will end in the misery and destruction of its own people.

Currently, our federal government, contrary to the wishes of our Founding Fathers, is becoming both too totalitarian and too permissive. In some cases, it has usurped the position of God Himself, in that people are taught that if something is wrong, let government fix it. Government now has invaded all of life until we have laws on everything except moral decency. The liberals in government today try to justify their intolerant, morally permissive actions by the Constitution. As one theistic historian said:

> The basic error of liberalism at this point has been its insistence that human government is a social institution, responsible to those men who created it and is primarily concerned with the preservation of human rights as they were defined by Jefferson and others of that day. This error is very popular among Christian people as well as the nation at large and it has been productive of great error for it has allowed the forces of political liberalism to extend the operations of government into those spheres where it has no right to be, and in so doing it has actually become a menace to the human liberty which the liberals insist that it must protect. But above and beyond this, when human government extends its powers and operations to those spheres of human life which God did not render subject to it, government then finds itself in oppo-

sition to its divinely bestowed purposes for it takes unto itself powers into these forbidden areas which has created
the modern totalitarian state. When human government
enters into the field of labor relations, education, mental
and physical health, agriculture, housing, and those
many other areas of legislation so characteristic of the
federal government today, it leaves its proper functions
and enters into those areas of life which God has either
ordained that the church or the family should have as
their particular sphere of responsibility, or that they
should be the concern of some human institution which
man may erect for his own civil purposes under God's
common grace.[211]

America: One Nation Under Man or God?

The most burning issue in America today is whether this is
"One nation under God," based on the Bible and Judeo-
Christian principles, or a secular nation without fixed moral
absolutes that functions independent of any god other than
human reason.

Lest you think that's an oversimplification of the issues, let
me point out that for 150 years this nation was built on Biblical
principles that assured freedom, community decency, and
domestic tranquility. Today, particularly since the Supreme
Court has resolutely misinterpreted the Constitution so as to increase the scope and power of the federal government and to
separate it almost entirely from God and Biblical principles, it
has become both secular and hostile to religion.

As a result, laws have been relaxed regarding man's responsibility to control his violent or perverse instincts, and we have
become the crime capital of the world. Capital punishment has
been deemed "cruel and inhuman treatment" and has been practically eliminated (although this is beginning to change somewhat). Consequently, murder has increased at an alarming rate,
and some murderers have been paroled in time to murder still
other helpless victims.

Rights have gradually become more important than respon-
sibilities, so that the right to print pornographic literature has
since the '70s been considered by our Supreme Court more im-

portant than moral responsibility to our fellow man. Consequently, we have become the porno capital of the world.

Forty years ago, when I was a boy, pornography was non-existent in this country, yet, we had plenty of "freedom of speech" and "freedom of the press." Today, thanks to secularist decisions by humanist Supreme Court justices, twenty-eight Mafia-controlled companies (according to the attorney general's pornography commission) produce $8 billion worth of porn annually. Partly as a result, millions of women are raped, and other millions of children are molested. It is estimated that twenty-five percent of all girls will be sexually molested before their eighteenth birthday, thanks to the "enlightened" decisions of secularism. This is a total distortion of the intents of our Founding Fathers.

Whatever forces of secularism existed in the colonies in 1787 had very little influence on the founding of the United States. Thomas Jefferson, chief among the eighteenth-century secularizers, was not even in the country at the time but was being humanized in France, where he served as minister of the new nation. Yet even Jefferson is touted by today's secular humanist historians for writing the Declaration of Independence as though he were the greatest genius of the colonial period. Dr. McDonald, however, has made clear that there were many gifted intellects living during that period.

The truth is, Jefferson has been touted for the past seventy-five years by the secularist scholars not just because of his genius, but also because some of his often-quoted humanist statements are more in line with their own philosophy, which they like to advance by attributing them to him. One example is his famous "wall of separation" principle between church and state. They represent Jefferson as though he taught that the church should not get involved with government, when in fact he meant the wall of separation kept the government from intruding into matters of religion, according to the first amendment. In fact, Jefferson had nothing to do with the writing of the first amendment.

The Wall of Separation — Irony

Jefferson's "wall of separation" statement is quoted by ACLU attorneys, secular humanist debaters, and secularism educators so often the average citizen thinks it is in the Constitution. Actually, he was not one of the fifty-five Founding Fathers, and as we've just noted, he had nothing to do with it. But that didn't hinder him from giving his interpretation to a group of Danbury Baptists—eleven years after the Constitution had been written—in which, he made the now-famous "wall of separation" statement. Doesn't it strike you as strange that the humanists had to skip all the Founding Fathers when trying to get an opinion they could agree with, and had to resort to a contemporary who hadn't even been a part of the constitutional deliberations? And even then, they went to a man who was out of the country at the time the Constitution was being debated, and one who was so hostile to Christianity that while in the White House, he made his own Bible by cutting out all the miracles of Jesus Christ because they emphasized His supernatural nature.

The truth is, there is no "wall of separation" in the Constitution, unless it is a wall intended by the Founding Fathers to keep the civil government totally out of the church.

Yet even Jefferson was a far cry from the modern secularizers and secular humanists. He obviously believed in God and recognized the need for a meaningful religion in the life of the nation, even though he opposed a governmentally established church and deplored the hypocrisy of some liberal clerics. To give you some idea of his recognition of a personal God, note these famous quotations etched in marble on the walls of the Jefferson Monument in Washington, D.C.

> Almighty God hath created the mind free. All attempts to influence it by temporal punishments or burdens . . . are a departure from the plan of the Holy Author of our religion. . . . No men shall be compelled to frequent or support any religious worship or ministry or shall otherwise suffer on account of his religious opinions or belief, but all men shall be free to profess and by argument to maintain, their opinions in matters of religion. I know but no one code of morality for men whether acting singly or collectively.

> I have sworn upon the altar of God eternal hostility against every form of tyranny over the mind of man.

God who gave us life, gave us liberty. Can the liberty of a nation be secure where we have removed a conviction that these liberties are a gift of God? Indeed I tremble for my country when I reflect that God is just. That His justice cannot sleep forever. Commerce between master and slave is despotism. Nothing is more certainly written in the Book of Life than that these people are to be free.

The Constitution was Intended for a Religious and Moral People

It is no accident that the majority of the few free nations that exist today are in the Western world and have their roots in the Christian religion. As Will and Ariel Durant, world-acclaimed historians, have said:

There is no significant example in history, before our time, of a society successfully maintaining moral life without the aid of religion. France, the United States, and some other nations have divorced their governments from all churches, but they have had the help of religion in keeping social order.[212]

Pat Robertson put it this way:

The framers believed that the Constitution could not survive a people who did not believe in God or His laws. Whether Anglican or Pilgrim, Puritan or Baptist, Presbyterian, Catholic, or Quaker, our forefathers knew well those Biblical passages that describe the sinful, fallen nature of man. In fact, the balance of power between people and government, between state and federal governments, and between the legislative, executive, and judicial branches of the federal government bears eloquent testimony to the Founding Fathers' belief in sinful man who should not be entrusted with too much power. "In God We Trust" was their motto, not "In Humanity We Trust."

They had just survived a bloody war with a king who talked of justice while forcing tyranny upon them. In that war they saw what men were made of, good and bad, and they concluded that without a people governed individually by God's laws, the nation would self-destruct.

George Washington said in his presidential farewell address that religion and morality are the two "great pillars of human happiness" and indispensable to "private and public felicity."

John Adams, our second president, said it this way: "We have no government armed with power capable of contending with human passions unbridled by morality and religion. Avarice, ambition, revenge or gallantry would break the strongest cords of our Constitution as a whale goes through a net. Our constitution was made only for a moral and religious people. It is wholly inadequate to the government of any other."

Thomas Jefferson, the third president, repeated the theme: "Can the liberties of a nation be sure when we remove their only firm basis, a conviction in the minds of the people, that these liberties are the gift of God? That they are not to be violated but with His wrath?"

Do you realize how helpless the police would be to prevent crime or to protect its victims if everybody suddenly decided to break the law? What would happen to the solvency of government if we all chose not to pay our taxes? Our neighborhoods would be transformed into armed camps if we decided that nothing is wrong with stealing our neighbors' goods, raping our neighbors' wives, abusing or kidnapping our neighbors' children. Alone, the laws of this land cannot hold society in check. All the policemen, sheriffs' officers, and highway patrolmen in the nation couldn't stop us if we all decided to disobey them.

Add together all the crimes and all the criminals reported in the past year (and they are many), and you will still find that most people have made it through the year without seriously breaking the law. The people, most of us, have policed ourselves. Why? What keeps most of us in order? What holds us back during those times of lust or anger or disappointment?

Our free society depends on one essential element, the self-restraint of its citizens. And the self-restraint of the citizens in turn depends on one primary belief, that God exists and that one day He will judge us and reward or punish us according to His divine standard. Believing in the just and powerful God of the Old Testament makes a tremendous difference in a society. Believing in the ancient promise of eternal rewards or eternal punishments helps foster self-control.

Jesus introduced a new dimension to the Old Testament law. Christians' desire to live by God's standards is reinforced by the presence of the Holy Spirit and by the comfort and discipline of the church. And though the New Testament presents the good news of God's love and forgiveness in the life, death, and resurrection of Jesus, grace motivates the Christian to want to obey God even more.

Both Old and New Testament standards create a law of the heart. Whether one lives life by the Ten Commandments of the Old Testament or the fruit of God's Spirit in the New, the law of the heart helps regulate your response to the laws of this nation. Imagine how different the world would be without these Biblically-based constraints. Imagine what might happen to this nation without them.[213]

While the Framers believed in and observed what they meant by the first amendment (that government should not establish one of the religious sects of the nation over all the others), they had a deep and abiding realization that government had a vested interest in making "religion, morality, and knowledge" available to the people. Today our public schools are in chaos because they are afraid of invoking morality for fear that they might be accused of promoting religion, and our young people are being destroyed by permissivism in the fields of sex, drugs, and character.

Our Founding Fathers knew that you could not have a free people very long without Biblical morality. Let them speak for themselves.

> Our Constitution was made only for a moral and relig-ious people. It is wholly inadequate to the government of any other. — John Adams

> Only a virtuous people are capable of freedom. As na-tions become corrupt and vicious, they have more need of masters. — Benjamin Franklin

> Neither the wisest constitution nor the wisest laws will secure the liberty and happiness of a people whose man-ners are universally corrupt. — Samuel Adams

Clinton Rossiter, in his introduction to the *Federalist Papers*, wrote,

> No happiness without liberty, no liberty without self-gov-ernment, no self-government without constitutionalism, and no constitutionalism without morality — and none of these great goods without stability and order.[214]

As a contemporary conservative, Cleon Skousen, has written:

> . . . freedom belongs only to people who are morally re-sponsible. It is not possible for a people to be corrupt and conniving liars, cheaters, and thieves, stealing from one another, and still remain free. To have a good country we have to build a nation of good people.[215]

If we as a nation do not soon return our official public policy to the Christian consensus of our Founding Fathers and the Bib-lical principles of law that have provided the freedoms we've en-joyed for over two hundred years, it is just a matter of time be-fore we lose those freedoms.

With that concern in mind, let me suggest ten governmental policies based on the Constitution that could return this nation to traditional moral values in one decade. These ten policy suggestions are well within the intent of the Founding Fathers. This would require a rollback of the oppressive power that some in government have taken to themselves in an attempt to do for the people what was not intended by the writers of the Constitution, those who ratified it, the officials who administered it for the first 150 years, or by the American citizens who first submitted to it. The state of the union would enjoy much better health if these ten principles were made current governmental policy.

Governmental Policy and Traditional Values
Statement of Principles

1. Public policy-making by the federal government in a free society (that is predominately Judeo-Christian in makeup) should reaffirm its commitment to religious freedom and should begin with the axiom "What strengthens the family strengthens the nation."

2. It shall not be the purpose of any of the agencies of government to control the family, but to recognize that parents have the responsibility and the freedom to bear, train, and educate their own children.

3. It shall be the purpose of all agencies of government to pass only those laws and regulations that will contribute to the creation of a culture that is supportive of the values and objectives of the traditional family, bringing governmentally approved policy into conformity with traditional family values.

4. This government should recognize that a monogamous marriage is the foundation to a lasting family and require that all agencies exalt that ideal and encourage only sexual behavior based on fidelity, commitment, and maturity, placing sexuality within the context of marriage.

5. All governmentally sponsored education programs and curricula should reinforce the principles and ideals parents strive to impart to their children and should assist parents, not only in the teaching of basics, but also in character development. The Department of Health and Human Services and the Department of Education should encourage all local school districts to disregard value-neutral materials.

6. Traditional family values should be recognized as official public policy by this government for education and entertainment in a secular society. These should include honesty, loyalty, patriotism, courage, industry, hard work, self-discipline, generosity, kindness, compassion, service to others, politeness, respect for both adults and children, and sexual expression reserved for adulthood and confined to marriage. Promiscuity of all kinds should be discouraged for the sake of health, emotional and mental well-being, and the protection of our society.

7. The Federal Communications Commission should be instructed to renew the radio, television, and cable license of only those stations that conform all programming to the above policy.

8. Governmental pro-family policy must be built upon a foundation of economic growth, declining taxation, reasonable expenditures, and welfare only to those who cannot provide for themselves. Nonetheless, attempts should be made to help the needy toward self-sufficiency and, wherever possible, should encourage self-ownership of homes.

9. All forms of obscenity and pornography that violate traditional family values, promote the exploitation of children or the rape or degradation of women should be condemned and, wherever legally possible, be prohibited.

10. In addition to our present social security system, additional aid to the poor, elderly, and lonely should be encouraged on a voluntary basis as part of the civic responsibility of all citizens, corporations, and religious and humanitarian organizations.

Summary

The genius of the American Constitution and the special contribution it made to the establishment of government, both in this country and in those where it has been copied, stems from our Founding Fathers' Biblical understanding of human nature and their Biblical view of government. As we have seen, the famous check and balance system was based on their recognition of the fallen nature of humanity. Consequently, they knew most people cannot be trusted without someone to watch over them, particularly when they have the power of government with which to play.

Our Founding Fathers also understood that government is of divine origin, not human. Therefore, it is responsible to God for the use of that power. Daniel Webster, the great statesman who followed the Founding Fathers by one generation, was once asked, "What is the greatest thought that ever passed through your mind?" He responded, "My accountability to God." The purpose of government is not to provide all man's needs but to provide a social climate in which he can, in quiet peace and safety, fulfill his duties to his Creator and earn his own living.

The purpose of government, according to the Founding Fathers, was to "promote domestic tranquility and to provide for the common defense." Today's secularist-style government does neither. We are a violent society internally, and for forty-five years we have consistently retreated in the face of an inferior Soviet enemy whose relentless intention to conquer the world is well known. Instead of protecting its citizens and those of our own hemisphere from barbarous attacks through the use of the Monroe Doctrine, established by our Founding Fathers and our sixth president, we have abandoned millions of Cubans, Nicaraguans, and others in Central and South America to the spread of godless communism.

The Founding Fathers, most of whom qualified to attend the Constitutional Convention by their heroic participation in the Revolutionary War of 1776 and who opposed England again in 1812, would hold our present House of Representatives, Senate, and Supreme Court in contempt for not guaranteeing the peace and safety of the people of the United States. They probably would have called for the impeachment of those who were responsible for abandoning the Monroe Doctrine. Yet our present secularist leaders in government lionize them.

What Can We Do?

The solution to the relentless secularization of our "one nation under God" is really not difficult — if a majority of our citizens, most of whom have deep religious and moral yearnings, can be enlisted. In fact, there are five things we can do that can return this nation to the base it was originally founded upon and that will assure peace and tranquility for both our nation and our hemisphere in the twenty-first century.

1. Like our Founding Fathers, pray for America. Pray for a moral, spiritual, and social revival. Pray that an army of God-fearing men and women will be inspired to run for the almost one hundred thousand elective offices of this land on the local, state-wide, and national levels. From school board to city council to state legislature to congress, we need elected officials who realize they are responsible to God for the way they rule their city or this country.

Pray also that we will elect God-fearing presidents in 1988, 1992, and 1996 who will appoint only "strict constructionists" to the Supreme Court so the Constitution will be interpreted as our Founding Fathers intended.

2. Register all born-again Christians and our fellow religious-minded citizens to vote. Then inform them on the moral issues of our day and the voting record of all politicians so they can vote intelligently. Wise voters of the future will vote for the moral commitment of candidates, not party or personality.

3. Recruit more Christians to become politically active. If just ten percent of the "born-again," who are forty percent of the population, and a similar percentage of the other forty-five percent of Americans who also claim to be religious would either run for public office or volunteer to campaign for someone who shares their moral values, we would see a return to the principles of our Founding Fathers in just one decade.

4. Get all Christians out to vote on Election Day. In 1984, less than sixty percent of the eligible voters exercised their God-given freedom to vote. In 1986, it was a disgraceful 38.5 percent—which is why so many liberals were elected to office. If all Christians had gone to the polls that day, both houses of Congress would be controlled by conservatives today. That is why I say the reason our federal government is controlled by liberals is the apathy of Christians.

The future of America is up for grabs and will be determined before the twenty-first century. It could go either way—to the left and let an elitist minority of secularists continue to lead this nation into impotence, stagnation, and slavery—or to the right and return it to the control of those who continue the spirit of our Founding Fathers, who like them would lead this nation to respect for God and man, moral sanity, true religious freedom, national strength, prosperity, and opportunity. As has been well said: "Now is the time for all good men to come to the aid of their country."

Our Founding Fathers did their part. They gave us a Constitution for the ages. Now it is up to us to do everything we can to keep it.

THE OTHER DELEGATES WHO SIGNED THE CONSTITUTION

The following Founding Fathers were among the thirty-nine who signed the Constitution. Most of them were religious men, as well as political leaders and professional men. However, because their personal religious views, which may have been very real and important to them, have not survived the passage of time, they are included in this appendix. You will find most of them were dedicated to preserving the Christian cultural consensus they had inherited. Some were ordinary citizens, some extremely gifted. Many were colorful personalities, and almost all made some contribution to the founding of this country. All Americans owe them a tremendous debt of gratitude.

William Blount of North Carolina

At the Convention, he said "almost nothing" during the debates. Known to have little faith in the Union, he signed the final document reluctantly. He did not participate in the first ratification attempt in his own state, and only after eleven other states ratified it did he finally endorse it. One year into his term as U.S. senator he was impeached and expelled under very questionable circumstances that reek of unfair politics relating to his efforts to secure navigation rights for his state on the Mississippi River. Upon his return to Tennessee (his adopted state after the Convention; it had been a western part of North Carolina), he was warmly greeted as a hero and immediately elected

WILLIAM BLOUNT
(1749-1800)

NORTH CAROLINA, PRESBYTERIAN: PLANTER; SOLDIER; MERCHANT;
LAND SPECULATOR; POLITICAL LEADER OF BOTH NORTH CAROLINA
AND TENNESSEE; STATE LEGISLATOR; MEMBER OF THE CONTINENTAL
CONGRESS; TERRITORIAL GOVERNOR OF TENNESSEE; U.S. SENATOR
FROM TENNESSEE; A FOUNDER OF THE UNIVERSITY OF TENNESSEE;
ENLISTED AS PAYMASTER OF THE NORTH CAROLINA FORCES IN 1776
AND FOR THE REST OF HIS LIFE ENGAGED IN PUBLIC SERVICE.

to the state senate, then selected by the senators as Speaker.
Had he not suddenly died one year later at the age of fifty, he
would doubtless have been the next governor of the new state.
Little is known about his religious background other than that
he was raised by Episcopalian parents. Due to the remoteness
of their home, they were only able to attend worship when the
Reverend James Reed came to a small chapel in Ayden. Blount
is on record as opposing the doctrines of the French Jacobins,
which were fashionable in some secularist circles, indicating
that he recognized the need for the teaching of religion and
morality in order to preserve a democratic society. At least we
know that he was a member of the Continental Congress in
1787 when religion and morality were requirements in the
western territorial lands.

PIERCE BUTLER
(1744-1824)
SOUTH CAROLINA, EPISCOPALIAN: SOLDIER; POLITICAL LEADER; WEALTHY PLANTER; ADJUTANT GENERAL OF SOUTH CAROLINA; MEMBER OF CONTINENTAL CONGRESS; UNITED STATES SENATOR IN THE FIRST CONGRESS.

Born into a wealthy family in Ireland, Butler chose to enter the British army at age twelve. He was sent to Canada, where he rose to the rank of major and resigned from British service in 1773.

Following his marriage to the daughter of a wealthy military man, Butler moved to South Carolina and immediately identified with the patriot cause in his adopted state. He poured money and goods into the Revolutionary War and was involved in the defense of Charleston, from which he and his family had to flee after its fall. With a loan which he arranged in Amsterdam, Butler rebuilt his fortune while at the same time serving in political office.

M. E. Bradford says of him,

In the Great Convention Pierce Butler (always addressed as "the Major") spoke on at least fifty occasions. And the mode of his discourse there was usually impressive — cautious, prudent, and full of the information provided by a cosmopolitan experience. Agreeing to a firmer connection to the Northern states was difficult for this Carolina nabob. For from his first coming to the New World as a soldier of King George III, Butler had acquired a distaste for New England manners and New England ideas. Nor did most of the Middle Colonies suit him any better. As early as 1782 he had concluded, from observing sectional tensions in the Continental Congress, that the Northern politicians meant to control the Union and to acquire influence and authority over the future development and internal life of the Southern states. . . .

Of the Framers, none was so suspicious of the dangers to liberty in an elaborate system of Federal courts, empowered with a vague authority over questions of constitutional interpretation as was Pierce Butler, or more determined that the new national legislature represent and protect property instead of some general notion of individual rights. [216]

He assailed the French Revolution as a possible influence on this country and made constant reiterations that "the powers of the General Government are [in the fundamental law] so defined as not to destroy the Sovereignty of the Individual States." [217]

After Aaron Burr's duel with Alexander Hamilton, in which Hamilton was fatally shot, Butler harbored Burr at his lavish plantation on St. Simeon Island. Aside from his membership in the Episcopal church, little is known of Butler's religious life.

Daniel Carroll of Maryland

Daniel Carroll, one of the senior Founding Fathers, was a very quiet man of considerable wealth. He was described by his colleague Pierce as "a man of large fortune, and influence in his State. He possesses plain, good sense, and is in the full confidence of his countrymen." [218]

Once he arrived at the Convention, he was in almost constant attendance. An ardent advocate of a strong central govern-

DANIEL CARROLL
(1730-1796)

MARYLAND, CATHOLIC: PLANTER; INFLUENTIAL MEMBER OF THE STATE'S POLITICAL ESTABLISHMENT; LEGISLATOR AND PRESIDENT OF STATE SENATE; MEMBER OF CONTINENTAL CONGRESS; UNITED STATES CONGRESSMAN; COMMISSIONER OF COMMITTEE TO DEFINE WASHINGTON, D.C.

ment (with limitations) to offset the anarchy of the times, he spoke on at least twenty occasions — "clearly the voice of authority within the Maryland delegation to the Great Convention."[219] Upon returning to his state after signing the Constitution, Carroll worked diligently for its ratification.

Carroll entered the first Congress as a member of the House of Representatives, where he was active in the passage of the Bill of Rights and was particularly zealous in his advocacy of religious freedom. He voted in favor of locating the national capital in his part of Maryland and was appointed by President Washington as one of the three commissioners directed to survey and define the District of Columbia. He was a very religious man of high character, one of only two Roman Catholics to serve as Framers of the Constitution. His brother, John Carroll, was archbishop of Baltimore. Daniel Carroll was devoted to his church, had a strong belief in its chief doctrines, and was very generous in support of it throughout his life.

George Clymer
(1739-1813)

PENNSYLVANIA, QUAKER/EPISCOPALIAN: MERCHANT; BANKER; LEADER IN THE MOVEMENT TOWARD THE REVOLUTION; SIGNER OF THE DEC-LARATION OF INDEPENDENCE.

Said one historian, "Probably no man in America so closely resembled the Father of his Country, in many respects, as the quiet 'Quaker merchant of Philadelphia.' "[220]

Anyone who looks at his picture can see that Clymer did bear a striking physical resemblance to his friend George Washington. And as we examine his life and character, we will identify other similarities. He has been described by writers as

a thoroughbred gentleman; never, in his conversation, making the most remote allusion to any subject or circumstance that might injure the feelings of any one present. In all his relation, whether domestic or public, he was worthy of imitation; he filled the spheres of husband, father, friend and citizen in the fullest manner and highest sense, and to do good seemed to be the entire aim of his existence. Eminently original in thought and invention, he shunned applause and notoriety. With no pretension to oratorical powers, he yet had the faculty, by the earnestness of his manner and the logic of his reasoning, to hold entire attention. Punctuality was a remarkable trait in his character; he never kept any one waiting.[221]

Best known for his work in financing the American war effort and for his role as a leader of the Continental Congress after the independence of the Colonies had been declared. A man of great wealth, but possessed of a genuine popular touch. Religious, and probably Quaker by origin, but a member of the Episcopal church during his maturity.[222]

During the discussions of the Convention, it is said that "in general he was silent, ever present and supportive of whatever his friend George Washington seemed to approve."[223] But "a careful man, he illustrates the pattern of American leaders who were 'radicals' for the Revolution, but did not expect independence to disturb the internal order of their society. In his old age, he was one of Philadelphia's most honored citizens, respected by all ranks of society."[224]

JONATHAN DAYTON
(1760-1824)
NEW JERSEY, EPISCOPALIAN: SOLDIER; LAWYER; CONGRESSMAN; U.S. SENATOR AND LAND SPECULATOR.

The Youngest of the Framers. Elected to sit in the Great Convention in his father's place. Educated at the College of New Jersey. . . . A Soldier in the Continental Army, rising to the rank of Captain at the age of nineteen. Served under his father [General Elias Dayton] and the Marquis de Lafayette. Captured, but exchanged, and returned to service in time for the Battle of Yorktown. . . .

Jonathan Dayton, perhaps in consequence of his youth, said very little during the Constitutional Convention, but faithfully followed the leadership of William Paterson and Governor William Livingston, the acknowledged spokesmen for his state. He did, however, speak on a few occasions and was one of the Framers who announced that he would sign the Constitution while objecting to some of its provisions.[225]

Fascinated by western land development after the Convention, Dayton became involved in land speculation that saw him indicted for treason. Though he was not convicted, it ruined him politically. His development of western lands gained him the honor of having the city of Dayton, Ohio, named after him.

Little is known of his religious beliefs other than that he was a member of the Episcopal church and must have given assent to the doctrine of the Trinity and inspiration of the Scriptures in order to get elected as a delegate from New Jersey, an affirmation required by the constitution of that state. He had little influence on the formulation of the Constitution.

William Few of Georgia

William Few was a "silent presence at the Great Convention [and] . . . the only genuine frontiersman among the Framers."[226] He vigorously supported the views of the Georgia delegation and was active in getting his state to ratify the Constitution upon its completion. In his autobiography, written in 1817, Few emphasized the importance of that Constitutional Convention by saying, "It was an awful and critical moment. If the convention had then adjourned, the dissolution of the union of the States seemed inevitable. This consideration no doubt had its weight in

WILLIAM FEW
(1741-1811)

GEORGIA, METHODIST: FARMER; SELF-TAUGHT LAWYER; WARTIME
SOLDIER; BANKER; POLITICAL LEADER OF GEORGIA; MEMBER OF THE
CONTINENTAL CONGRESS; UNITED STATES SENATOR.

reconciling clashing opinions and interests."[227]

Few must have had a brilliant and inquisitive mind to have
advanced so far without formal training. It is said that in his
youth he read every book in his father's small library, including
the Bible, which he perused several times.

Although little is known of his personal religious faith
(typical of many leaders in Georgia during that period), there is
nothing in his history to indicate that he ever forsook his
Methodist roots. One historian said of him, "Senator Few was
described as 'tall, erect, slender, and well-proportioned,' in appearance. His manner was 'grave and dignified.' He was deeply
religious, and gave what he could to charity."[228]

His Georgia colleague William Pierce reported that he
"possesses a strong natural genius, and from application has acquired some knowledge of legal matters; he practices at the Bar
of Georgia, and speaks tolerably well in the legislature. He has
been twice a member of Congress, and served in that capacity
with fidelity to his State, and honor to himself."[229]

THOMAS FITZSIMONS
(1741-1811)
PENNSYLVANIA, ROMAN CATHOLIC: WEALTHY MERCHANT OF PHILA-
DELPHIA; MILITIA OFFICER; CONGRESSMAN.
[portrait not available]

Born in Ireland, Thomas Fitzsimons migrated to Philadelphia, joined the trades, married the daughter of a wealthy family, and was regarded by his peers as "an aristocrat."[230]
During the Revolutionary War he commanded a militia
that he recruited himself and is said to have given between five
thousand and twenty-five thousand pounds to the support of
the Continental army (historians differ). He was a "pious
Roman Catholic, one of only two in the Great Convention."[231]
Fitzsimons "said little to distinguish himself in the debates of
the Framers."[232]

NICHOLAS GILMAN
(1755-1814)
NEW HAMPSHIRE, CONGREGATIONALIST: MERCHANT; CAPTAIN IN THE
REVOLUTIONARY ARMY; STATE POLITICAL LEADER; U.S. REPRESENTA-
TIVE AND U.S. SENATOR.

Nicholas Gilman, brother of the famous governor of New Hampshire, John Taylor Gilman, was a silent man who never married but made public service the pursuit of his life. Though a man of wealth, Gilman was still able to maintain a close relationship with the common people, who looked upon him as their representative.

While inconspicuous at the convention, he was very supportive of his good friend John Langdon, with whom he concurred philosophically and religiously.

Gilman was a member of the Second Congregational Church of Exeter. After service at the Constitutional Convention, he helped in the New Hampshire ratification process and then became a member of the first House of Representatives, surrendering that position for election to the U.S. Senate, where he served until his death.

His obituary testifies to his character and religious convictions.

It is but justice to the deceased to say, that in every situation in which he has been placed, he has conducted with honor to himself and fidelity to the public. In private life his virtues were equally conspicuous. He was the friend of the widow and the fatherless, and the hearts of the poor were made glad by his unnoticed magnificence. In all his dealings, he was honest, honorable, and just. Those who knew him can well appreciate his virtues — the breach which this death has made in the family of the deceased must be grievous — as a brother he was amiable, affectionate, and kind; united to his brothers and sister, by all the ties that can bind together the hearts of mortals. The loss to this town, and the religious society to which he belonged is very grieved. He was ever ready to contribute liberally to the support to all public expenses and particularly to the support of religious worship.[233]

Nathaniel Gorham of Massachusetts

At fifty years of age, Gorham was the oldest Massachusetts delegate at the Constitutional Convention, where he spoke "on over forty occasions."[234] Pierce eulogized him as a "vigorous, active participant in the debates of the Great Convention; of a

NATHANIEL GORHAM
(1748-1796)
MASSACHUSETTS, CONGREGATIONALIST: MERCHANT; STATE POLITICAL
LEADER; HELPED WRITE STATE CONSTITUTION; FINANCIER; LAND
SPECULATOR; DELEGATE TO THE CONTINENTAL CONGRESS, WHERE
HE SERVED AS PRESIDENT.

'lusty . . . agreeable and pleasing manner.' "[235] "A merchant in
Boston, high in reputation, and much in the esteem of his countrymen. He is a man of very good sense."[236]

Religiously, he was a Congregationalist of old Puritan stock
whose personal faith was clearly acceptable to Samuel Adams,
for otherwise he probably would not have been appointed to
serve as a delegate to the Constitutional Convention. As a writer
of the Massachusetts constitution, which required personal
faith,[237] we are assured that he was a man who revered the word
of God, even though little has survived about his personal faith.

Jared Ingersoll, Jr. of Pennsylvania

Unlike many of the other Founding Fathers, Ingersoll, at
thirty-eight years of age, was not politically active prior to the
Convention. He was the son of a famous father who did not
support the revolution and was in Europe when the Declaration was signed.

According to a contemporary,

Jared Ingersoll, Jr.
(1749-1822)

PENNSYLVANIA, PRESBYTERIAN: LAWYER; POST REVOLUTIONARY POLITICAL LEADER; VICE-PRESIDENTIAL CANDIDATE IN 1812; FREQUENTLY PRACTICED BEFORE THE SUPREME COURT.

No man that I ever knew, lived further away from the fault or the toleration of a dishonorable act. His personal virtue was as straight-upward and erect as his person; but he was a religious man also, in open and full communion with the Presbyterian Church, of which he was a member to his death, and made as humble an estimate of his own moral attainments, as if the life he led had been anything but what it was in close correspondence with his duties.[238]

As a graduate of Yale in 1766, he was probably influenced by the spiritual life of the school that still reflected the effects of the Great Awakening. He moved to Philadelphia and became a member of the bar in 1771, attended law school in England from 1774-76, and met Benjamin Franklin and spent some time with him in France. During those years he apparently saw and experienced things on the continent that kindled the fires of patriotism within him.

A very cautious person, Ingersoll was also an able attorney, numbering among his clients some of the outstanding people of the day, even though he practiced in a city that boasted some of the greatest lawyers in the nation.

In 1791, Ingersoll was admitted to practice before the United States Supreme Court. And in that arena he participated in some of the most famous of the early cases to be tried there, including *Chisholm v. Georgia* (1792) and *Hylton v. United States* (1796). In these actions, Ingersoll contended generally for a strict construction of the Constitution and against the doctrine of "implied powers." He was attorney for Senator William Blount of Tennessee when his old colleague and fellow Framer was threatened with impeachment for his role in a Western plan to get Britain to conquer Louisiana and Spanish Florida.[239]

Ingersoll spoke only once in the Convention, and that during the closing days.

Daniel Jenifer
(1723-1790)
MARYLAND, EPISCOPALIAN: PROFESSIONAL POLITICIAN; PERENNIAL STATE OFFICEHOLDER; MEMBER OF CONTINENTAL CONGRESS.

Born of a wealthy, English-Swedish family, Daniel Jenifer was educated in finance and represented Maryland's old aristocracy. Historians generally are not kind to Jenifer. For example,

Always a friend to those in authority, at least until their power began to wane. . . . A convivial man, with an eye to the main chance. An unscrupulous, charming opportunist, a great host and giver of parties, but devious nonetheless. A person of genuine social skill and aplomb, called upon throughout his life to perform in offices of trust. . . . During the Convention his presence was constant, his position constant, and his voice almost unheard. At 64, he was one of the oldest of the men there.[240]

Little is known of Jenifer's religious life except that he was an Episcopalian. He had little influence on the Constitution other than voting with the majority in the Maryland delegation. He died three years after the Convention.

THOMAS MIFFLIN
(1744-1800)
PENNSYLVANIA, QUAKER/LUTHERAN: MERCHANT; SOLDIER OF THE REVOLUTION; PENNSYLVANIA LEGISLATOR; PRESIDENT OF PENNSYLVANIA CONSTITUTIONAL CONVENTION; GOVERNOR.

Thomas Mifflin was an extremely popular man in his home state but not very respected throughout the rest of the country. His life is a pathetic illustration of what uncontrolled indulgence in strong drink can do to a potentially capable person. Born of

Quaker parents and educated in Quaker schools, his love for politics brought him into conflict with his religious roots because of Quaker pacifism. As the Revolutionary War came into view, the Quakers withdrew from the political arena, forcing Mifflin to choose between them and politics. He entered the political arena and became a Lutheran of convenience. Quite probably his enormous political base that endured throughout most of his life was due in part to the fact that the voting Quakers always regarded him as one of their own. Their vote, together with his own political following, consistently gave him a majority and got him elected to almost every position he desired, including the first governorship of Pennsylvania.

Mifflin became General George Washington's aide-de-camp in 1775 and was appointed by him to be quartermaster general of the entire Continental Army until 1778. It is suspected by some historians that his love for strong drink rendered him less than effective at Valley Forge and may have been the cause for the lack of supplies that would have cost us the war had not God intervened to save Washington and his army in answer to the prayers of the general and many others. In spite of this and his many sicknesses, Mifflin's powerful personality and clever wits enabled him to rise to Major General before his return to private life. He used his uniform, which he frequently wore as if on parade, to garner popularity in his hometown of Philadelphia. He amassed and lost a great fortune during his life, yet was loved by the people of his state.

Though an outgoing and gregarious person, either his drinking kept him from meaningful participation in the Constitutional Convention debates or he was intimidated by Washington, who did not trust him, and others, who did not respect him. According to one historian, Mifflin was "perhaps the most popular political figure in his state at the time of the Constitutional Convention, but of no influence on its deliberations."[241]

His contemporaries recorded a variety of unfortunate incidents in the life of Mifflin.

One has stated that the Governor, while commanding the Pennsylvanians at Carlisle during the Whiskey Rebellion, unwisely issued orders that almost precipitated a battle between his own men and the New Jersey troops. Mifflin "was charged with being in a shameful state of intoxication, and was obliged publicly to ask pardon of some officers and make that excuse." (David Ford, *Journal of an Expedition Made in the Autumn of 1794. Proceedings of the New Jersey Historical Society,* VIII, 85-86.) In his memoirs Jonathan Roberts describes him as "a worn out debauchee whose face showed signs of deep dissipation." (Philip S. Klein, "Memoirs of Jonathan Roberts," PMHB, LXII (1938), 89.) Another contemporary, Oliver Wolcott, told Hamilton that the Governor was drunk every day and that "Dallas and Judge McKean possess[ed] the efficient powers of government." (Wolcott to Hamilton, April 1, 1799, Hamilton, *Works* VI, 106, cited in Peeling, "McKean," 204.) Finally, in reference to Mifflin's death, a Pennsylvania historian has flatly stated that he "drowned himself in drink." (Ferguson, *Early Western Pennsylvania Politics*, 211.)[242]

His death, like his life, was a testament to the destructive nature of "demon rum." As one of his biographers put it, "Lacking was the ceremony attending the death of a fallen hero or great statesman. It was described as the burial of a pauper."[243]

ROBERT MORRIS

(1734-1806)

PENNSYLVANIA, EPISCOPALIAN: GREAT FINANCIER OF THE REVOLUTION; MERCHANT; BANKER; LAND SPECULATOR; SIGNER OF THE ARTICLES OF CONFEDERATION AND THE DECLARATION OF INDEPENDENCE.

Like so many of the Founding Fathers, Morris was quite young when his father died. He apprenticed his way into business until he became one of the wealthiest men in America.

During the Revolutionary War, he performed incredible feats of financial wizardry to purchase munitions for the patriot cause. "When Washington needed to pay the army under his command in order to march it south to Virginia, Morris, in person, rushed coin to motivate the uneasy Northern regiments into cheerful assent to a long campaign far away from home."[244]

When the expedition was planned by Washington against Cornwallis at Yorktown, the government treasury was empty, and her credit shivering in the wind. The army was in a destitute situation: the means of prosecuting a siege were to be provided, and Mr. Morris informed the commander-in-chief that unless he arrived at the conclusion that the necessary supplies could be raised on his (Mr. Morris's) credit, the expedition must fail. Washington expressed his entire confidence in the ability of the financier, and immediately took up the line of march.

In the short space of four weeks, Mr. Morris, aided by the patriotic Richard Peters, furnished near eighty pieces of battering cannon and one hundred pieces of field artillery, and all other necessary supplies not furnished from other sources, and became personally responsible to the amount of ONE MILLION FOUR HUNDRED THOUSAND DOLLARS, upon his own notes, which were promptly paid at maturity. This, united with aid from Virginia and some of the other states, enabled the American army to give the finishing stroke to the revolution, and triumph, in victory complete, over a proud and merciless foe.[245]

From 1781 to 1784, Morris served as the superintendent of Finance, the highest office under the Articles of Confederation, working tirelessly and successfully to keep the infant nation from going bankrupt.

At the time of the Constitutional Convention, it is said that "he was the most influential member of the Pennsylvania delegation."[246] One historian described him as,

> large and florid, bright eyed, pleasant faced, magnetic, just as we see him in his portrait, and in the very prime of his noble manhood. He was a fluent and impressive orator, and whether in public speaking or in private conversation, overflowed with a rich fund of political knowledge and general and trustworthy information. But for his magnanimity and fertility of invention, it is doubtful whether, after all, the Independence so dearly bought could have been maintained.[247]

Somehow, due either to his optimism concerning the future of the new nation or greed for personal gain (it is difficult to say which), he became enamored with enormous land speculations. At one time he apparently owned more land than any man in the colonies, and through many land companies and investors he controlled as much as six million acres in Pennsylvania alone. But the depression of the late 1790s destroyed him financially, and he went to debtor's prison (where General Washington personally called on him) in 1798 for failure to pay his debts after declaring bankruptcy. He owed almost three million dollars to his creditors, not counting the fortunes that other investors lost with him.

After being released from prison in 1801, he was nursed back to health by his good friend Gouverneur Morris, who made an annual endowment to Mrs. Morris and set him up in a small home in Philadelphia, where the former "merchant prince of Philadelphia" lived out his life in modesty. In spite of the bankruptcy, the following statement made before Congress in his prime reflects his character and the view held of him by his colleagues of better days: "The United States may command everything I have except my integrity, and the loss of that would effectually disable me from serving them more."[248]

Although he was a member of the Episcopal church and was married at Christ's Church, little is known of his spiritual life, and he seems to have had little influence on the actual formation of the Constitution.

Once in the Great Convention, Robert Morris was surprisingly silent for a man of such self-confidence and obvious influence over the proceedings. But Morris knew his limitations. Moreover, Gouverneur Morris and James Wilson were both present to speak for him, except when Wilson sounded too "democratic." And General Washington was in the chair. To these particulars, Morris had addressed himself. Prior to the formal opening of the Convention, he had unsuccessfully argued that the vote of the states should be weighted according to their population and their property. Morris seconded a motion that United States Senators be appointed to serve "on good behavior"—for life. Otherwise he kept silent and worked behind the scenes as host for much of the social activity of the gathering. Moreover, once the Constitution was signed, Morris put the great resources of his influence to work in supporting ratification, especially among public creditors—security holders who, as a group, had an interest in the establishment of the proposed Federal government.[249]

CHARLES PINCKNEY III
(1757-1824)

SOUTH CAROLINA, EPISCOPALIAN: PLANTER; SOLDIER; LAWYER; POLITICAL LEADER; MEMBER OF CONTINENTAL CONGRESS; GOVERNOR; UNITED STATES SENATOR; U.S. CONGRESSMAN, DIPLOMAT TO SPAIN.

[*portrait not available*]

While related by blood to his older cousin, Charles Cotesworth Pinckney, Charles III was more outgoing and aggressive. Some say that his father's betrayal of the Revolution after the fall of Charleston to the British while he was a prisoner of war drove him relentlessly in public service to repair the image of the family name.

Although not trained in Europe like his illustrious cousin, he was very brilliant, may have been a better speaker, and was extremely forceful. After listening to him during the Convention, delegate William Pierce said of him, "A young gentleman of the most promising talents. . . . He is in possession of a very great variety of knowledge. Government, law, history and philosophy are his favorite studies, but he is intimately acquainted with every species of polite learning, and has a spirit of application and industry beyond most men."[250]

He arrived at the Constitutional Convention with a conviction that a stronger central government was essential, but he was never interested in giving up slavery in the South to gain it. On that subject he always voted with the rest of his delegation, but on many others he was often a maverick who was outvoted by the other three delegates. Consequently he had little influence on the outcome of the Convention.

JOHN RUTLEDGE
(1737-1800)

SOUTH CAROLINA, EPISCOPALIAN: LAWYER; JURIST; STATE ATTORNEY GENERAL; MEMBER OF CONTINENTAL CONGRESS AND STAMP ACT CONGRESS; GOVERNOR; CHIEF JUSTICE OF SOUTH CAROLINA'S SUPREME COURT; U.S. SUPREME COURT JUSTICE.

Affectionately called "Dictator John" by the people of his state, Rutledge was easily the most powerful figure in the Southern delegation. One historian even termed him "the Father of the Republic." Another described his influence as follows:

Oliver Ellsworth reportedly said to his son that Rutledge played as important a role as himself, James Wilson, Alexander Hamilton, and James Madison in the convention, and Madison's biographer Irving Brant gives him credit with both Madison and Wilson for the "actual construction of the government." There is some justification for these claims. Rutledge was the South Carolina delegate to the select committee which brought in the Great Compromise, giving the states equal voice in the Senate, with the lower house apportioned according to population (five slaves considered three persons) and requiring all revenue measures to originate in the lower house. He proposed the supremacy clause in substantially the form in which it stands in the Constitution. He also served as chairman of the Committee on Detail which composed the first draft of the Constitution.[251]

John Rutledge was born in Charles Town, the son of Dr. John Rutledge, a physician, and Sara Hext Rutledge, the only daughter of the very wealthy Colonel Hugh Hext. John Rutledge's uncle (and eventually his role model) was Andrew Rutledge, Speaker of the Commons House of Assembly and the leader of the South Carolina bar. . . . John Rutledge lost both his father (1750) and his uncle (1755) while still a child. He was educated by his mother, by the Episcopal minister of Christ Church Parish, and by Dr. David Rhind, a respected tutor. Later he read law with James Parsons, also speaker of the house. In 1757 he journeyed to Great Britain, where, according to the pattern with South Carolinians of his class, he studied in the Middle Temple, and was called to the English bar in 1760, trying and winning two cases in London courts before his return home. Within two years of his first appearance in the courts of South Carolina, Rutledge had become one of the three most successful attorneys in the province. In 1761 he was elected to the Commons House from Christ Church Parish and continued to carry out that assignment until, during the Revolution, he rose to be the president and governor of an independent and sovereign nation and state.[252]

Rutledge attended most of the important conventions that produced this nation and always represented the interests of his state, economically and socially. When it came time to elect delegates to the Constitutional Convention, it was a foregone conclusion that Rutledge would not only be a delegate but would also head the delegation. Some believe that the "triumvirate" of power—Rutledge and the two Pinkneys, who controlled state politics—made that decision. He was forty-eight years of age when he arrived at the Convention.

Rutledge made it clear from the outset that slavery was not a negotiable subject at the Convention and that if it were brought up, the South Carolina delegation and most of the South would bolt. All proceedings were based on this basic affirmation. According to one of his classic statements early in the proceedings, "The true question at present is whether the Southern States shall or shall not be parties to the Union."[253] His meaning was clear, and though many compromises were made to meld the independent colonies into "one nation," the removal of slavery was not one of them. It took a civil war seventy-three years later to do that. On August 6, Rutledge presented his report as chairman of the committee on detail, completing his work on the Constitution. Although most South Carolinians disapproved of the U.S. Constitution, they held him in such high regard that they ratified it.

Religiously, Rutledge was an Episcopalian, with the typical background and training to be a vestryman. Retaining his membership in the church all his life, he was respectful toward God, the Bible, and the need for religion as a life force in this nation. In fact, if he had shown signs of infidelity or hostility to the Protestant religion common to the region, he would not have won election in 1761 as a member of the Commons House of the state from Christ Church Parish. We would probably not consider him an evangelical by today's standards, however.

Richard Dobbs Spaight of North Carolina

Born in New Bern, North Carolina, of Irish parentage, Spaight was orphaned at eight. Educated at Glasgow University, upon graduation in 1778 he returned to America and immediately accepted a military commission, rising to the rank of

RICHARD DOBBS SPAIGHT
(1758-1802)
NORTH CAROLINA, EPISCOPALIAN: SOLDIER; PLANTER; STATE LEG-
ISLATOR; MEMBER OF CONTINENTAL CONGRESS; GOVERNOR; U.S.
CONGRESSMAN.

lieutenant colonel. He served the military until 1781, when he
was elected to the House of Commons; he then worked for two
years in the Continental Congress. After the convention he was
ill for four years, then became the first native-born governor of
North Carolina. Following this he was elected to the U.S. Congress. Only twenty-nine years old at the Constitutional Convention, Spaight attended every session, establishing himself as
a strong federalist. Historians claim that he was:

> devoted to the idea of union of sovereign states preserv-
> ing their civil liberties and connected together by such
> ties as to preserve permanent and effective government,
> though he doubted the possibility of such balance. Of the
> opinion that those gathered with him in Philadelphia had
> assembled to produce "a system not described, . . . that
> has not occurred in the history of man."[254]

Noted for his hot temper and short fuse, Spaight was involved in a stormy election in 1802 (which he won), taking

offense at an opponent who called him "a liar and a crook." When satisfaction was demanded, he challenged his opponent to a duel. Ordinarily one miss by both parties would settle the matter, but their confrontation included three misses, and Spaight was killed on the fourth attempt. He was listed as an Episcopalian by religious preference, but little else is known of his religious beliefs.

JAMES WILSON
(1742-1798)
PENNSYLVANIA, EPISCOPALIAN-DEIST: LAWYER; POLITICAL PHILOSOPHER; LAND SPECULATOR; STATESMAN; SUPREME COURT JUSTICE.

Born in Scotland of deeply religious parents, Wilson was granted a scholarship to St. Andrews, a Church of Scotland college, where he was expected to study for the ministry. When his father died in 1762, he left his theological studies and took up tutoring to support himself. The neighbors helped to provide him with a financial stake in the new world (Philadelphia), from which he never returned. He read law with John Dickinson and in 1767 was admitted to the bar, after which he moved to Reading, Pennsylvania. Two years later he married the daughter of a wealthy family. He was a brilliant orator, speaking 168 times at the Constitutional Convention.

Of all the Founding Fathers, James Wilson is the greatest enigma in that he is both adored and despised by historians. As a general rule, those who lean toward Deism tend to lionize him and cover up many of the charges against him. Those of a strong Christian persuasion point out his character flaws. As one historian has written of him:

> As a constructive statesman Wilson had no superior in the Federal Convention of 1787. He favored the independence of the executive, legislative and judicial departments, the supremacy of the Federal government over the state governments, and the election of senators as well as representatives by the people, and was opposed to the election of the President or the judges by Congress. His political philosophy was based upon implicit confidence in the people, and he strove for such provisions as he thought would best guarantee a government by the people. When the Constitution had been framed, Wilson pronounced it "the best form of government which has ever been offered to the world," and he, at least, among the Framers regarded it not as a compact but as an ordinance to be established by the people. During the struggle for ratification he made a speech before a mass meeting in Philadelphia which has been characterized as the ablest single presentation of the whole subject. In the Pennsylvania ratification convention (Nov. 21 to Dec. 15, 1787), he was the Constitution's principal defender.[255]

It is suggested by another that he was adversely influenced by political theorists-philosophers Viscount Bolingbroke, "the brilliant, opportunistic Jacobite," and Anthony Ashley Cooper Shaftesbury, who "secularized the idea of moral content in the world . . . by divorcing it from theology. . . . If Shaftesbury stood closer to the skeptical, rationalistic spirit of his age, Bolingbroke wrote more in the orthodox Anglican tradition."[256]

> Although Bolingbroke might resist the secularization of political theory, he contributed toward it. To him "sociability is the foundation of human happiness." Society cannot be maintained without benevolence, justice, and other moral virtues. "These virtues, therefore, are the

foundations of society, and self-love underlies them all. . . ."

Archdeacon Paley was the great Deist who adapted Newtonian physics to moral philosophy and envisioned the universe as a giant watch, wound and set in motion by a God who was then relegated to the role of a first cause. Paley, in common with Shaftesbury and Bolingbroke, accepted happiness as the end of individual life.[257]

Another writer may be suggesting that James Wilson was a closet forerunner of modern liberal secularists.

The common denominator among all the English *illuminati* to whom Wilson turned for inspiration or for confirmation of his own ideas was found in their concern with the organization of society and their agreement on happiness as the end of life and object of government. It is not hard to trace in Paley's cry of protest for the ninety-nine who labor to create a surplus for the one tones of social aspiration that will find voice in Marx. The ideas of all these men, so much a part of Wilson's intellectual equipment, partook in a generous measure of the skeptical, adventuring spirit of the age. In the American politician and his fellows they formed an amalgam which entered into history.[258]

That may be why one careful researcher describes him in the following manner:

Wilson came to the deliberations of the Convention with a set of assumptions concerning American politics and the meaning of the Articles of Confederation not shared by many of his colleagues. First of all, Wilson never accepted the historic and well established multiplicity of cultural identities reflected in the thirteen state governments as a given of any viable plan for a stronger union. Indeed, Wilson denied, in the face of all evidence and opinion, that the states were sovereign in their connection through the Articles of Confederation.[259]

Though he served on the Committee of Detail, whose members composed the first draft of the Constitution, the theory that he was a major influence on the final form of the document is unsupported, a myth of those scholars who prefer his teaching to that of the Framers of genuine importance. Wilson is perhaps most useful in directing our attention to what the authors of the Constitution did not intend for it to mean.

Though often disappointed in the Great Convention, James Wilson was the dominant figure in the Pennsylvania ratifying convention of 1787.[260]

With the installation of President George Washington and the formation of the government under the new Constitution, James Wilson did not receive the highest judicial honor within its gift. Though he directly solicited the post of Chief Justice of the Supreme Court, and though the most important Federalist in Pennsylvania, Robert Morris, had lobbied to win him the job, Washington recognized the problems that might issue from Wilson's passion for speculation, from the rumor of his debts, and from riots like the one in Carlisle, Pennsylvania, in January of 1788—where the capstone was a burning of Wilson in effigy in a town which had once been his home. Therefore, Washington wisely turned away from the proud, learned Scot, called by his enemies "lieutenant-General of the Myrmidons of power," and appointed John Jay of New York. Wilson was, however, offered the position of Associate Justice, which he accepted.[261]

Between 1792 and his death in 1798, James Wilson plunged more and more deeply into land speculation. He was a large investor in the Illinois-Wabash Company. He bought an interest in one of the infamous Yazoo companies, as well as other lands in Pennsylvania and New York.

He bought on option, and then tried to hold on, while at the same time adventuring in other commercial and manufacturing schemes. Depression and war in Europe—a war that cut off immigration—dried up investment funds and lowered the value of all frontier properties. Still, Wilson came up with larger and larger designs, asking Dutch investors to buy 500,000 acres through him and to ship over their own immigrants to purchase the land. . . . In the end, creditors began to call in his notes. The United States Congress still refused to shore up his claims. Hundreds of thousands of dollars were due. Wilson, though a justice of the United States Supreme Court, fled, "hunted," in his own words, "like a wild beast." Twice he was arrested. As he had deceived others, now it became clear that he had also deceived himself.

Ironically, he found final shelter in the South, with his friend Justice James Iredell at Edenton, North Carolina. There, of a "nervous fever," crying out in remorse, he died in shame—one of the most curious, brilliant, gifted, and distressing figures in the political history of his country.[262]

In fairness, if these historians are accurate, and it certainly seems that they are, Wilson was a pathetic example of one who turned his back on his family's God, then their ways, and finally the family itself—only to lose all in the quest to gain all. We can only be grateful that his old-world, skeptically based ideas were out of step with the other Founding Fathers and that he had little to do with the Constitution's final construction.

APPENDIX B

THE DELEGATES WHO DID NOT SIGN THE CONSTITUTION

Sixteen delegates (including George Mason, who was discussed in chapter 6) did not sign the Constitution because they faced ill health or family difficulties, the press of personal business encumbered them, or they were also members of the Continental Congress and had to leave the Convention early before signing the final document. A few didn't sign because they disagreed with the development of the new government, and some refused to sign because it didn't contain a bill of rights. However, several of those who did not or could not include their signatures on the document did have a significant influence on the final product. Their inclusion in this appendix does not suggest they were unimportant players in this cause or were not active Christians, for several were. They are included here simply because they did not sign the final document.

William Richardson Davie of North Carolina

William Davie graduated from Princeton the year the Declaration of Independence was signed. He immediately volunteered for military service and established himself as a hero. Wounded in the war, he eventually rose to the rank of brigadier general.

Raised in a godly Presbyterian home, this patriot lawyer returned from the war as one of the most popular men of North Carolina. He was a natural selection to be one of his state's delegates to the Constitutional Convention. One nineteenth-century historian described him as follows:

WILLIAM RICHARDSON DAVIE
(1756-1820)
NORTH CAROLINA, PRESBYTERIAN: LAWYER; SOLDIER; PLANTER;
STATESMAN; A FOUNDER OF THE UNIVERSITY OF NORTH CAROLINA;
GOVERNOR; SPECIAL MINISTER TO FRANCE.

The youngest man from North Carolina was William
Richardson Davie, then but thirty-one, of commanding
presence, an accomplished orator, with a voice of peculiar melody, and remarkably winning and handsome fea-
tures. He was a general favorite; one of the most affable,
hospitable and delightful of companions.[263]

M. E. Bradford wrote of him,

Davie left the Constitutional Convention late in
August, convinced that most of the great questions had
been decided. And with James Iredell he led the fight for
ratification in North Carolina. . . . In 1798, he was
elected governor of North Carolina by a legislature dominated by a large majority of Jeffersonians — a measure
of his great popularity. President Adams appointed
Davie as brigadier general in the regular army during
the mobilization against France and in 1799 sent him as
part of a peace commission to Paris, where he was

instrumental in negotiating the Convention of Montefontaine in October, 1800.[264]

As a Christian, William Davie "hated Jacobins and electoral condescension."[265] In reaction to the French Revolution, he recommended for the federal service only officers "untainted in any manner by French politics or principles."[266] Davie said of the Jacobins that "these mad men possess nothing upon which you can certainly calculate, no moral principle, no fixed political data: they seem to have no system but anarchy, no plan but plunder."[267]

It is interesting to note that the very philosophy Davie and other anti-Enlightenment founders warned our nation against more than two hundred years ago has jumped the Atlantic Ocean as they feared and today has become the prevailing thought in our schools, government, and media. Today secular humanism is opposed to almost everything our Founding Fathers fought to build into our nation.

Bradford wisely said of Davie, "he was one of those . . . who gave to our nation its original political configuration and impetus, a man of such impressive rectitude that even the passage of two centuries cannot obscure his stature."[268]

OLIVER ELLSWORTH
(1745-1807)
CONNECTICUT, CONGREGATIONALIST: LAWYER; JUDGE; LEGISLATOR; DIPLOMAT; LAND ENTREPRENEUR; STATE ATTORNEY; JUSTICE OF THE STATE SUPREME COURT; MEMBER OF CONTINENTAL CONGRESS; UNITED STATES SENATOR; CHIEF JUSTICE OF SUPREME COURT; SPECIAL MINISTER TO FRANCE.

[*portrait not available*]

Ellsworth was born into a godly Connecticut home. Hoping that he would enter the Congregationalist ministry, his father hired a minister, the Reverend Joseph Bellamy, to prepare him. Oliver attended Yale but wasn't comfortable there, so he transferred to Princeton, where he met many other theological students with an interest in law and politics — thanks to the Reverend John Witherspoon's influence. Like many other Christians who understood the dangers of French Enlightenment theories, Ellsworth was "utterly alarmed at the influence of the French Revolution on some of his countrymen."[269]

He was "an active member of the Constitutional Convention, where he spoke 84 times."[270] He believed very strongly in state's rights and insisted that the federal government should not impose its will on the sovereign states.

> "We know," Ellsworth said in Philadelphia, that "the people of the states are strongly attached to their own constitutions. If you hold up a system of government destructive of their constitutional rights, they will oppose it. The only chance we have to support a general government is to graft it on the state governments," so that "the United States are sovereign on their side of the line dividing jurisdictions — the states on the other" — with both having "power to defend their respective sovereignties.". . .

> Throughout his lifetime he opposed disestablishment of the churches in Connecticut. Moreover, in the Continental Congress he had supported a proclamation against "evil amusements," such as "play going, gaming, and horse races." But such godly sentiments were only *advisory*. Ellsworth was unusual among his New England "brethren" in recognizing that all Americans did not and would not share in one system of values. . . . On or about the 25th of August, with most of the discussion complete, he left Philadelphia — knowing that Sherman and Johnson could represent his views while he saw to his judicial duties in Connecticut.

> In the struggle over ratification of the Constitution in Connecticut, Oliver Ellsworth played a central role. In the state convention of January, 1788, called upon to judge of that document, Ellsworth made the principal address, in which he argued that under the terms of the Federal compact "this is a government of strictly defined pow-

ers," in which the "particular states retain their sovereignty" where it is not clearly surrendered. . . . During his years in the Senate, he was perhaps its most influential member and is to be remembered for his role in creating the instruments and agencies of a new government under the Constitution. He believed in judicial review as a means of preserving the Constitutional balance of powers between the individual states and the United States. In 1796, President Washington appointed Oliver Ellsworth Chief Justice of the United States Supreme Court, in which office he continued until 1800. . . . Throughout his life he was an orthodox Congregationalist and disapproved of the Deism of such advanced spirits as the new President, Thomas Jefferson. . . . At the time of his death, Oliver Ellsworth was Connecticut's leading citizen.[271]

His colleague William Pierce said of him, "He is a gentleman of a clear, deep, and copious understanding; eloquent, and connected in public debate; and always attentive to his duty. . . . A man much respected for his integrity, and venerated for his abilities."[272]

ELDRIDGE GERRY
(1744-1814)

MASSACHUSETTS, EPISCOPALIAN: MERCHANT; SIGNER OF THE DEC-
LARATION OF INDEPENDENCE AND THE ARTICLES OF CONFEDERA-
TION; LEADER OF THE PATRIOT CAUSE IN HIS STATE; MEMBER OF THE
FIRST U.S. CONGRESS; SPECIAL ENVOY TO FRANCE; GOVERNOR OF
MASSACHUSETTS; VICE PRESIDENT OF THE UNITED STATES.

Said M. E. Bradford of Gerry, "Few Americans of his generation had so much to do with the nation's history, performed on so large a stage, and yet retained so intense an identity with their provincial origins as did Eldridge Gerry."[273] He never lost sight of his mission to represent the state of Massachusetts. Although he refused to sign the Constitution because it did not contain a bill of rights, he was nevertheless very influential in its formation. He gave 119 speeches during the Convention, offered several motions and seconds, and successfully modified many of the provisions from the original Virginia Plan.

"No one in that Philadelphia meeting spoke more forcefully for the Bill of Rights than did Gerry."[274] He considered a bill of rights necessary to restrain the federal government's authority. While Gerry recognized that total democracy leads to anarchy, he also realized that a limited government was essential. If he could see our present government of over three million bureaucrats and employees, he would probably be tempted to proclaim, "I told you so!" However, all our Founding Fathers would probably say the same.

Educated by local clergymen and at Harvard, Gerry was a man of deep faith who believed God had called Massachusetts to be an example to the nation (and the United States to be an example to the world) of self-government on a representative basis. Two of his best friends in government, Samuel Adams and John Adams, were dedicated Christians who believed that self-government is only possible for a people with a religious perspective on life.

WILLIAM CHURCHILL HOUSTON
(1746-1788)
NEW JERSEY, PRESBYTERIAN: EDUCATOR; LAWYER; POLITICAL LEADER
OF HIS STATE; MEMBER OF CONTINENTAL CONGRESS; DELEGATE TO
ANNAPOLIS CONVENTION.

[*portrait not available*]

William Houston was a devout Presbyterian, trained at the Poplar Tent Academy by Presbyterian ministers.[275] He attended

Princeton College, where he returned to teach math and natural philosophy.

Houston was so highly respected by the citizens of his state that he was elected, "health willing," to represent them even though he was deathly ill with tuberculosis. His health permitted him to attend only two weeks of the Convention, where he "contributed nothing." He was able, however, "to sign the report of the New Jersey delegates to their state legislature."[276]

WILLIAM HOUSTOUN
(1757-1813)
GEORGIA, EPISCOPALIAN: PLANTER; LAWYER; MEMBER OF GEORGIA'S LEGISLATURE AND OF THE CONTINENTAL CONGRESS.
[portrait not available]

Houstoun was called "a gentleman of family . . . of an amiable and sweet temper, and of good and honorable principles."[277] Raised in a wealthy Episcopalian home, he remained a member of that church throughout his fifty-five years of life. He spoke only seven times during the Convention, though he served as a member of the "Grand Committee" that at first tried to make changes to the Articles of Confederation.

Although favorable toward slavery, he endorsed a strong federal government as a means of providing protection for his state, which was the most underdeveloped of the thirteen. Without fanfare he left the Convention about the time his fellow delegate, William Few, returned. Upon his return, Houstoun provided representation for his state in the Continental Congress at New York.

After the Convention, little was heard of Houstoun except that he married in 1788, was admitted to practice law before the United States Supreme Court in 1790, and spent his time between New York and Georgia.

John Lansing of New York

Born into a Dutch Reformed home, Lansing read law under fellow delegate Robert Yates. After the Revolutionary War, in

JOHN LANSING
(1754-1829)

NEW YORK, DUTCH REFORMED: LAWYER; JURIST; MEMBER OF STATE LEGISLATURE; MAYOR OF ALBANY; MEMBER OF CONTINENTAL CONGRESS AND STATE RATIFYING CONVENTION; CHIEF JUSTICE OF STATE SUPREME COURT; CHANCELLOR OF NEW YORK.

which he acted as aide-de-camp to General Philip Schuyler, he served in the New York state assembly. Like his colleague Judge Yates, he was precommitted to minor change in the Articles of Confederation—so much so that he couldn't keep faith with those who sent him if he went along with the decision to write a new Constitution.

Lansing was an "Anti-Federalist" more concerned about loss of civil liberties than about the anarchy and rebellion that caused the majority to recognize the need for at least a limited federal government. Wrote Bradford:

> Lansing made only one major speech in Philadelphia, an attack on "consolidation" delivered on June 16. His point was that the distinct sovereignties of the states should be preserved; and that "all reasoning on systems unaided by experience has generally been productive of false inferences." He accused the centralizers of being "theoretic" and of desiring "a perfection which never existed.". . . Once certain that their associates would attempt some-

thing more ambitious [than minor changes in the Articles of Confederation], the two New York Anti-federalists [Lansing and Yates], on July 10, went home, explaining their reasons for withdrawal in a long epistle in apology to Governor George Clinton.[278]

Lansing worked hard to defeat ratification by his very influential state. He was no match for the brilliant and indefatigable Alexander Hamilton, however, the driving force behind *The Federalist Papers*, which more than anything else turned the tide in New York (and in several other states) for ratification. John Lansing did, however, secure promises that a bill of rights would be included soon after ratification.

ALEXANDER MARTIN
(1740-1807)

NORTH CAROLINA, EPISCOPALIAN: MERCHANT; LAWYER; PLANTER; SOLDIER; STATE AND NATIONAL POLITICAL LEADER FOR THIRTY-FIVE YEARS, INCLUDING SPEAKER OF THE STATE SENATE, GOVERNOR, AND U.S. SENATOR.

[portrait not available]

Alexander Martin graduated at only sixteen years of age from Princeton College and three years later received an M. A. from the same school. He was born of godly, Scotch-Irish parents. His father, the Reverend Hugh Martin, was a Presbyterian minister in Hunterdon County, New Jersey. He went into the North Carolina continental regiment as a lieutenant colonel, retiring after three years and then being elected to his first state office. He was acting governor and then governor of North Carolina before the Union, the first to become governor after the new state constitution was approved.

Martin was not a good public speaker, but he was a wise lawyer. At the Convention he made no speeches or motions, seconded only three proposals, and had little influence on the Convention's outcome. He left Philadelphia late in August before the signing, "doubting the value of the Constitution that was emerging, but changed in his opinion within a few months of his return to the Salisbury/Guilford County region of North Carolina which was his base of power."[279]

Martin was a committed Christian who joined the Episcopalian Church in later life. He identified the Enlightenment philosophy that produced the French Revolution as a threat to the American way of life.

LUTHER MARTIN
(1748-1826)

MARYLAND, EPISCOPALIAN: TEACHER; LAWYER; ATTORNEY GENERAL; ELECTED TO CONTINENTAL CONGRESS.

Born to "pious evangelical Protestants of English stock whose ancestors had come to New Jersey and Massachusetts,"[280] Martin graduated from Princeton with honors after only two years and passed the Virginia bar exam before George Wythe, the teacher of so many colonial lawyers. For twenty-eight years, Luther Martin held the position of attorney general of his state (longer than anyone in American history) while simultaneously becoming one of America's most eminent lawyers.

Martin was an antifederalist and became a "tireless champion of the Sovereignty of the States."[281] One historian described him this way:

the most Prominent of the Maryland delegates . . . a lawyer of commanding influence, and a violent politician.

. . . In his celebrated report to the Maryland legislature on the doings of the Convention, he said there was "a distinct monarchical party" in that body. He opposed the Constitution with all his strength. Twenty years later, at the age of sixty-three, he was a firm personal and political friend of Aaron Burr, whose acquittal he was instrumental in procuring when he was tried for treason in 1807.[282]

During the Convention, he gave fifty-three speeches and promoted the "small state" or "New Jersey Plan." He was also responsible for proposing the electoral college system for selection of the President, finally adopted by the Convention. "He served amicably on the committee that produced the compromise on representation in the United States Senate."[283]

Luther Martin did all he could to provide a weak central government. When he failed, he deliberately waited until the document was completed and then left so he wouldn't have to sign it. Failing to keep it from being ratified by his own state, he spent the rest of his life opposing a strong central government, even contravening Thomas Jefferson, a member of his own party. Like many other northern Christians, he was suspicious of Jefferson. Religiously he was an Episcopalian who said of himself that he had been devoted to "the sacred truths of the Christian Religion."[284]

James McClung of Virginia

Born into the home of a highly successful and wealthy family, McClung followed his father into the medical profession. Graduated from William and Mary at the age of sixteen, he attended medical school at the University of Edinburgh, receiving his M.D. degree in 1772. He became physician-general and director of hospitals for his state, a highly respected leader of the medical profession. McClung was probably not a good appointee for the Convention. In fact, his appointment was arranged by General Washington to make up for Patrick Henry and Richard Lee, who both refused to attend because they didn't approve of a strong federal government. He had little influence on the outcome of the Convention and left Philadelphia the last week of July. As a medical doctor, he probably found it difficult

James McClung
(1746-1823)

VIRGINIA: PHYSICIAN; BANKER; SPECULATOR AND MINER; STATE POLITICIAN.

to justify his time in such a debating society. Religiously, nothing is known of his beliefs.

John Francis Mercer
(1759-1821)

MARYLAND, EPISCOPALIAN: SOLDIER; LAWYER; STATE POLITICIAN; MEMBER OF CONTINENTAL CONGRESS AND THE UNITED STATES HOUSE OF REPRESENTATIVES; PLANTER; GOVERNOR.

It is hardly worth mentioning that John Mercer attended the Constitutional Convention. A fiery fighter during the Revolution who rose from lieutenant to lieutenant colonel, he bitterly opposed the Convention and the Constitution.

Mercer only attended eleven days of the Convention in early August, yet he spoke twenty times. On his first occasion he bluntly stated that "the plan under consideration was 'objectionable,' followed by the statement that 'it never could succeed.' He mocked the solemn deliberations of his associates and sneered, 'It is a great mistake to suppose that the paper we propose will govern the United States.' "[285]

He left for "home, convinced that the entire proceedings were an 'aristocratic' or monarchist plot against the liberties of the people."[286] Upon his return to Maryland, Mercer did everything in his power to defeat the ratification of the new Constitution. And history has proved how out of step he was with his generation. His opinionated disposition and fiery judgment, which may have served him well on the battlefield, kept him from participating in the creation of the greatest constitutional document in the history of mankind.

WILLIAM PIERCE
(1740-1789)
GEORGIA, EPISCOPALIAN: SOLDIER; MERCHANT; MEMBER OF THE CONTINENTAL CONGRESS; AUTHOR OF THE ONLY CHARACTER SKETCHES MADE OF THE FIFTY-FIVE CONSTITUTIONAL CONVENTION DELEGATES.

[*portrait not available*]

Little is known of Pierce's parentage and background, though it is thought that he was born in Virginia. Pierce showed evidence of a good education, served with distinction as an officer in the Continental army, moved to Savannah, Georgia, after the war, and opened a trading company.

Pierce spoke four times during the Convention but, like his colleague William Few, he was a member of the Continental Congress and had to leave the Convention to represent his state in the debate over disposition of western lands and Indian problems. Consequently, he wasn't on hand to sign the Constitution when it was finished. However, his affirmation of the document was demonstrated by his vote for its approval in the Congress. He personally carried a copy of it back to Savannah, where he diligently worked for its ratification.

We are indebted to Pierce for his sketches of each delegate at the Convention. Not discovered and printed until forty years after his death, they contain the only personal evaluations by an insider of each of our Founding Fathers at work.

Frail in health, Pierce contracted an illness and died only a few months after the ratification of our Constitution. In his sketches he included this modest description of himself:

> I am conscious of having discharged my duty as a soldier through the course of the late Revolution with honor and propriety; and my services in Congress and the convention were bestowed with the best intention towards the interest of Georgia, and towards the general welfare of the Confederacy. The . . . flattering opinion which some of my friends had of me . . . gave me a seat in the wisest council in the world.[287]

Edmund Jennings Randolph of Virginia

Edmund Randolph was born an aristocrat and inherited the most prominent name in Virginia politics (a prominence dating back to early colonial days). He was educated at William and Mary, read law with his famous father, James Randolph, and was clerk of the House of Burgesses and the British crown's Attorney General. At twenty-three, he was faced with his most traumatic decision. When Virginia decided to disestablish the colonial government and break with the mother country, John Randolph decided to sell out and return to England. It is said that he told his son he was going home, inviting Edmund to accompany him. To this the younger Randolph supposedly responded, "I *am* home, father!" Ten years later, young Edmund Randolph was elected governor of Virginia.

Randolph had the major role in selecting the Virginia delegates to the Philadelphia meeting, was personally responsible for persuading his old commander in chief,

EDMUND JENNINGS RANDOLPH
(1753-1813)

VIRGINIA, EPISCOPALIAN: LAWYER; AIDE-DE-CAMP TO GENERAL
WASHINGTON; STATE ATTORNEY GENERAL; MEMBER OF STATE CON-
STITUTIONAL CONVENTION; MAYOR OF WILLIAMSBURG; GOVERNOR
OF CONTINENTAL CONGRESS; FIRST U.S. ATTORNEY GENERAL; SECRE-
TARY OF STATE.

General Washington, to attend, and was present himself
to speak "officially" for the Old Dominion. The strategy
followed by the Virginia delegation as a whole was well
considered. It was decided during their private deliberations that the best course was to have governor Randolph,
well-spoken and a fine figure of a man, move the consideration of a plan of government essentially the handiwork
of James Madison. For Madison held no great office, was
not a powerful speaker, or, at this point in his career, a
person of presence. . . . On May 29, once the Great Convention had been properly organized, Edmund Randolph
rose and proposed a formula for a completely new government, not a revision of the Articles. More or less, what he
proposed concerning the purpose and structure of the Federal power was in the end adopted by the Convention.[288]

Although he was an enthusiastic advocate of a very limited
federal union, he became fearful that without a bill of rights, the

bureaucratic growth of government would steal the liberties of the individual.

On September 10, 1787, Edmund Randolph announced that without these and other changes in the document as proposed, and without provision for a second convention, following recommendations for amendment from the states, he would not be a party to the business now almost complete. With Eldridge Gerry of Massachusetts and George Mason of his own state, Randolph attended the entire Constitutional Convention and still refused to sign the proposed instrument of government. According to his apology, he could not endorse a plan that would "end in Tyranny."[289]

His friends George Washington and James Madison counseled with him after the Convention and finally obtained his approval for ratification, even after he had written a tract against the Constitution. With Washington and Madison leading the proratification group and George Mason and Patrick Henry leading the opposition, Virginia probably experienced the most fiercely debated ratification convention of any state. It was Randolph's change of heart (upon the assurance of Madison that the first work of the Congress would be a bill of rights protecting the individual from a strong federal government) that provided one of the key votes assuring the four-vote victory for ratification.

Some say that his change of heart earned his appointment by President Washington as the first United States attorney general and later secretary of state. Others believe that Washington knew and respected his previous attorney general's experience with the state of Virginia, and valued Randolph because he was jealously committed to protecting the liberties of the individual.

Caleb Strong of Massachusetts

In an age that placed a high priority on character in its political leaders, Caleb Strong stood tall. He didn't separate his old-school Puritanism from politics, as evidenced in 1780 when he helped write the state constitution and the article on religion.

Strong so intensely felt that religion should have a high place

CALEB STRONG
(1745-1819)
MASSACHUSETTS, CONGREGATIONALIST: LAWYER; STATE POLITICAL
LEADER; UNITED STATES SENATOR.

in a community that he helped establish the Congregational church as the state church. While he made no attempt to include such a policy in the national Constitution, neither did that body address the subject or forbid it for the states. The current imposition of a federally mandated separation of powers for all the states was foreign to the Framers of the Constitution.

While I am not advocating national recognition of any particular religion in our presently pluralistic nation, I am suggesting that the current antireligious policies of our present government (which has totally secularized anything it touches) represent a significant departure from the intents of our Founding Fathers—particularly men like Caleb Strong.

Raised in a Christian home, Strong graduated from Harvard just twenty years after the Great Awakening. Sickness in his family forced him to return home late in August after most of the work of writing the document was completed. Following the Convention, he was elected to the United States Senate, where he served six years, after which he was elected governor of Massachusetts, an office he held for twelve years. President John Adams referred to him as "so good and unexceptionable a man."[290]

GEORGE WYTHE
(1726-1806)

VIRGINIA, EPISCOPALIAN: LAWYER; JUDGE; LAW PROFESSOR; ATTORNEY GENERAL OF VIRGINIA COLONY; MEMBER OF HOUSE OF BURGESSES; MAYOR OF WILLIAMSBURG; MEMBER OF CONTINENTAL CONGRESS; SIGNER OF THE DECLARATION OF INDEPENDENCE.

William Pierce identified Wythe as

> One of the most learned legal characters of the present age. . . . He is remarked for his exemplary life and universally esteemed for his good principles. No man, it is said, understands the history of government better than Mr. Wythe — nor anyone who understands the fluctuating conditions to which all societies are liable than he does. . . . He is a neat and pleasing speaker, and a most correct and able writer.[291]

Described by an historian as "one of the most distinguished men elected to be a delegate to the Constitution,"[292] Wythe had a profound impact as a teacher of the law on the thinking of many lawyers in Virginia — some of whom were delegates to the Constitutional Convention. What the Reverend John Witherspoon was to law students at Princeton, George Wythe was to law students in Virginia.

His personal contributions to the Constitution were few,

however, because of the illness of a close family member, that forced him to retire from the Convention just a few days after his arrival.

Wythe was raised in the Episcopal church, and he maintained membership throughout his lifetime. Like many intellectuals of faith, he became so obsessed with his chosen field of law that he spent little time cultivating his faith or communicating it. In the later years of his life, however, he again pursued the practice of his faith.

ROBERT YATES
(1738-1801)
NEW YORK, DUTCH REFORMED: LAWYER; JUDGE; LEADER OF REVOLUTION IN NEW YORK; MEMBER OF PROVINCIAL CONGRESS; JUSTICE AND CHIEF JUSTICE OF SUPREME COURT OF NEW YORK.

[*portrait not available*]

Judge Yates was fifty years of age when commissioned as a delegate to the Constitutional Convention by the same anti-federalist forces (led by the powerful governor of the state, George Clinton) that appointed his colleague, John Lansing, to see that New York did not surrender her sovereignty to a federal government.

Born into a strong Dutch Reformed family, Robert Yates embraced that faith, and after his education in New York City he studied law under the godly William Livingston. He arrived at the Convention with a thorough understanding of the law and had the experience of being one of the thirteen men who drafted the New York State constitution. He was considered "one of the most popular men in New York, being unanimously elected to the great Convention."[293]

With his colleague John Lansing (who had been his pupil in the study of law), he bolted the Convention on July 10. Judge Yates was the floor leader of the "antifederalists" during New York's ratification convention, but, as Bradford describes it he "did not play his part well."[294]

It was Robert Yates and John Lansing who defined the Anti-federalist position in their state, maintaining that the Framers had exceeded their authority, that their document would be "destructive of the political happiness of the citizens of the United States," and that state sovereignty was a better security for civil liberty than consolidated government. . . .

In view of his party's large majority among the delegates elected to the New York ratifying convention, Robert Yates was over-confident of victory. And among the Anti-federalists he was not alone. Though he had a full set of notes on what had been said in Philadelphia before his departure on July 10, 1787 (notes first published in 1821), Yates had great difficulty in preparing the "previous amendments" which were supposed to be attached as preconditions of a ratification, and thus revise or prevent the creation of a consolidated government. Yet, after Virginia had ratified it might have accomplished nothing if Yates, Melancton Smith, and Lansing had been better organized. Robert Yates voted against ratification of the Constitution, knowing that with the threat of New York City's secession from the state the document would win approval. Yet, once ratification was complete and amendments recommended subsequently, he called for acceptance of the new government.[295]

The heated debates in both New York and Virginia were not without purpose, however. They served as guidelines for the Bill of Rights and federal policy during the formative stages of the new national government.

THE DIVERSITY
OF RELIGIOUS LIFE
AT THE TIME OF
THE REVOLUTION

One historian describes the enormous influence of the diversity of religious patterns at the end of the colonial period as follows:

Roughly speaking, in New England outside Rhode Island the Congregational church was favored by the State, though British authority had no predilection for it. In the Middle Colonies the Church of England and the Friends divided a place of slight advantage over other sects; the Anglicans having certain special statutory privileges in a part of New York and in Maryland, and the Quakers enjoying real though not nominal privilege in Pennsylvania and Delaware. In the South the Church of England was buttressed by the state, but it met a rising opposition from the increase of dissenters. Nowhere in British America were the Catholics wholly immune from religious disadvantages. . . .

In Massachusetts in 1776 the old Puritan Congregational Church was the established church. In every town the support of at least one place of worship in that Church was compulsory, and was maintained by public taxation of all estates and polls, special exceptions under certain conditions being made for Baptists, Quakers, and Episcopalians. The ministers were nominated by the church for each town or parish, and confirmed by the local political division. Those who were communicants of a minor sect which had not yet been given the privileges of the Baptists, Episcopalians, or Friends, had to support the Establishment. Catholic priests were liable to imprisonment for life; and the tithing men could arrest Sabbath breakers and hale truants off to church. The commonwealth was nothing if not religious. The Abbaa Robin says in his "New Travels" that Sunday was observed with such strictness that Boston was a mere desert, all business being "totally at a stand, and the most innocent recreations and pleasures prohibited"; while he tells how in 1781 a Frenchman who lodged with him in Boston and indiscreetly played his flute on Sunday, was almost mobbed. The first warm agitation in favor of religious liberty, after independence, took place in the Constitutional Convention of 1780, where it was the chief topic of debate.[296]

In New Hampshire the relation of the government to the churches when the Revolution began was similar to that in Massachusetts, and the Constitution of 1784 was not an iota more progressive than the Bay State's. Governor Benning Wentworth had reserved land, in every township he granted, for the support of the Church of England; but Episcopalians were few, and next to the Congregational Church the Presbyterian, introduced by Scotch-Irish immigrants from Londonderry, had the most communicants. It was the law in 1775 that all should attend church regularly, but it was not enforced as it once had been. During the colonial period all citizens were required to pay taxes to support the Congregational church except the Presbyterians, Quakers, and in later years the Baptists. The Constitution of 1784 placed religious affairs in the same posture as in Massachusetts. The Legislature was "empowered" to "authorize" the towns to lay taxes for the support of ministers.[297]

[In Connecticut] Methodist missionaries entered the State in 1780, made converts in spite of fines and impris-

onment, and were soon able to organize flourishing
churches. The irritation of these denominations had
much to feed upon, for the Congregationalists made use
of their control over the State government to obtain many
special privileges. Thus in 1785-86 the Legislature, ar-
ranging for the sale of the Western Reserve lands, and the
division of the proceeds among the various Protestant
sects, also enacted that there should be reserved in each
township sold 500 acres for the gospel, 500 for the
schools, and 240 acres "to be granted in fee simple to the
first gospel minister who shall settle in such town." The
wealthy Congregationalists, carrying out on a large scale
the planting of missions in the West, naturally received
the most benefit. . . .

In New York the Anglican Church enjoyed little beyond a
nominal establishment. The Dutch and English Calvinists were the most numerous sects, and just before the
Revolution they and the other dissenting bodies were estimated by a contemporary historian to outnumber the
Anglicans fifteen to one. "Hence partly arises the general
discontent on account of the ministry acts; not so much
that the provision made by them is engrossed by the
minor sect as because the body of the people are for an
equal universal toleration of Protestants, and utterly
averse to any kind of ecclesiastical establishment." It was
in New York City that the Episcopalians were strongest;
and there, at the middle of the eighteenth century, there
were two Episcopalian churches, two Dutch Calvinist,
two German Lutheran, and one each of the English Calvinist, Baptist, French Huguenot, Moravian, and
Quaker sects — besides a Jewish synagogue. In such a cosmopolitan Province religious toleration, like other kinds
of toleration, could not help flourishing.[298]

In New Jersey the equality of the different Protestant
faiths was quite clear, there being no statute for an Establishment. As in New York, the dissenters far outnumbered the Episcopalians. Samuel Smith, writing from his
own knowledge in 1765, tells us there were then about 160

churches in the Colony, representing a dozen different denominations. About one-third were Presbyterian; one-fourth were Dutch Calvinist; about one-fifth were Quaker, and the Baptist and Episcopal churches were each less than one-eighth of the whole. About 1730 an Episcopalian had admitted, speaking of Pennsylvania and New Jersey, that there were "such a prodigious number of sectaries that the Church of England is like a small twig growing under the spreading boughs of a mighty tree." Moreover, the Anglican clergy, as in New York, lived too freely, and spent too much money on wine and too little on books, to be much respected. Most dissenting ministers, on the other hand, were active and influential, and to the Presbyterians and Dutch Calvinists the Province owed most of its educational facilities. The assumption of independence confirmed religious freedom, for the Constitution of 1776 provided that no man should be required to support or attend a church against his will, and that there should be no establishment of one sect over another.

In Pennsylvania and Delaware, as in Rhode Island, religious freedom was as full and real as anywhere in the wide world; the only exception to the universal toleration lying in a sporadic and occasional tendency to deal harshly with Catholics. The Constitutional basis of government laid for the two Colonies in 1682 guaranteed a wide charity for all forms of belief, and non-interference by the government in matters of conscience. The Anglican Church has little vitality in the Quaker Colonies; the Calvinist Churches had much; and the Province was renowned in the Old World as well as new for the variety of its small religious groups, the German immigration alone furnishing a half dozen distinct and eccentric sects. The immigration tended slowly but steadily to reduce the dominant strength of the Quakers. The Scotch, Scotch-Irish, and many of the Welsh supported the Calvinist churches, the Germans maintained the Lutheran congregations of the small societies like the Dunkards, Mennonites, and Ridge Hermits, and the Baptists and the Anabaptists were numerous. There were certain religious tests for office, which many of these sects strongly supported. The Irish and German Catholics, strengthened by the Acadians, formed a small but growing body by the outbreak of the Revolution.

But if the state had nothing to *do* with the church in Pennsylvania, the church often had much to do with the state. By their numerical superiority and great wealth, their energy and intellectual ability, the Quakers during most of the eighteenth century previous to the Revolution controlled the Assembly.[299]

In Maryland, Virginia, and the Carolinas the Church of England enjoyed a recognized supremacy as the state church, its establishment in all four Colonies being explicitly fixed by law. In Maryland general taxes were levied in support of the Church, and as its communicants were in a minority in the Province, it became much disliked by a large part of the population. Only one fact enabled the sects of dissenting Protestants to reconcile themselves to the Establishment — their dread of the numerous, able, and wealthy Catholics.[300]

The Anglican Church at the beginning of Virginia history had firmly entrenched itself through the immigration of the Cavaliers. The leading statesmen — Washington, Jefferson, Madison, Mason, Pendleton, the Lees, the Randolphs — of the Revolution were of families which had supported the Church ever since their forbears had come from the mother land. However, the unquestioned supremacy of the Establishment had been somewhat shaken in pre-Revolutionary days by two factors: the disrepute into which many of the horse-racing, fox-hunting, wine-drinking clergy fell, and the fact that the immigration of Presbyterians, Quakers, Lutherans, and above all, Baptists, had reduced its communicants to a minority of the Colony's church-members. The newer denominations grew especially strong west of the Blue Ridge, and about 1765 their moral position was improved by the persecutions to which the Episcopalian party tried to subject them. A familiar anecdote tells how in 1768, when three Baptist ministers were being tried in Spottsylvania County, the deep voice of Patrick Henry, who had come for miles on horseback, was heard lifted from the rear of the room in protest. "May it please your lordships," he interrupted, "What did I hear read? Did I hear an expression that these men, whom you worships are about to try for misdemeanor, are charged with preaching the gospel of the Son of God?"[301]

Henceforth the "general assessment" was the chief religious question before the Legislature. Our available evidence shows that by the end of 1783 the plan of taxing everyone for the support of all Christian ministers had gained wide favor, and was approved by a majority of Episcopalians, Methodists, and perhaps Presbyterians; but it was opposed by the Baptists and many in all other denominations who agreed with Jefferson that any link whatever between church and state was an evil.[302] . . . A majority both of the Legislature and the people appeared to believe that unless the obligation to support religion were made unescapable, stinginess and indifference would let many churches die; and Henry showed with his convincing oratory how nations had declined when religion decayed.[303]

The Anglican Church of North Carolina was wrecked in the Revolution. Most of the ministers remained loyal to the Crown, were deprived of their cures, and returned home; and as a majority of the communicants were also Tory, the disappearance of the Establishment meant almost the disappearance of Episcopalianism. The Constitution and Bill of Rights adopted by the fifth Provincial Convention in the fall of 1776 ensured perfect religious freedom, providing that "there shall be no establishment of any one religious church or denomination in this State in preference to any other."[304]

In South Carolina the Episcopal Church was in comparatively prosperous circumstances, its condition being the best in America. Just before the Revolution there were twenty parishes; the ministers were remarkably well educated, talented, and upright.[305]

The next legislature decided for disestablishment. With the new and better Constitution which it adopted in 1778, the progressives won the day. This instrument declared that all Protestant sects, demeaning themselves peaceably and faithfully, should enjoy equal religious and civil privileges, and that any church-society might be incorporated. The Episcopal churches, however, were confirmed by the Constitution in the property they already held.

Georgia fell in with the whole Southern movement. The Established Church there was weak, for it was comparatively young. The first permanent missionary had entered upon his duties in 1733; and it will be remembered that John Wesley arrived in 1736, labored diligently as an Episcopalian, and returned to England in consequence of an unfortunate love affair. Under the royal government all dissenters were given complete toleration, and they quite outnumbered the Anglicans. A certain Puritan element entered into the legislation of the Colony, for all persons were compelled to attend church, work and play on Sunday were forbidden, and the constables patrolled the streets, as in New England, to see that the taverns were closed and that all were at service. At the time of the Revolution there were only a few Anglican clergymen settled in the Province. Several of them took the part of the mother land, and left America; and as their places were not supplied, their denomination languished. The dissenters took advantage of their opportunity to overturn the Establishment. By the Constitution adopted in February, 1777, it was declared that all persons should have the free exercise of their religion, provided that it was not repugnant to the peace and safety of the State.[306]

END NOTES

Chapter 1 — Help! We've Been Robbed!

1. Dr. Ed Rowe, *The ACLU and America's Freedom* (Washington: Church League of America, 1984), pp. 20-21.
2. A. James Reichley, *Religion in American Public Life* (Washington: The Brookings Institution, 1985), pp. 54-55.

Chapter 2 — Who Secularized America?

3. James Hitchcock, *What is Secular Humanism?* (Ann Arbor: Servant Books, 1982), p. 39.
4. Ibid., p. 40.
5. Francis A. Schaeffer, *A Christian Manifesto* (Westchester, IL: Crossway Books, 1981), p. 29.
6. Hitchcock, pp. 40-41.
7. C. Gregg Singer, *A Theological Interpretation of American History* (Phillipsburg, NJ: Presbyterian and Reformed, 1975).

Chapter 3 — Who Fathered America?

8. M. E. Bradford, *A Worthy Company* (Marlborough, NH: Plymouth Rock Foundation, 1982), p. viii.
9. Benjamin Franklin, "Advice on Coming to America," *America in Person*, ed. George D. Youstra (Greenville, S.C.: Bob Jones University Press, 1975), p. 109.
10. Robert G. Ferris, ed., *Signers of the Constitution* (Washington, D.C.: National Park Service, 1976), pp. 136-37.
11. Vincent Wilson, Jr., ed., *The Book of Great American Documents* (Brookville, MD: American History Research Associates, 1982), p. 27.

Chapter 4 — Interesting Historical Events to Keep in View

12. Michael Farris, "The Real Meaning of the Declaration of Independence," *Concerned Women for America News*, Vol. 8 (July, 1986), pp. 3, 16.
13. Andrew M. Allison, ed., "America's First Constitution," *The Constitution* (March, 1986), pp. 21-22.

14. John Sexton and Nat Brandt, *How Free Are We?* (New York: M. Evans and Co., 1986), pp. 20-21.
15. Isaac Asimov, *The Birth of the United States* (Boston: Houghton Mifflin, 1974), pp. 125-26.
16. Daniel L. Marsh, *Unto the Generations* (Buena Park, CA: ARC, 1968).
17. Sexton and Brandt, p. 21.
18. Ibid., pp. 21-22.
19. Marsh, p. 51.
20. W. Cleon Skousen, *The Making of America* (Washington, D.C.: The National Center for Constitutional Studies, 1985), p. 162.

Chapter 5 — The Writing of the Constitution

21. Bruce Catton and William B. Catton, *The Bold and Magnificent Dream* (Garden City, NY: Doubleday, 1978), p. 330.
22. *The Worldbook Encyclopedia*, vol. XVIII (Chicago: World Book of Chicago, 1959), p. 8636.
23. W. Cleon Skousen, *The Making of America* (Washington, D.C.: The National Center for Constitutional Studies, 1985), p. 136.
24. Ibid., pp. 157-59.
25. For a complete reading of Franklin's plea for prayer at the Convention, see chapter 8, pp. 123-24.
26. Daniel L. Marsh, *Unto the Generations*.
27. Peter Marshall and David Manuel, *The Light and the Glory* (Old Tappan, NJ: Fleming H. Revell, 1977), p. 349.
28. Marshall and Manuel, p. 343.
29. Verne Paul Kaub, *Collectivism Challenges Christianity* (Winona Lake, IN: Light and Life Press, 1946), p. 58.
30. U.S. Constitution.
31. Marsh, p. 51.

Chapter 6 — The Christian Consensus of America in 1787

32. Bruce Catton and William B. Catton, *The Bold and Magnificent Dream* (Garden City, NY: Doubleday, 1978), p. 170.
33. Norman Cousins, *In God We Trust* (New York: Harper & Bros., 1958), pp. 9-10.
34. John W. Whitehead, *The Second American Revolution* (Elgin, IL: David C. Cook, 1982), p. 96.
35. Francis Newton Thorpe, *The Federal and State Constitutions, Colonial Charters, and Other Organic Laws of the States, Territories, and Colonies Now or Heretofore Forming the United States of America*, Vol. III (St. Clair Shores, MI: Scholarly Press, 1968).
36. H. R. Warfel, *Noah Webster, Schoolmaster to America* (New York: Octagon Press, 1966), pp. 11-13.
37. Ibid., pp. 181-82.
38. Verna M. Hall and Rosalie J. Slater, *The Bible and the Constitution of the United States of America* (San Francisco: Foundation for American Christian Education, 1983), p. 27.
39. Gaillard Hunt, *James Madison and Religious Liberty* (Washington: Government Printing Office, 1902), p. 166.

Chapter 7 — The Christian Understanding of Civil Law

40. C. Gregg Singer, *A Theological Interpretation of American History* (Phillipsburg, NJ, Presbyterian and Reformed, 1975).
41. John W. Whitehead, *The Second American Revolution* (Elgin, IL: David C. Cook, 1982), p. 75.
42. Ibid., p. 74.
43. Ibid., pp. 76-77.
44. Ibid., p. 78.
45. Ibid., pp. 78-81.
46. Ibid., pp. 28-30.
47. Ibid., pp. 30-32.
48. W. Cleon Skousen, *The Making of America* (Washington: The National Center for Constitutional Studies, 1985), p. 195.
49. Verna M. Hall and Rosalie J. Slater, *The Bible and the Constitution of the United States of America* (San Francisco: Foundation for American Christian Education, 1983), p. 17.
50. William Benton, *The Annals of America*, Vol III (Chicago: Encyclopedia Britannica, 1968), pp. 194-95.
51. John C. Fitzpatrick, ed., *The Writings of George Washington*, Vol. 35 (Washington: Government Printing Office, 1940), p. 229.
52. Preamble of the Constitution of North Carolina, 1868.
53. Preamble of the Constitution of New Jersey, 1844.
54. Preamble of the Constitution of Rhode Island, 1842.
55. Preamble of the Constitution of New York, 1846.
56. From an unabridged, printed sermon by D. James Kennedy, Ph.D., "Church and State," used by permission.
57. The six men who *signed* both the Declaration of Independence and the Constitution were Benjamin Franklin, Robert Morris, and James Wilson, all of Pennsylvania, George Read of Delaware, Ed Rutledge of South Carolina, and Roger Sherman of Connecticut.
58. Peter Marshall and David Manuel, *The Light and the Glory* (Old Tappan, NJ: Fleming H. Revell, 1977), p. 307.
59. George D. Youstra, ed., *America in Person* (Greenville, SC: Bob Jones University Press, n.d.), p. 109.
60. *Journals of the Continental Congress, 1774-1789*, Vol. VIII (Washington: Government Printing Office, 1907), pp. 731-35.
61. Alexis de Tocqueville, *Democracy in America*, Volume I (New York: Vintage Books, 1945), p. 319.
62. Ibid., p. 316.
63. Ibid., pp. 314-15.

Chapter 8 — The Two Most-Honored Founding Fathers

64. John F. Schroeder, ed., *Maxims of Washington* (Mt. Vernon: Mt. Vernon Ladies Association, 1942), p. 274.
65. Idem.
66. *The World Book Encyclopedia*, Vol. XVIII, (Chicago: Field Enterprises Education Corp., 1959), p. 8628.
67. George Washington, *Programs and Papers* (Washington: U.S. George Washington Bicentennial Commission, 1932), p. 33.
68. Schroeder, p. 406.

69. Ibid., p. 275.

70. Idem.

71. Idem.

72. Ibid., p. 280.

73. Ibid., pp. 280-81.

74. Ibid., p. 281.

75. Ibid., p. 287.

76. Idem.

77. Ibid., pp. 286-87.

78. Ibid., pp. 287-88.

79. Ibid., pp. 298-99.

80. Ibid., p. 299.

81. Ibid., p. 302.

82. Saul Padover, ed., *The Washington Papers* (New York: Harper and Bros., 1955), pp. 410-11.

83. Schroeder, p. 303.

84. Ibid., pp. 301-2.

85. W. Herbert Burk, B.D., *Washington's Prayers,* (Norristown, Penn.: Published for the Benefit of the Washington Memorial Chapel, 1907), pp. 87-95.

86. W. Cleon Skousen, *The Making of America* (Washington: The National Center for Constitutional Studies, 1985), p. 139.

87. *The Autobiography of Benjamin Franklin* (New York: Books, Inc., 1791) p. 146.

88. Albert Henry Smyth, ed., *The Writings of Benjamin Franklin* (New York: Macmillan, 1905-7), Vol. 10, p. 84.

89. Skousen, p. 677.

90. Ibid., pp. 677-78.

91. Leonard Labaree, ed., *The Papers of Benjamin Franklin* (New Haven: Yale University Press, 1959), Vol. I, p. 103.

92. Brackets in the manuscript.

93. Brackets in the manuscript.

94. Labaree, pp. 104-5.

95. Ibid., p. 108.

96. Ibid., p. 109.

97. Ibid., p. 213.

98. *Autobiography of Benjamin Franklin* (Note: Franklin's epitaph, written by himself, is engraved on his gravestone), p. 401.

99. Carl Becker, *Benjamin Franklin* (New York: Cornell University, 1946), p. 7.

100. Ibid., p. 81.

101. Idem.

102. Gaillard Hunt and James B. Scott, ed., *The Debates in the Federal Convention of 1787 Which Framed the Constitution of the United States of America, reported by James Madison* (New York: Oxford University Press, 1920), pp. 181-82.

103. William B. Willcox, ed., *The Papers of Benjamin Franklin* (New Haven: Yale University Press, 1972), Vol. 15, p. 301.

Chapter 9 — The Five Most Influential Founding Fathers

104. Irving Brant, *James Madison, Father of the Constitution, 1787-1800* (New York: Bobbs-Merrill, 1950), Vol. III, p. 84.

105. Gaillard Hunt, *James Madison and Religious Liberty* (Washington: American Historical Association, Government Printing Office, 1902), p. 166.

106. Bishop William Meade, *Old Churches, Ministers and Families of Virginia* (Philadelphia: J. B. Lippincott, 1910), Vol. II, p. 99.

107. Hunt, p. 167.

108. Idem.

109. William C. Rives, *History of the Life and Times of James Madison* (Boston: Little, Brown), Vol. I, pp. 33-34.

110. Hutchison and Rachal, *The Papers of James Madison* (Chicago: University of Chicago, 1912), Vol. I, p. 52.

111. Ibid., p. 7.

112. Madison to William Bradford, November 9, 1772; reprinted in *The Papers of James Madison*, William T. Hutchinson, ed. (Chicago: University of Chicago Press, 1962), Vol. I, p. 75.

113. James Madison, *Religious Freedom, A Memorial & Remonstrance to the General Assembly of Virginia, Session of 1785* (Boston: Lincoln and Edmands, 1819), p. 7.

114. A. D. Wainwright, ed., *Madison and Witherspoon: Theological Roots of American Political Thought* (The Princeton University Library Chronicle, Spring, 1961), p. 125.

115. A. M. Schlesinger, *The State of the Union Messages of the Presidents, 1790-1966* (New York: Chelsea House-Robert Hector, 1966); Adrienne Koch, *Madison's "Advice to My Country"* (Princeton: Princeton University Press, 1966), p. 43.

116. J. Eidsmoe, *Christianity and the Constitution: The Faith of our Founding Fathers* (Grand Rapids: Baker Book House, 1987), p. 13.

117. M. E. Bradford, *A Worthy Company* (Marlborough, NH: Plymouth Rock Foundation, 1982), p. 91.

118. Henry C. Lodge, *Historical & Political Essays* (Salem, NC: Ayer Co., 1952), p. 68.

119. C. F. Adams, ed., *Familiar Letters of John Adams and His Wife* (1876), p. 251.

120. Martha J. Lamb, ed., *The Framers of the Constitution, A Magazine of American History* (New York: Historical Publishing Co., 1885), Vol. 13, p. 337.

121. W. Cleon Skousen, *The Making of America* (Washington: The National Center for Constitutional Studies, 1985), p. 151.

122. Lewis Henry Boutell, *The Life of Roger Sherman* (Chicago: A. C. McClure & Co., 1896), p. 269.

123. Ibid., p. 271.

124. Ibid., pp. 272-73.

125. Ibid., p. 213.

126. Bradford, p. 41.

127. Idem.

128. Idem.

129. Allan M. Hamilton, *The Intimate Life of Alexander Hamilton* (Philadelphia: Richard West, 1979).

130. Ibid., p. 335.

131. Bradford, p. 48.

132. Ibid., p. 49.

133. Lamb, pp. 322-23.

134. Skousen, p. xxiii.

135. Bradford, pp. 157-58.

136. Ibid., p. 162.

137. Ibid., p. 163.

Chapter 10 — Outstanding Christians Among the Founding Fathers

138. M. E. Bradford, *A Worthy Company* (Marlborough, NH: Plymouth Rock Foundation, 1982), p. 214.
139. Martha J. Lamb, ed., *The Framers of the Constitution, A Magazine of American History*, Vol. XIII (New York: Historical Publishing Co., 1885), p. 330.
140. Charles C. Jones, *Biographical Sketches of the Delegates from Georgia* (Tustin, CA: American Biography Service), p. 61.
141. Ibid., pp. 6-7.
142. W. Cleon Skousen, *The Making of America* (Washington,: The National Center for Constitutional Studies, 1985), p. xv.
143. Bradford, pp. 110-11.
144. Allen Johnson, ed., *Dictionary of American Biography* (New York: Charles Scribner's, 1964), I:123.
145. Frederick Horner, *History of the Blair, Banister and Braxton Families* (Philadelphia: J. B. Lippincott Co., 1898), pp. 68-69.
146. Dorothy McGee, *Framers of the Constitution* (New York: Dodd, Mead, 1968), p. 133.
147. Bradford, p. 63.
148. McGee, p. 132.
149. Rev. William Campbell, *Papers of the Historical Society of Delaware* (Wilmington: Historical Society of Delaware, 1909), p. 8.
150. Idem.
151. Ibid., p. 27.
152. Ibid., p. 35.
153. Ibid., p. 27.
154. Bradford, p. 113.
155. Skousen, p. xv.
156. Bradford, p. 103.
157. Skousen, p. xviii.
158. Charles Stille, *The Life and Times of John Dickinson* (New York: Burt Franklin, 1968), p. 93.
159. Forrest McDonald, ed., *Empire and Nation* (Englewood Cliffs, NJ: Prentice-Hall, 1962), p. 15.
160. Ibid., p. 17.
161. Ibid., p. 20.
162. Ibid., p. 28.
163. Ibid., p. 83.
164. Stille, p. 185.
165. Ibid., pp. 187-88.
166. Bradford, p. 30.
167. Molone, ed., *Dictionary of American Biography* (New York: Charles Scribner's Sons, 1964), V:131.
168. Skousen, p. xxi.
169. John Irving, *A Discourse of the Advantages of Classical Learning* (New York: G. & C. & H. Carvill, 1830), pp. 141-43.
170. Skousen, p. xxxi.
171. Bradford, p. 12.
172. Ibid., p. 15.
173. David C. Mearns, *The Story Up to Now* (Washington: The Library of Congress, 1947), p. 19.

174. Bradford, p. 2.
175. Idem.
176. R. P. Bristol, *The American Bibliography of Charles Evans, Vol. 14* (Portsmouth [1785] Broadside: LOC Microfilm Library, Nov. 24, 1785), #19115, 19116.
177. McGee, p. 45.
178. John Langdon of New Hampshire, p. 285.
179. Ibid., p. 286.
180. Bradford, p. 60.
181. Skousen, p. xxii.
182. Vincent Wilson, Jr., *The Book of the Founding Fathers* (Brookeville, MD: American History Research Associates, 1974), p. 44.
183. J. A. Stevens, *The Magazine of American History* (New York: A. J. Baines & Co., 1878), Vol. 22, p. 485.
184. Wilson, p. 44.
185. Idem.
186. McGee, p. 125.
187. Bernard Steiner, *One Hundred and Ten Years of Bible Society in Maryland* (Maryland: Maryland Bible Society, 1921), p. 14.
188. Bradford, p. 56.
189. Brantz Mayer, *Baltimore Past and Present, 1729-1970* (Washington: Library of Congress, n.d.), p. 403.
190. Skousen, p. xxv.
191. Bradford, pp. 205-6.
192. Ibid., p. 207.
193. Ibid., p. 206.
194. Idem.
195. Francis Williams, *The Pinckneys of South Carolina* (New York: Harcourt, Brace, Jovanovich, 1978), p. 21.
196. *A Sermon Preached at St. Phillips Church, August 21, 1825, by Christopher E. Gadsen, On the Occasion of the Decease* (Charleston: published by the vestry, printed by A. E. Miller, 1825), pp. 20-21.
197. Ibid., p. 11.
198. Alex Garden, *Eulogy of Charles Cotesworth Pinckney* (Charleston: Printed by A. E. Miller, 1825), pp. 42-43.
199. Lamb, p. 326.
200. J. C. Judson, *A Biography of the Signers of the Declaration of Independence* (Philadelphia: Dobson & Thomas, 1839), p. 85.
201. Bristol, #01291, Reel 224.
202. Skousen, p. xxvi.
203. Francis Newton Thorpe, *The Federal and State Constitutions* (St. Clair, MI: Scholarly Press), Vol. I, p. 142.
204. Bradford, p. 109.
205. John Neal, *Trinity College Historical Society Papers, Series 13* (New York: AMS Press, 1915), p. 62.
206. Ibid., pp. 62-63.
207. Bradford, pp. 184-85.

Chapter 11 — A Constitution for the Ages — If We Can Keep It

208. Theo Stamos, "Speaking of our Founding Fathers," *The Washington Times*, May, 1987.

209. Pat Robertson, *America's Dates With Destiny* (Nashville, TN: Thomas Nelson, 1986), pp. 89-91.
210. Ibid., p. 92.
211. C. Gregg Singer, *A Theological Interpretation of American History* (Phillipsburg, NJ: Presbyterian and Reformed, 1975), pp. 340-41.
212. Will and Ariel Durant, *The Lessons of History* (New York: Simon & Schuster, 1968), pp. 63-64
213. Robertson, pp. 93-95.
214. W. Cleon Skousen, "Writing a New Constitution," *The Constitution* (December 5, 1985), p. 8.
215. Idem.

Appendix A — The Other Delegates Who Signed the Constitution

216. M. E. Bradford, *A Worthy Company* (Marlborough, NH: Plymouth Rock Foundation, 1982), p. 209.
217. Ibid., p. 211.
218. W. Cleon Skousen, *The Making of America* (Washington: The National Center for Constitutional Studies, 1985), p. xvii.
219. Bradford, p. 121.
220. Wharton Diedenson, "George Clymer — The Signer," *The Magazine of American History* (New York: A. S. Barnes, 1880), Vol. 5, p. 202.
221. Ibid., p. 203.
222. Bradford, p. 96.
223. Ibid., p. 98.
224. Ibid., p. 98.
225. Ibid., pp. 61-62.
226. Ibid., p. 219.
227. Dorothy McGee, *Framers of the Constitution* (New York: Dodd and Mead, 1968), p. 344.
228. Ibid., p. 346.
229. Skousen, p. xviii.
230. Bradford, p. 99.
231. Idem.
232. Idem.
233. *Constitutionalist and Weekly Magazine* (Exeter, NH, May 10, 1814).
234. Bradford, p. 20.
235. Ibid., p. 19.
236. Skousen, p. xix.
237. The Massachusetts constitution stated that "the governor shall be chosen annually; and no person shall be eligible to this office, unless, at the time of his election . . . he shall declare himself to be of the Christian religion." The oath required for taking office read, "I, A. B., do declare, that I believe the Christian religion, and have a firm persuasion of its truth; and I am seized and possessed, in my own right, of the property required by the constitution, as one qualification for the office or place to which I am elected." From the Massachusetts Constitution as copied from Francis Newton Thorpe, ed., *The Federal and State Constitutions, Colonial Charters, and other Organic Laws of the States, Territories, and Colonies Now or Heretofore Forming the United States of America,* (Washington: Government Printing Office, 1909), Vol. III, pp. 1900, 1908.

238. Horace Binney, *The Leaders of the Bar of Philadelphia* (Philadelphia: Henry Ashmead, printer, 1886), p. 91.
239. Bradford, p. 102.
240. Ibid., pp. 127-28.
241. Ibid., p. 93.
242. H. M. Timkcom, *The Republicans and Federalists in Pennsylvania* (Philadelphia: University of Pennsylvania, 1950), p. 310.
243. K. R. Rossman, *Thomas Mifflin* (Chapel Hill, NC: University of North Carolina Press, 1952), p. 307.
244. Bradford, p. 78.
245. J. C. Judson, *A Biography of the Signers of the Declaration of Independence* (Philadelphia: Dobson & Thomas, 1839), pp. 94-95.
246. Bradford, p. 76.
247. McGee, p. 318.
248. Bradford, p. 78.
249. Ibid., pp. 79-80.
250. Skousen, p. xxv.
251. Leon Friedman and Fred Israel, *The Justices of the United States Supreme Court, 1789-1969* (New York: Chelsea House Publishing, 1969), Vol. I, p. 40.
252. Bradford, pp. 197-98.
253. Ibid., p. 200.
254. Ibid., p. 193.
255. *Encyclopaedia Britannica*, 11th Ed., "James Wilson" (New York: The Encyclopaedia Britannica Co., 1911), vol. 28, p. 693.
256. C. P. Smith, *James Wilson* (Chapel Hill, NC: University of North Carolina Press, 1956), pp. 334-35.
257. Ibid., p. 335.
258. Idem.
259. Bradford, p. 84.
260. Ibid., p. 85.
261. Ibid., p. 86.
262. Ibid., pp. 86-87.

Appendix B — The Delegates Who Did Not Sign the Constitution

263. Martha Lamb, ed., *A Magazine of American History* (New York: Historical Publication Co., 1885), Vol. 13, p. 329.
264. M. E. Bradford, *A Worthy Company* (Marlborough, NH: Plymouth Rock Foundation, 1982), p. 181.
265. Idem.
266. Idem.
267. Ibid., p. 182.
268. Idem.
269. Ibid., p. 35.
270. Idem.
271. Ibid., pp. 37-40.
272. W. Cleon Skousen, *The Making of America* (Washington: The National Center for Constitutional Studies, 1985), p. xviii.
273. Bradford, p. 11.
274. Ibid., p. 9.
275. Ibid., p. 64.

276. Ibid., p. 65.
277. Skousen, p. xx.
278. Bradford, p. 51.
279. Ibid., p. 189.
280. Ibid., p. 115.
281. Ibid., p. 114.
282. Lamb, p. 340.
283. Bradford, p. 117.
284. Ibid., p. 114.
285. Ibid., p. 124.
286. Ibid., p. 123.
287. Skousen, p. xxv.
288. Bradford, p. 167.
289. Ibid., p. 168.
290. Ibid., p. 18.
291. Skousen, p. xxix.
292. Bradford, p. 175.
293. Ibid., p. 53.
294. Idem.
295. Ibid., p. 54.

Appendix C — The Diversity of Religious Life at the Time of the Revolution

296. Allen Nevins, *The American States During and After the Revolution: 1770-1789* (New York: Macmillan, 1924), pp. 420-21.
297. Ibid., p. 423.
298. Ibid., p. 426.
299. Ibid., pp. 427-28.
300. Ibid., p. 429.
301. Ibid., pp. 431-32.
302. Ibid., p. 434.
303. Ibid., p. 435.
304. Ibid., pp. 437-38.
305. Ibid., p. 438.
306. Ibid., pp. 439-40.

COLOPHON

The typeface for the text of this book is *Baskerville*. Its creator, John Baskerville (1706-1775), broke with tradition to reflect in his type the rounder, yet more sharply cut lettering of eighteenth-century stone inscriptions and copy books. The type foreshadows modern design in such novel characteristics as the increase in contrast between thick and thin strokes and the shifting of stress from the diagonal to the vertical strokes. Realizing that this new style of letter would be most effective if cleanly printed on smooth paper with genuinely black ink, he built his own presses, developed a method of hot-pressing the printed sheet to a smooth, glossy finish, and experimented with special inks. However, Baskerville did not enter into general commercial use in England until 1923.

Substantive editing by Larry Weeden
Copy editing by James B. Jordan
Manuscript preparation by Karen Grant

Typography by Thoburn Press, Tyler, Texas